Summa of the Christian Life

Cross and Crown Series of Spirituality

GENERAL EDITOR

Very Reverend John L. Callahan, O.P., S.T.M.

LITERARY EDITOR

Reverend Jordan Aumann, O.P., S.T.D.

NUMBER 5

This translation was made from the Spanish edition of *Obra Selecta: Una Suma de la Vida Cristiana,* published by La Editorial Católica, Madrid, Spain, 1947, under the auspices of the Biblioteca de Autores Cristianos.

SUMMA OF THE CHRISTIAN LIFE

SELECTED TEXTS FROM THE WRITINGS OF

Venerable Louis of Granada, O.P.

VOLUME TWO

Translated and Adapted

by Jordan Aumann, O.P.

TAN BOOKS AND PUBLISHERS, INC.
Rockford, Illinois 61105

NIHIL OBSTAT:

James R. Gillis, O.P., S.T.M.
James J. McDonald, O.P., S.T.B.

IMPRIMI POTEST:

Edward L. Hughes, O.P., S.T.M.
Provincial

NIHIL OBSTAT:

Thomas G. Kinsella, O.P.
Censor Librorum

IMPRIMATUR:

Edward A. Fitzgerald, D.D.
Bishop of Winona
April 11, 1955

Originally published in English by B. Herder Book Co.,
St. Louis, Missouri in 1955.

Printed and bound in the United States of America

TAN BOOKS AND PUBLISHERS, INC.
P. O. Box 424
Rockford, Illinois 61105

1979

Contents ✍

BOOK FIVE

The Moral Virtues

BOOK THREE

The Quest for Happiness

CHAPTER 1 🖋

Man's Final End

ONE of the facts that clearly proves the insufficiency of philosophy for the formulation of rules of good living is the ignorance of the philosophers themselves concerning man's final end. In order to understand man's true goal, we must know that all men are born with a desire to reach a state in which they will be so completely satisfied that nothing remains to be desired. Such a state is called happiness or beatitude. The philosophers did not doubt that it was possible to arrive at such a state, for they agreed that the Author of nature would not impress on our hearts a natural desire for something that is impossible of attainment. God does not do things in vain.

Convinced as they were of this fact, the philosophers expended all their diligence to discover what class of goods will provide this perfect happiness, for they realized that they could not order their lives well unless they knew the ultimate end to which human life is ordained. In things that are directed to an end, the rule of action must be taken from that very end. Thus, he who pilots a ship must know the port to which the ship should be directed, so that a voyage may be charted accordingly. So also, the proper direction of human life first requires that a man know his ultimate end so that he may direct all his steps toward that end. Hence Aristotle, when attempting to formulate the rules for a good life, treated first of man's ultimate end, for the final goal of human life determines the counsels and rules that must be proposed for attaining that goal.

All the philosophers who professed to be masters of the good life exerted every effort to discover in which class of goods man's ultimate end was to be found. But they were so much at variance with one another that Marcus Varro counted more than two hundred different opinions concerning man's ultimate end. Varro himself, observing that man is neither pure spirit nor merely a body, but a body-soul composite, concluded that man's happiness is to be found in a blending of the goods of body and soul. And since the soul possesses two principal faculties—the intellect and the will—Varro would require perfect wisdom in the intellect (for that is its proper good) and consummate virtue in the will (so that the passions which war against this faculty may be completely subjugated and controlled). In the body he would require health, power, proper disposition of parts, and good temperament. To all this, Aristotle adds that it is also necessary that man should have a portion of temporal goods which will be placed at the service of virtue. Lastly, the happiness described by these two philosophers presupposes freedom from all the evils and miseries of this life, for such things would disturb the soul and be prejudicial to the goods of the body that are required for perfect happiness.

St. Augustine refers to the opinion of Marcus Varro in his *City of God,* but he scoffs at the folly of placing man's true happiness in a life that is surrounded by misery and misfortune. For if happiness consists in certain goods of body and soul and in freedom from all evils, where shall we ever find a man who is perfectly happy? This life is a sea of constant change, a vale of tears, wherein there are more miseries than there are hairs on a man's head. Man is plagued by infirmities of the body and inordinate desires in the soul. He experiences anger and hatred because of injuries received and disappointment in not attaining the goods he desires. His life is made sorrowful by the death of loved ones, the injuries endured at the hands of wicked neighbors, the betrayals and deceptions by false friends, and the injustices from false judges. How can he find perfect happiness in a life where there is so little truth, so little faith, so little loyalty; where malice and ambition rule; where virtue is neglected and forgotten; where money means everything and a son sometimes desires the death of his own father in order to come into the inheritance? And what shall we say of the constant war of the flesh against the spirit, the temptations of the devil, the cruel wars on land and sea that destroy the peace and tranquillity of men and nations, the intrigues and false testimony of perverse men, the tyranny of the powerful, and the oppression of the weak? Observing the sufferings of this life, Solomon considered the dead to be in a happier state than the living,[1] and Job, a man well experienced in suffering, states that "the life of man upon earth is a warfare and his days are like the days of a hireling." [2]

Moreover, if perfect wisdom is required for perfect happiness, how many years and how much study will be necessary to attain it! Plato observes that they are fortunate indeed who have succeeded in acquiring true wisdom by the time they reach old age. If, in addition to wisdom, perfect virtue is required—and for this it is necessary to mortify the passions and have them under perfect control—who could reach such a state without divine grace? And if, besides these perfections of intellect and will, perfect happiness demands certain perfections of the body, when and where shall we find all these perfections together? Sometimes, indeed, one deficiency can make a man more misera-

[1] Eccles. 4:2 f.   [2] Job 7:1.

ble than all the other perfections can make him happy, as is clearly demonstrated in Scripture, where we read that Aman, in spite of all his wealth, his multitude of children, and the great honor that had been paid to him by Esther, felt that he had nothing, as long as Mardochai refused to show him honor and reverence.[3]

If it is so difficult to find all these perfections in one man, who will be truly happy? And yet, if all animals succeed in attaining their proper ends, it would be a cruel irony if man alone, for whom this visible universe was created, were unable to reach his ultimate goal.

The philosophers who have erred in this matter deserve both pardon and blame. They can be excused to the extent that they knew nothing about the happiness of the next life and were forced to seek for it in this life. Therefore, some philosophers placed happiness in one line of goods and others in another, depending upon their personal inclinations and tastes. But pressed as they were to find a solution, they are deserving of blame for not seeking light from the Creator so that they could arrive at the truth. Relying on their own ingenuity, they not only believed that they could understand in what true happiness consists, but that they could attain this happiness by their own efforts.

From all that we have said, we can draw two conclusions that are worthy of consideration. The first is that man is able to attain the state of perfect happiness, but since this happiness is not to be found in this life, it must be found in the life to come; otherwise man's natural desire for beatitude would be fruitless and vain. The knowledge of this truth is so important that the Apostle makes it the very foundation of Christianity: "He that cometh to God

---

[3] Cf. Esther 5:9–13.

must believe that He is and is a rewarder to them that seek Him." [4]

The second conclusion pertains to the fact of a divine revelation. Philosophy is not sufficient either to teach us the true religion or to give us the rules for a good life. For if philosophers have been unable to discover the true end of life, they cannot teach us the means for arriving at that end, since the means are determined by the end. On the other hand, if divine providence is not deficient in the care of the animals, how could it be lacking to the most noble of all God's visible creatures in regard to the one thing that is most necessary? For it is most important for man to know how he should honor and serve God and that he should know the end for which he was created and the means of attaining that end. Therefore, it is not fitting that the Creator should fail man in this great need of his soul, while providing for the needs of the body, for it would be contrary to His wisdom and providence if He were to have a care for those things that are inferior and be unmindful of that which is more noble. Such a disorder is incompatible with God's infinite goodness and wisdom. We conclude from this that it pertains to the perfection of divine providence to reveal to us this truth concerning His glory and our beatitude and to teach us the way to happiness and salvation.

[4] Heb. 11:6.

CHAPTER 2 ✍

False Happiness of This World

IF we consider the happiness of this world, we shall discover that it is accompanied by many kinds of evil. In the first place, the happiness of this world, of whatever kind, is at the most very brief. Man's earthly happiness cannot last any longer than his life, and however long his life may be, it rarely reaches a hundred years. "Let us," says St. John Chrysostom, "devote a hundred years to the pleasures of this world, then another hundred, and then twice again another hundred; how does all this compare with eternity?" "If a man live many years," says Solomon, "and have rejoiced in them all, he must remember the darksome time and the many days, which when they shall come, the things past shall be accused of vanity." [1]

Even evil men have admitted this: "So we also being born, forthwith ceased to be, . . . but are consumed in our wickedness." [2] Consider how short the entire span of their lives will appear to the wicked when they enter eternity. It will seem to them that they have lived scarcely a day, as if they had been carried from the womb to the tomb. The pleasures of this world will then seem to them merely a dream of joys that seemed to be but never really were. "And as he that is hungry dreameth and eateth, but when he is awake his soul is empty, and as he that is thirsty dreameth and drinketh, but after he is awake his soul is yet faint with thirst and his soul is empty, so shall be the

[1] Eccles. 11:8.   [2] Wisd. 5:13.

multitude of all the Gentiles that have fought against Mount Sion." [3]

"Where," says Baruch, "are the princes of the nations and they that rule over the beasts that are on the earth, that take their diversion with the birds of the air, that hoard silver and gold wherein men trust and there is no end of their getting, who work in silver and are solicitous and their works are unsearchable? They are cut off and are gone down to hell, and others are risen up in their place." [4] Where is the wise and educated man? Where is the investigator of the secrets of nature? What has become of the glory of Solomon? Where is the powerful Alexander the Great? Where are the famous Caesars of the Romans? Where are the other kings and princes of the earth? Of what avail were their glory, worldly power, great wealth, legions of soldiers, and companies of flatterers? All this was but a shadow and a dream, a happiness that passed in a moment.

Another evil that accompanies this world's happiness is the multitude of miseries in this vale of tears. Truly, the miseries of man are more numerous than the days or hours of his life. Each day brings its cares and each hour threatens us with its misery. Who could count the variety of illnesses that affect the body or the annoyances caused by our neighbors? One person disputes with you, another persecutes you, and a third blackens your good name. Some afflict you with hatred, others with envy, deceit, and false testimony, and others with desire for revenge. All of them make war against you unto death.

In addition to these miseries there is an infinite number of unexpected disasters and misfortunes. One man loses his sight, another breaks an arm, another falls from a high place, another drowns, and yet another loses his wealth. And

[3] Isa. 29:8. [4] Bar. 3:16–19.

if you wish to hear of other miseries, ask the men of the world how their brief pleasures have brought many griefs in their wake. For if the two were to be weighed in the balance, you would see that the one far outweighs the other and that for one hour of pleasure there are a hundred hours of grief.

But these miseries are common to both the good and the bad, for all men traverse the same sea of life and are subject to the same storms. There are other miseries that afflict only evil men, for they are the daughters of the evil deeds these men commit. A consideration of such miseries is more to our purpose, for it will manifest how abhorrent is the life of the sinner. The sinners themselves admit the magnitude of their misery, as we read in the Book of Wisdom: "We wearied ourselves in the way of iniquity and destruction, and have walked through hard ways, but the way of the Lord we have not known. What hath pride profited us? Or what advantage hath the boasting of riches brought us? All those things are passed away like a shadow . . . and as a ship that passeth through the waves, whereof when it is gone by, the trace cannot be found nor the path of its keel in the waters; or as when a bird flieth through the air, of the passage of which no mark can be found, but only the sound of the wings beating the light air, and parting it by the force of her flight; . . . or as when an arrow is shot at a mark, the divided air presently cometh together again so that the passage thereof is not known. So we also being born, forthwith cease to be and have been able to show no mark of virtue, but are consumed in our wickedness." [5] Consequently, as the good in this life enjoy a kind of paradise and yet look forward to another, so the sinners have a hell in this life and await another in the life to come.

[5] Wisd. 5:7–13.

If it were merely a question of the pains and labors of the body in this life, that would not be cause for excessive fear, but there are also dangers to the soul, and these are much harder to bear because they touch us more vitally. Thus, we read in Scripture: "He shall rain snares upon sinners." [6] Since sinners have so little guard over their hearts and senses, are so careless in avoiding the occasions of sin, and are so slothful in making use of spiritual remedies, how can they avoid walking into countless dangers? For this reason does God rain snares upon the wicked; snares in their youth and snares in their old age; snares in riches and in poverty; snares in honor and snares in dishonor; snares in their association with other men and snares in solitude; snares in adversity and snares in prosperity.

Who, then, will not fear such a dangerous world? Who will not be afraid to walk unarmed among so many enemies and unprotected amid so many occasions of sin? Who will consider himself secure? "Can a man hide fire in his bosom, and his garments not burn? Or can he walk upon hot coals, and his feet not be burned?" [7] "He that toucheth pitch shall be defiled with it; and he that hath fellowship with the proud shall put on pride." [8]

To this multitude of snares and dangers is added yet another misery which makes them even greater: the blindness and darkness of worldly persons, which is fittingly symbolized by the darkness recorded in the land of Egypt during the time of Moses.[9] So dense was this darkness that for three days no man could see his neighbor nor move out of the place where he was. Such is the darkness which the world suffers, only it is much worse. What greater blindness than for so many men to believe as they do and yet to

[6] Ps. 10:7.   [7] Prov. 6:27–28.   [8] Ecclus. 13:1.
[9] Exod. 10:21.

live as they do? What greater blindness than to think so much of men and take so little notice of God? To be so solicitous about the laws of the world and so negligent about the laws of God? To work so energetically for the body, which is but dust, and so little for the soul, which is an image of the divine Majesty? To store up so many riches for this life, which may end tomorrow, and lay aside nothing for the next life, which will endure forever? Knowing for certain that we must die and that the moment of death will determine our state for all eternity, what greater blindness than to live as carelessly as if we were to remain on earth forever? What greater blindness than to forego the heritage of heaven for the satisfaction of a passion; to have such regard for possessions and so little for conscience; to want all one's things to be good but not to worry whether one's life is good? Men have eyes sharper than lynxes for the things of this world but are blinder than moles in regard to the things of heaven.

Since there are so many snares in the world, what can be expected but many sins and falls? Cast your eyes on the palaces, cities, and nations of the world; you will see so many sins, such forgetfulness of God, and such disregard for one's own salvation that you will be astonished at so much evil. You will see that the greater part of men live like animals, following the impulse of their passions, without any more regard for the laws of justice than heathens who have no knowledge of God and think that there is nothing for man but birth and death. You will see the innocent mistreated, the guilty excused, the good despised, sinners honored and praised, the poor and humble oppressed, and human respect esteemed above virtue. You will see that laws are flouted, truth is ignored, shame is lost, the arts are corrupted, offices are abused, and the states of life are perverted. You will see how evil men, by means of theft, deceit, and other unlawful deeds, acquire great wealth and are feared and praised by all, while others, who scarcely deserve to be called men, hold high offices. You will see that men love and worship their money more than they do God and for its sake they violate every human and divine law, so that nothing remains of justice but its name.

When you have witnessed all these things, you will understand with what good reason the Psalmist could say: "The Lord hath looked down from heaven upon the children of men, to see if there be any that understand and seek God. They are all gone aside; they are become unprofitable together. There is none that doth good; no not one." [10] Likewise did Osee complain: "There is no truth and there is no mercy and there is no knowledge of God in the land. Cursing and lying and killing and theft and adultery have overflowed, and blood hath touched blood." [11]

Who would not wish to abandon such a world? Certainly Jeremias had such a desire when he said: "Who will give me in the wilderness a lodging place of wayfaring men, and I will leave my people and depart from them? Because they are all adulterers, an assembly of transgressors, and they have bent their tongue, as a bow, for lies and not for truth; they have strengthened themselves upon the earth, for they have proceeded from evil to evil, and Me they have not known, saith the Lord." [12]

These and many others are the miseries and evils that accompany the wretched happiness of this world, and through them you can perceive how much more bitterness than sweetness it carries with it. Besides being brief and wretched, the happiness of this world is also filthy, because it makes men carnal and impure; it is brutish, because it

[10] Ps. 13:2-3.   [11] Osee 4:1-2.   [12] Jer. 9:2-3.

makes men beasts; it is foolish, because it makes men fools and often deprives them of reason; it is inconstant, because it never remains the same; it is faithless and treacherous, because when we are enjoying it most, it leaves us and vanishes into the air.

One final evil which I cannot neglect to mention is that this world's happiness is false and deceptive. It appears to be what it is not and it promises to give what it cannot, and in this way it lures many souls to eternal ruin. Just as there are true gold and false gold, true jewels and paste jewels, so there are true goods and apparent goods, true happiness and that which appears to be happiness but is not. Such is the happiness of this world. Aristotle observed that there are some lies which, in spite of their falsehood, have more the appearance of truth than truth itself, and that there are some evils which, in spite of being truly evil, have more the appearance of good than things that are really good. Such is the happiness of this world, and for that reason ignorant persons are easily deceived, as birds are decoyed and fish are caught with the bait. It is the nature of corporeal things to present themselves to us under a pleasant guise and with an attractive appearance which promise joy and contentment, but when experience undeceives us, we feel the hook beneath the bait.

Accordingly, what is all the happiness of the world but a siren's song which lulls one to sleep? If it delights, it is to deceive us; if it lifts us up, it is to cast us down again; if it gladdens us, it is to sadden us. It gives pleasure at an exorbitant rate of interest. Its tranquillity is distressing, its security is without foundation, its fear is without cause, its labors without fruit, its tears without purpose, its projects without success, its hope vain, its joy fictitious, and its sorrow true.

In all this you can see how much this world is like hell itself, for if hell is a place of pain and torment, what else abounds more in this world? This is the fruit of the world; this is the merchandise that it sells; this is the treatment that one receives on every side. So St. Bernard said that were it not for the hope we have of obtaining a better life, this world would seem little better than hell itself.

CHAPTER 3

Man's True Happiness

HAVING seen how wretched and deceitful is the happiness of this world, it remains for us to consider that true happiness can be found only in God. If worldly men understood this well, they would not pursue mundane pleasures as they do. Therefore, I intend to prove this all-important truth, not only by the authority and testimony of faith, but also by arguments from reason.

No creature can enjoy perfect happiness until it attains its ultimate end, that is, the last perfection that is due to it according to its nature. Until it arrives at this state, it is necessarily restless and discontented, as is anyone who feels a need for that which he yet lacks. Now, what is the ultimate end of man, the possession of which constitutes his complete happiness? Undoubtedly, it is God, who is man's first beginning and last end. And just as it is impossible for man to have two beginnings, it is likewise impossible that he have two ultimate ends, for that would necessitate the existence of two gods.

Moreover, if God alone is man's last end and true happiness, it is impossible for man to find true happiness outside of God. As the glove is made for the hand and the scabbard for the sword, and they serve for no other purpose than that for which they were made, so the human heart, created as it is for God, cannot find rest in anything outside of God. In Him alone is it content; without Him it is poor and needy. The reason for this is that man's perfect happiness especially consists in the operation of his most noble faculties, intellect and will, and as long as these are restless, man himself cannot be tranquil and content. But these two faculties can never be at rest except in God alone. St. Thomas says that our intellect cannot know and understand so much as not to be capable and desirous of knowing more, if there is more to be known, and our will cannot love and enjoy so many goods as not to be capable of more, if more can be given. Therefore, these two faculties will never be satisfied until they find a universal object wherein are to be found all things and which, once it is known and loved, will leave no more truths to be known and no more goods to be loved. It follows from this that no created thing, not even the possession of the entire universe, can satisfy our heart, but only Him for whom it was created—God.

In order that you may understand this truth more clearly, consider the needle on a compass. The needle has been touched with a magnet and as a result it always points to the north. Observe how restless this needle is and how it fluctuates until it points to the north. Once this is done, the needle stops and remains fixed. So also, God created man with a natural inclination to Himself, and as long as man is separated from God, he remains restless, even though he possess all the treasures of the world. But once he has turned to God, he finds repose, as does the needle when it turns north, for in God man finds all his rest. Hence, he alone is happy who possesses God and he will be the closer to true beatitude who is closer to God. And since in this life the just are closer to God, they are the more happy, although the world does not understand their happiness.

Another argument, no less convincing than the former, is based on the principle that much more is required to make a thing perfect than to make it imperfect, for perfection requires that a thing be completely perfect, but imperfection requires only one defect. Moreover, perfect happiness requires that a man have all that he desires, and if only one thing is missing, this may contribute more to his unhappines than do all the other things to his happiness. I have seen people in high places and with great possessions who in spite of these things were most unhappy because they were made more wretched by the lack of something they yet desired and could not obtain than they were made happy by all that they had. However much a man may have, it will not give him satisfaction as long as he is tormented by a desire for something. It is not the possession of many things that makes a man happy, but the satisfaction and fulfillment of all his desires.

St. Augustine explained this beautifully when he wrote: "To my way of thinking, no man can be called truly happy who has not attained what he loves, whatever be the thing that he loves. Neither is he happy who does not love what he possesses, although the thing itself possessed be very good. For he who yet desires something he cannot obtain, remains wretched and tormented; he who desires that which is not worth desiring, deceives himself; and he who does not desire what deserves to be desired, is sick. From this it follows that our happiness consists in the possession and love of the supreme good and apart from this no man can be happy." Therefore, these three things, possession and love and the supreme good, make a man happy. Apart from this no man can be happy, no matter how much he possesses.

If this be true, rightly could the Psalmist exclaim: "O ye sons of men, how long will you be dull of heart? Why do you love vanity and seek after lying?" [1] He does well to refer both to vanity and to lying, for if the things of this world were merely vanity, which is to be nothing, this would be a small enough evil, but what is worse, they are also lies and deception, for they make us believe they are something when in reality they are nothing. Hence, Solomon says: "Favor is deceitful and beauty is vain." [2]

All this is proof of the hypocrisy of the world, for as hypocrites strive to cover up their faults, so worldly men try to dissimulate the true misery that they suffer. The first try to pass themselves off as saints, when in reality they are sinners; the second try to appear happy, when in reality they are wretched. If you look upon the grandeur of their state and the splendor of their homes, you will think they are the happiest of men, but if you approach more closely, you will find that they are quite different from what they appear to be. As a result, many who were once desirous of attaining a high station in life or great possessions, later reject all such things when they have had the opportunity to discover the thorns that lie hidden beneath the flower.

O sons of men, created in the image of God, redeemed by His blood, and destined to become companions of the angels, why do you love vanity and seek after lies, thinking that you can find rest in those false goods that never have given happiness and never will? Why have you left the banquet of the angels for the food of beasts? Why have you left the delights and perfumes of paradise for the bitterness

[1] Ps. 4:3.   [2] Prov. 31:30.

and stench of this world? Have not the calamities and disasters of daily life made you want to escape from the cruel
tyranny of this world?

We sometimes act like certain perverse women that have
fallen in love with a man who is worthless, who dines and
frolics with them at his good pleasure and beats and mis-
treats them every day, and yet in spite of such wretched
subjection and slavery, they still pursue him. If we cannot
find true happiness in this world but only in God, why do
we not seek it in Him? "Encircle the earth and sea and
travel where you will," says St. Augustine, "wherever you
go, you will be miserable if you do not go to God."

CHAPTER 4 ✄

The Path of Virtue

TO understand the function of the virtues, it is well to
recall that virtuous acts can be reduced to two classes: the
first are spiritual and internal, the second are visible and
external. In the first class we place the acts of the theological
virtues, which have God as their object and of which charity
has the first place as queen of all the others. To these we
may add acts of humility, chastity, mercy, patience, discretion, devotion, poverty of spirit, contempt of the world,
denial of self-will and love of the Cross, and similar virtuous acts. We call them spiritual and internal because they
are immanent operations, although they may also be manifested externally.

The second class of virtues comprises acts that are visible

and external, such as fasting, the discipline, silence, solitude, spiritual reading, prayer, chanting, pilgrimages, hearing Mass, listening to sermons, and all the observances and bodily ceremonies of the Christian and religious life. Although these acts also are primarily in the soul, their proper acts are more external than those of the first class of virtues, whose acts are often hidden and invisible, such as to believe, to love, to hope, to contemplate, to humble oneself interiorly, to sorrow for one's sins, to judge prudently, and so forth.

Of these two classes of virtuous acts there is no doubt that the first is more excellent and more necessary than the second. As Christ said to the Samaritan women: "The hour cometh, and now is, when the true adorers shall adore the Father in spirit and in truth. For the Father also seeketh such to adore Him. God is a spirit, and they that adore Him must adore Him in spirit and in truth." [1] Even the pagan philosophers understood this truth, for Aristotle has written that if the gods have a concern for human affairs, as it is reasonable to believe that they do, it is probable that they are most pleased with that which is best and most like themselves, namely, the mind or spirit of man. Therefore, they who adorn their spirit with the knowledge of truth and the correction of their appetites are undoubtedly most pleasing to the gods. Galenus, the prince of doctors, was also aware of this truth, for in writing of the composition and structure of the human body, he arrived at a point where the wisdom and providence of God was manifested in a remarkable manner. Overwhelmed by admiration at such great marvels and forgetting his profession as a doctor and becoming for the moment a theologian, he exclaimed: "Let others honor the gods with their sacrifices of a hundred oxen; I shall

[1] John 4:23–24

honor them by recognizing the greatness of their wisdom by which they have so wonderfully disposed all things, and the greatness of their power by which they have effected that which their wisdom ordained, and the greatness of their goodness so that they have given each of their creatures all that was necessary."

These are the words of a pagan philosopher, but what more could a perfect Christian say? What more could Galenus say if he had read the words of Osee: "For I desired mercy and not sacrifice, and the knowledge of God more than holocausts?" [2]

Notwithstanding the praise that is given to the internal acts of virtue, the external acts, although of lesser excellence, are very important. This can be seen by considering some of the external acts we have already mentioned. Solitude and the cloister prevent a man from seeing, hearing, and discussing a thousand things that would be dangerous not only for his peace and tranquillity, but also for his chastity and innocence. Silence is a great aid to devotion and prevents many sins of speech, as we read in Scripture: "In the multitude of words there shall not want sin; but he that refraineth his lips is most wise." [3] Fasting, besides being an act of the virtue of temperance and a satisfactory and meritorious work, if done under the impulse of charity, subdues the body, lifts the spirit, lessens the power of the adversary, disposes us for prayer, spiritual reading, and contemplation, saves us from the excesses of those who are overly fond of eating and drinking and from the reproaches, loquacity, and quarrels that arise after men are satiated. The reading of holy books, attendance at sermons, participation in prayer, singing hymns, and assistance at Divine Office are acts of religion and incentives to devotion and

[2] Os. 2:2.   [3] Prov. 10:19.

they serve to enlighten the intellect and inflame the will for spiritual things.

If you adhere to the doctrine we have expounded, you will avoid two extremes: that of the Pharisees and that of the heretics.[4] The Pharisees, a carnal and ambitious group who could see nothing but the external observance of the law, took no account of true justice, which is a spiritual and internal virtue. For that reason they had only the appearance of virtue without its substance, appearing good externally while within they were abominable. The heretics, on the other hand, having seen the error of the Pharisees, fled from one extreme to the other and rejected and disdained all external acts of virtue. But Catholic doctrine avoids these two extremes by giving proper recognition to both the internal and the external virtues, but it gives the internal virtues first place while not neglecting to give the external virtues the importance that is due them.

What is more deserving of love than virtue, in which all perfections are to be found? What is more deserving of honor than virtue? And if it is a question of beauty, Plato says that if the beauty of virtue could be seen, it would draw the whole world after it. If it is a question of utility, what is more useful and a greater basis for hope than virtue, by means of which we attain our highest good? If it be delight that we seek, then what greater delight than that of a good conscience? What greater delight than the consolations of the Holy Ghost which accompany virtue? If it is immortal fame that we desire, the just man will be remembered for all eternity but the name of the wicked will corrupt and disappear like smoke. If we desire wisdom, there

---

[4] Translator's note: Fray Louis is here referring to the Pharisaic doctrine of justification by external works alone and the Lutheran teaching on justification by faith alone.

is no greater wisdom than to know God and to know how to travel through life, using the right means to attain one's ultimate end. If it is a pleasant thing to be esteemed by men, the virtuous life causes a beauty that is pleasing not only to God and the angels but even to the wicked and one's own enemies.

The good of virtue is so absolute that it has nothing of evil in it. "Say to the just man that it is well." [5] Tell him that he was born in a propitious hour and that he will die in a propitious hour. Tell him that he shall be blessed in his life as well as in his death and in that which will follow after death. Tell him that he shall prosper in all things, in his pleasures and pains, in his labor and rest, and in his honors and dishonors, because for those who love God all things work together unto good. Tell him that although all the world be evil, he has nothing to fear, because the day of his redemption is at hand. Tell him that it is well, because the greatest of all goods, God Himself, is prepared for him and he is freed from the devil, who is the greatest of evils and man's worst enemy.

Tell the just man that it is well, for his name is written in the book of life. God the Father has taken him as His son, God the Son has taken him as His brother, and the Holy Ghost has taken him as His living temple. Tell him that it is well, for the path that he has taken and the resolution he has followed have worked out to his good: good for his soul and good for his body; good in the estimation of God and of men; good for this life and good for the life to come, because to those who seek first the kingdom of God, all things else shall be added. And even if some temporal affairs do not go well with the just man, they also will be to his greater good if they are borne with patience, because

[5] Isa. 3:10.

to those who have patience, losses become gains, sufferings bring merit, and battles win crowns.

Why will you be so cruel to yourself and so much your own enemy that you do not embrace something that is in every way to your own advantage? What better counsel could you take than the following? "Blessed are the undefiled in the way, who walk in the law of the Lord. Blessed are they that search His testimonies; that seek Him with their whole heart." [6] If, as the philosophers say, good is the object of our will and if better things are more deserving of our love, who has so vitiated your will that you do not embrace the great good of virtue? If you consider your obligation, is there any greater than that which you owe to God simply because He is what He is? If you look for benefits, what greater benefits than those we have received from God, for not only did He create us and redeem us with His own blood, but everything we have, body, soul, life, health, grace, good desires and resolutions, everything proceeds from Him who is the source of goodness. If you are motivated by self-interest, let all the angels and men declare whether there is anything more profitable to us than eternal glory and freedom from everlasting torment, which is the reward of virtue.

Having seen the perfection and beauty of virtue, repeat the words that were spoken of wisdom: "Her have I loved, and have sought her out from my youth and have desired to take her for my spouse, and I became a lover of her beauty. She glorifieth her nobility by being conversant with God; yea, and the Lord of all things hath loved her. For it is she that teacheth the knowledge of God and is the chooser of His works. And if riches be desired in life, what is richer than wisdom, which maketh all things? And if sense do

[6] Ps. 118:1-2.

work, who is a more artful worker than she of those things that are? And if a man love justice, her labors have great virtues, for she teacheth temperance and prudence and justice and fortitude, which are such things as men can have nothing more profitable in life. . . . I purposed, therefore, to take her to me to live with me, knowing that she will communicate to me of her good things, and will be a comfort in my cares and grief." [7]

We shall conclude this matter by quoting from a beautiful letter written by St. Cyprian: "There is but one peaceful and secure tranquillity and but one firm and perpetual security: when a man, freed from the storms and tempests of this world and placed in the secure haven and port of salvation, lifts his eyes from earth to heaven and, already admitted to the grace and companionship of the Lord, delights to see how all that which was esteemed in the opinion of the world has fallen to ruins in his heart. Such a man cannot desire anything of the world because he is now above the world. . . . It is not necessary to have many riches or ambitious projects to obtain this happiness; it is a gift of God which is bestowed on the devout soul. . . . Whence you, my brother, who are already enlisted in this heavenly army, work with all your energy to observe faithfully the discipline of this army by means of the Christian exercises. Take as your constant companions spiritual reading and prayer; sometimes speaking to God and at other times letting God speak to you. Let Him teach you His commandments; let Him dispose and order all the affairs of your life. Whomever God enriches, let no one consider poor. . . . All the edifices made of precious marble or laid over with gold will appear to you as dung when you understand that it is you who should first be adorned and that

[7] Wisd. 8:2–9.

this is a much more magnificent structure wherein God reposes as in a living temple and which the Holy Ghost has taken as His dwelling place. Let us, then, decorate this house with innocence; let us brighten it with the light and splendor of justice. . . . It will not deteriorate or tarnish, but will become even more beautiful with the resurrection of the body."

CHAPTER 5

The Gifts of the Holy Ghost

BY means of His gifts, the Holy Ghost governs the just and strengthens and sustains them in their spiritual life. It is fitting, therefore, that we should consider those gifts—what they are and how many they are—for it is important that the Christian have a clear knowledge of such matters.

The gifts of the Holy Ghost are seven in number: wisdom, understanding, counsel, fortitude, knowledge, piety, and fear of the Lord. In showing how these seven gifts were perfectly blended in Christ and in His mystical body, the Church, Isaias says: "There shall come forth a rod out of the root of Jesse, and a flower shall rise up out of His root. And the Spirit of the Lord shall rest upon Him: the spirit of wisdom and of understanding, the spirit of counsel and of fortitude, the spirit of knowledge and of godliness, and He shall be filled with the spirit of the fear of the Lord." [1]

The gifts proceed in an orderly fashion and gradually ascend by degrees. From the fear of the Lord, the soul

[1] Isa. 11:1–2.

rises to the other gifts, one after the other, to arrive at the most lofty and excellent of all, which is the gift of wisdom. Fear of the Lord arouses and awakens in us a fear of God; not the servile fear which the Apostle calls the spirit of bondage,[2] but a fear proper to the adopted sons of God. Such a fear enables the Christian to venerate his merciful Father with filial reverence, striving conscientiously never to offend Him in the slightest way nor to lose His grace and love. St. Augustine calls it a chaste fear which is born of charity.

The gift of piety teaches and inclines us to honor God with ardent and joyful affection and to love our neighbor for the love of God, even when he is not deserving of our love. The gift of knowledge impels us to recognize our defects and learn how to live innocently and prudently in this evil world without committing sin. The gift of fortitude enables us to remain strong and constant in Christ, so that neither the pleasures nor the difficulties of this world can separate us in any way from the honor and service of God. It makes us yearn and thirst for the just life.

The gift of counsel teaches, advises, and directs us so that we may diligently put into effect those things which we prudently judge to be most conducive to our salvation and for the greater glory of God. The gift of understanding discloses to us the true and Catholic meaning of divine things. Through the gift of wisdom the soul is completely detached from all temporal and earthly things so that it may enjoy the contemplation of God and experience the most tender consolation and a taste for divine delights.

We should beg God to actuate these gifts in our souls through the merits of Jesus Christ, His Son, from whom they flow as from an abundant spring. So the Savior tells

[2] Rom. 8:15.

us: "If you, then, being evil, know how to give good gifts to your children, how much more will your Father from heaven give the good Spirit to them that ask Him?" [3] And St. James says: "If any of you want wisdom, let him ask of God, who giveth to all men abundantly and upbraideth not, and it shall be given him. But let him ask in faith, nothing wavering." [4]

The gifts of the Holy Ghost also facilitate the operations of the virtues, animating and strengthening them so that they will always be ready for the performance of their proper acts. Faith, hope, and charity are perfected by the gifts of wisdom and understanding; prudence, by the gifts of knowledge and counsel; justice, by the gift of piety; fortitude, by the gift of fortitude; and temperance, by the fear of the Lord.

The gifts also help to destroy the seven evil inclinations which the prince of devils arouses in those who live according to the desires of the flesh and the law of sin. Thus, the fear of the Lord destroys pride and disposes for true humility, for Solomon says: "The fruit of humility is fear of the Lord." [5] The gift of piety, which makes us desire the good of our neighbor with a joyful heart, replaces envy, as St. Peter says: "In patience, godliness; and in godliness, love of brotherhood." [6] The gift of knowledge represses anger, which is usually accompanied by folly, as it is written: "Be not quickly angry, for anger resteth in the bosom of a fool." [7] He who has the gift of knowledge understands that he must not be angry at those who have unjustly offended him, but that he must treat them as one treats children, the sick, or those who are mentally ill. Thus, parents, friends, and

[3] Luke 11:13.   [4] Jas. 1:5–6.   [5] Prov. 22:4.
[6] Cf. II Pet. 1:5–8.   [7] Eccles. 7:10.

doctors are the objects of much abuse and recrimination, but they suffer it all with patience, and will even endure much more until the sick have regained their health or the demented have been restored to sanity.

The gift of fortitude dissipates the spirit of sloth and spiritual sadness and rids the soul of its morbid boredom. It brightens and gladdens the soul and sustains it in hope, as Isaias says: "In silence and in hope shall your strength be." [8] Likewise we read in the Book of Esdras: "Be not sad; for the joy of the Lord is our strength." [9] And St. James writes: "Is any of you sad? Let him pray. Let him sing." [10]

The spirit of counsel uproots avarice, because he who is instructed by this gift, readily selects what is better. He enriches his soul with spiritual goods and lays up treasures in heaven where they can never be lost, instead of gathering the riches of the earth, which the worms eat, the moths consume, or thieves steal. To this effect, the Savior asked: "What shall it profit a man, if he gain the whole world, and suffer the loss of his soul?" [11] The gift of understanding destroys gluttony, which enslaves those who give themselves to this vice, as we read in Scripture: "Do not become like the horse and the mule, who have no understanding." [12] The gift of wisdom destroys lust, for they who possess the spirit of wisdom delight in God and abhor the pleasures of carnal men, who are like beasts in their own excrement. [13]

Let us, therefore, beg God, our Father, to grant us these seven gifts through the merits of His Son, Jesus Christ, saying with the Psalmist: "Create a clean heart in me, O God, and renew a right spirit within my bowels. Cast me not away from Thy face and take not Thy Holy Spirit from me. Re-

[8] Isa. 30:15. [9] Cf. II Esdr. 8:10. [10] Jas. 5:13.
[11] Mark 8:36. [12] Ps. 31:9. [13] Cf. Joel 1:17.

store unto me the joy of Thy salvation and strengthen me with a perfect spirit." [14]

CHAPTER 6

Venial and Mortal Sin

SIN, says St. Ambrose, is the breaking of the law of God or disobedience to the divine commandments. In other words, there are two general classes of sin: sin of commission (the performance of an evil deed, such as robbery or murder), and sin of omission (the failure to perform some prescribed good work, such as not to fast or not to pray). The sin of commission, since it consists in performing an act, is very evident and easy to recognize; the sin of omission, since it is the neglect to perform an act, is not so clearly manifested. For that reason some spiritual persons, especially if they are simple people, find no sins of which to accuse themselves. Since they do not fall into many sins of commission and they do not readily perceive their sins of omission, they find nothing to confess.

Sins are also divided according to their gravity: those which are generally mortal sins, those which are generally venial sins, and those which may be either venial or mortal. It is expedient that we guard ourselves against all sin of any kind, but especially against mortal sins, because by such sins we lose sanctifying grace and all the infused virtues, except faith and hope, which are lost only by sins committed directly against these two virtues.

[14] Ps. 50:12–14.

In order to distinguish between mortal and venial sins, two rules should be kept in mind. The first and general rule is that mortal sin is directly opposed to charity, and by charity we here understand the love of God and neighbor. Accordingly, anything contrary to the honor of God or the good of one's neighbor in a serious matter is a mortal sin. Such sins are called mortal because they kill the spiritual life.

The second rule is more particular and it states that anything contrary to the Commandments of God or the Church is a mortal sin. But it is to be noted that a sin which is generally mortal may become venial under certain circumstances, if it is a question of light matter or if the act was defective through lack of deliberation or full consent of the will. In such instances that which in itself is mortally sinful is no more than a venial sin.

Venial sins are so named because they are more readily pardoned than mortal sins. Some persons commit venial sins in spite of their good resolutions, usually out of laziness or negligence or as the result of the remnants of evil habits that yet remain in the soul. Others have a lax conscience and do not make sufficient good resolutions. They are content merely to avoid mortal sin, and apart from that, they like to eat and drink and waste much time in talk and in other pastimes to which generally there are many venial sins attached. Such persons will never be pardoned these sins no matter how often they confess them, unless they make a true resolution to amend their lives, for they seem to have every intention of continuing to commit such sins. Such people live in constant danger because, as St. Thomas points out, he who does not have the firm determination to improve, is likely to become worse. A man who tries to remain stationary in the middle of a fast-flowing river will be carried away by the current; so also he is in much danger of falling back in the spiritual life who does not strive to advance. However, those who commit venial sins through carelessness or negligence are more quickly converted and more easily obtain pardon, for it is not in man's power, however perfect he be, to avoid all venial sins. "A just man shall fall seven times and shall rise again; but the wicked shall fall down into evil." [1] St. Augustine says that saintly men have reason to weep for their faults but in spite of this they are truly saints because they have a holy desire to do all that is required for perfect sanctity.

As to those sins that may be either venial or mortal, they are usually the more serious venial sins and very close to mortal sins. For that reason certain sins are to be avoided with greatest diligence. The first is envy, for although it frequently concerns light matter and is more a movement of the passions than a deliberate act of the will, it militates against charity, which is the very life of the soul. Therefore, a man ought to flee from this sin as from death itself. The second sin is anger, and although in the majority of instances it is not a mortal sin, it is nevertheless serious, for it upsets the soul and disturbs peace of conscience. The third sin is criticism, which sometimes becomes detraction, for when one begins to speak of the public and known faults of another, he easily proceeds to reveal another's secret sins and thus blackens the reputation of his neighbor. The fourth sin is ridicule or derision of one's neighbor, which has all the ugliness of the former sin but adds to it a certain pride, presumption, disdain, and contempt that are abominable to God and man.

The fifth sin is rash judgment of one's neighbor, that is,

[1] Prov. 24:16.

interpreting as evil that which could as easily be interpreted as good. This sin is found more often in women than in men. If they lack something in their home or are jealous of their husbands, their sorrow or distrust gives rise to suspicions and they pass judgments on others, however light the reasons for so doing. What is worse, they sometimes openly express what is in their heart and commit two sins: that of judging their neighbor and that of bearing false testimony. The sixth sin is lying and flattery, which may become mortal if it is a question of grave matter; moreover, if it is accompanied by damage to one's neighbor, there is an obligation to make restitution. Such are the sins into which people most frequently fall and we ought all to avoid them as much as possible.

Take care that you do not become one of those persons who, when they know that a sin is not a mortal sin, do not hesitate to commit that sin time after time. Heed the words of the wise man who tells you that he who disdains the little things will soon fall in the great things. Although it is true that neither seven nor seven thousand venial sins make one mortal sin, St. Augustine warns us: "Do not underestimate venial sins because they are small, but fear them because they are so numerous." However small they may be, they do much damage to the soul. They weaken devotion, disturb peace of conscience, make the heart torpid, smother the fervor of charity, soften the rigor of the ascetical life, and offer resistance to the Holy Ghost. There is no enemy, however small, which, if we ignore it, cannot do us much harm.

Let us take care to cleanse ourselves of the stains of venial sin, for St. John tells us that nothing stained can enter the heavenly Jerusalem. Therefore, if these stains are not purged in this life, they must be cleansed in the fires of purgatory which, although they are not eternal, are more painful than anything that we could suffer in this life.

The remedies against venial sin are the following: humble accusation of one's sins, fervent recitation of the Our Father, the use of bodily mortifications, and other pious practices. Every man must render an account on the day of judgment for every idle word. Therefore Job says: "I feared all my works, knowing that Thou didst not spare the offender." [2] And the Apostle tells us: "Therefore thou art inexcusable, O man, whosoever thou art that judgest. For wherein thou judgest another, thou condemnest thyself. For thou dost the same things which thou judgest. For we know that the judgment of God is, according to truth, against them that do such things. And thinkest thou this, O man, that judgest them who do such things, and dost the same, that thou shalt escape the judgment of God? . . . Knowest thou not that the benignity of God leadeth thee to penance?" [3]

We should notice, however, that there is a difference between imperfections and venial sins. Some things are imperfections but are not sins, as happens when one neglects to perform a good work that he could have performed, for we are not always obliged in each instance to perform the good work. One could give more alms than he does or pray more than he prays or fast more than he fasts, but to fail in such things is not always a sin; it may be only a weakness or imperfection. Nevertheless, the devout person does not fail to accuse himself of such things, because in so doing he humbles himself before the representative of Christ and endeavors to depart from his imperfections.

Turning now to a consideration of mortal sin, we should

[2] Job 9:28.   [3] Rom. 2:1–4.

observe that there are two deformities in every mortal sin: the disordered love of some created thing, which moves us to sin, and a disregard for God's laws, which we despise when we sin. The second deformity is more serious than the first, as David admitted when he accused himself of his sin: "To Thee only have I sinned." [4] What could be more unworthy of the great majesty of God than to place before it something so lowly as a created good? How similar to the action of the Jews who preferred Barabbas to Christ! What is this but to take from God the crown and glory that are due to Him and to attribute them to some created thing? For he who esteems any created thing more than he does God, places his ultimate end in that creature.

In order to avoid so great an evil, we should observe that a man descends to mortal sin by three steps: by suggestion, delight, and consent. By suggestion we mean that the world, the flesh, or the devil arouses in us some evil thought; by delight we mean the complacency and interest with which we receive the evil suggestion; by consent we mean that the will, moved by pleasure or the prospect of pleasure, deliberately consents to the evil. It is of great importance to understand this procession of evil, because he who wishes to avoid the last stages must also avoid the first inclinations. The first seed is the evil thought, which proceeds from the temptation, and if one suffocates this seed and uproots the first sprouts, all the branches and fruits that would have proceeded from it are likewise destroyed. Consequently, one of the principal counsels given to the Christian is that he should resist evil thoughts. But if he acts otherwise, he will offend God by dallying with the evil thought, and he will have to exert all the greater effort to rid himself of it if he has retained the thought for any length of time.

[4] Ps. 50:6.

Although the Christian should carefully avoid all mortal sin, he should be especially careful of the following, for they are frequently committed. The first sin is blasphemy, which is closely related to the three worst sins: infidelity, despair, and direct hatred of God. Women do not usually commit this sin, but they commit others that are very similar to it: they turn against God in the labors that He sends to them, they complain against Him and His providence, or they say that they do not like the kind of life He has bestowed on them.

The second sin, taking the name of the Lord in vain, is also directly against God and is for that reason more serious than sins committed against one's neighbor. It is true, however, that if a man does this through carelessness or without due consideration, he may be excused from mortal sin, for where there is no deliberation or full consent of the will, there is no serious sin.

The third sin which the Christian should especially avoid is every kind of lust. A man can fall into sins of this type by thought, word, deed, desire, or morose delectation. Morose delectation occurs when a man deliberately takes pleasure in a lustful thought, even if he has no intention of performing the deed. This is as much a mortal sin as the others. The man in such a position realizes what he is thinking and wishes to retain that type of thought. However, if such thoughts come to mind spontaneously and the man does not realize what he is doing, but later recollects himself and endeavors to rid himself of such thoughts, he is not guilty of mortal sin, because of the lack of deliberation.

The fourth sin is that of hatred, and it is usually accompanied by desires for revenge. If the animosity or hatred between persons does not reach the point of a desire for revenge, it is not usually a mortal sin, but otherwise it is generally serious. The fifth sin is willful possession of property against the will of the owner. As long as one retains another's goods in this fashion, he is in the state of sin, just as he would be if he were at enmity with another or were living in concubinage. For it is not only a sin to take the goods of another, but also to retain those goods against the will of the rightful owner. Nor does it suffice merely to have the intention of making restitution at some later date, when he is able to make restitution at once, for such a person not only has the obligation of making restitution but of doing so as soon as he can. But if a man cannot make restitution at all or if he cannot do so without reducing himself to abject poverty, then there is no obligation to restitution at that time, because God does not demand the impossible.

The sixth sin is that of violating the precepts of the Church, which oblige under serious obligation, for example, to attend Mass on Sundays and holy days, to confess once a year, to receive Holy Communion during the Easter season, and to fast or abstain on the days prescribed. As to the attendance at Mass on days of obligation, we must observe that parents are obliged to see to it that their children hear Mass on the prescribed days. Many parents are negligent in this matter and they will one day have to give God a strict account. It is true, of course, that if one is prevented from attending Mass because of some urgent and reasonable necessity, no sin is committed, because necessity excuses from the law.

Let us now consider the effects of mortal sin. First of all, the sinner loses the grace of the Holy Ghost, which is the greatest gift that God could give to any creature. Charity also is lost, as well as all the infused virtues (except faith and hope) and the gifts of the Holy Ghost. The sinner is deprived of the right to the kingdom of heaven, for this right proceeds from the possession of grace, as the Apostle tells us when he says that glory is given through grace. Having lost the status of an adopted son of God, the sinner no longer enjoys the special care of divine providence which is given to the just. Moreover, the man in mortal sin loses the peace and serenity of a good conscience, the consolations of the Holy Ghost, and the merit of all the good works that he has performed throughout his life. He also loses the full participation in the goods of the Church, to the extent that he cannot share in them as completely as he did while in the state of grace.

All this is lost by a single mortal sin. And what does the sinner gain by his sin? As long as he remains in sin he is a condemned man, doomed to suffer the pains of hell for all eternity. His name is erased from the book of life and instead of a child of God, he has become a slave of the devil. But of all the losses, the greatest by far is that the sinner has lost God, and this is the root and cause of all the other evil effects of sin. To lose God is to cease to have Him as one's Father and Good Shepherd and to make of Him a severe judge and an enemy. Should not one weep if he has lost so great a good?

How confounded he will be who has the misfortune to fall into so many evils! O miserable soul, consider what you were and what you are now. Formerly you were a spouse of the Most High, a temple of the living God, a chosen vessel, and an heir to the kingdom of heaven. All this you once were, and as often as I say that you were once these things, you have reason to weep.

What is the meaning of this great change? Why has the bride of God become an adulteress with Satan? Why has a temple of the Holy Ghost become a nest of vipers, the chosen vessel a cistern of corruption, and the fellow-citizen of the saints a companion of devils? She who once flew through the heavens like a dove, now crawls upon the earth like a serpent.

Weep, then, wretched soul, and free yourself from this sad condition. The angels weep for you, the heavens weep for you, and all the saints weep for you. The tears of St. Paul are shed for you because you have sinned and have not done penance. The prophets weep for you because they see that the fury of divine justice will descend upon you. For you, much more than for the fallen walls of Jerusalem, Jeremias weeps, because he sees that a daughter of Sion has lost her beauty.

No one can say in this life: "My heart is clean; I am free from sin." Therefore, it is well for us to know what are the remedies for sin. The first and principal remedy is the sacrament of penance, without which a man in mortal sin uses the other remedies in vain. After baptism, this is the most important medicine that has been prescribed for us by the divine Physician. The second remedy is sorrow for sin, the sacrifice of a contrite heart which God never despises. Thus David tells us that God looks upon the hearts of the humble and does not despise their prayers and St. Augustine says that it is not enough to turn away from our sins, but that we must add to this the weeping of humility, the sorrow of penance, and the performance of works of mercy. The third remedy is the atonement for sin by almsgiving which, as Tobias tells us, frees a man from every sin and from death and does not allow him to pass into darkness. The fourth remedy is to seek pardon for our sins by forgiving our neighbors' offenses against us, for Christ tells us that if we forgive our neighbors, the heavenly Father will forgive us. The fifth remedy is to give spiritual help for the salvation of our neighbors, for St. James teaches that he who converts a sinner from his evil way delivers his own soul from death and covers a multitude of his own sins. The sixth remedy is humble prayer, similar to that of the man who prayed: "O God, be merciful to me, a sinner." The seventh and last remedy is the love of God, which cleanses the soul as fire cleanses iron of its rust. "Many sins are forgiven her because she has loved much."

CHAPTER 7 ✒

Sins Against the Holy Ghost

THE sins against the Holy Ghost are those grievous sins of which Christ said that they will not be forgiven either in this life or in the next. God will not give His grace to those who do not abhor sin and resolve to lead a good life, and this is the condition of those who commit sins against the Holy Ghost, for out of pure malice they reject the mercy and grace that the Holy Ghost offers.

A man can sin in three ways: through sloth, willful ignorance, or malice. To sin through sloth is to sin against the Father, to whom is attributed power, and in this way St. Peter sinned when he denied Christ.[1] To sin through willful ignorance is to sin against the Son, to whom wisdom is attributed, and in this way St. Paul sinned when he persecuted the Church.[2] To sin through malice is to sin against the Holy Ghost, to whom we attribute goodness, and in this way the Pharisees sinned.

[1] Cf. Matt. 26:25.   [2] Cf. Gal. 1:13.

Theologians enumerate six sins against the Holy Ghost: presumption, despair, resistance of a known truth, envy of another's spiritual good, obstinacy in evil, and final impenitence. Presumption is an excessive confidence in divine mercy to the extent that a man puts aside all fear of the Lord and abandons himself recklessly to every kind of sin. Such is the attitude of those who are so confident of divine mercy that they expect to reach heaven without performing any works of penance. They are totally unmindful of the words of the Apostle: "And thinkest thou this, O man, . . . that thou shalt escape the judgment of God? Or despiseth thou the riches of His goodness and patience and longsuffering? Knowest thou not that the benignity of God leadeth thee to penance? But according to thy hardness and impenitent heart, thou treasurest up to thyself wrath, against the day of wrath, and revelation of the just judgment of God." [3] Ecclesiasticus also warns us against this sin in the following words: "Be not without fear about sin forgiven, and add not sin upon sin. And say not, 'The mercy of the Lord is great; He will have mercy on the multitude of my sins.' For mercy and wrath quickly come from Him, and His wrath looketh upon sinners." [4]

The second sin against the Holy Ghost is despair or lack of trust in divine mercy. This occurs when a man abandons all hope of obtaining pardon from God or of attaining eternal life. Cain sinned in this way when he said: "My iniquity is greater than that I may deserve pardon." [5] Judas also sinned in this way when he hanged himself. But we know that in this life it is never too late for repentance, as was manifested by the thief on the cross.

The third sin against the Holy Ghost is deliberate resistance of a known truth, not of any truth at all, but of a

[3] Rom. 2:3–5.   [4] Ecclus. 5:7.   [5] Gen. 4:13.

divine truth, with the result that the purity of faith is corrupted. In this way the Pharisees sinned, for they knowingly denied Christ even though they could not deny the truth of His miracles. The Psalmist refers to such sinners as those who sit "in the chair of pestilence"; [6] St. Peter calls them "lying teachers who bring in sects of perdition"; [7] and St. Paul says that they are heretics, corrupted in their intellects and reprobate in the faith, deceived by the spirit of error, and perverted and condemned by their own judgments.

The fourth sin against the Holy Ghost is envy of the spiritual goods of one's neighbor, and this occurs when a man is saddened at the virtues and gifts which God mercifully bestows upon another. This sin seems more proper to devils than to men, for Satan is exceedingly saddened to see grace preserved and increased in us. Some of the Jews sinned in this way, for they labored so strenuously to destroy the grace of the gospel at the very time that it was first being preached.[8]

The fifth sin against the Holy Ghost is obstinacy in evil and this takes place when a man clings so stubbornly to his evil ways that he cannot be made to depart from them. Such was the case with Pharao, who had so often been warned and punished by God but would not cease from his tyranny and died in his sin.[9] Such also are they of whom the Psalmist spoke when he said that they are "like the deaf asp that stoppeth her ears, which will not hear the voice of the charmers," that is, the teaching of the Church.[10] They seem to say: "Depart from us; your way of thinking be far from us." [11]

[6] Ps. 1:1.
[7] Cf. II Pet. 2:1.
[8] Acts 4:2.
[9] Cf. Exod. 5:6.
[10] Cf. Ps. 57:5.
[11] Cf. Job 22:17.

The sixth sin against the Holy Ghost is that of final impenitence, which happens when a man does not wish to put an end to his sins but proposes never to do penance and never to be converted from his evil ways. The death of such sinners is described by the Psalmist as "very evil," [12] for these men, although they may not say so in words, manifest by their deeds the words of Isaias: "We have entered into a league with death, and we have made a covenant with hell." [13]

Such are the sins against the Holy Ghost and since they are more grievous than any others and are seldom pardoned, we must be sufficiently armed against them, being mindful of the words of the Apostle: "Grieve not the Holy Spirit," [14] and the words of the Psalmist: "Today if you shall hear His voice, harden not your hearts." [15] For, as we read in the Book of Ecclesiasticus, "a hard heart shall fear evil at the last." [16]

In addition to the sins against the Holy Ghost, there are others that cry to heaven for vengeance. The first is the sin of murder, which was the sin of Cain, to whom God said: "The voice of thy brother's blood crieth to Me from the earth." [17] The second is the abominable sin of sodomy, of which God said: "The men of Sodom were very wicked, and sinners before the face of the Lord beyond measure." [18] And the angels said to Lot: "For we will destroy this place because their cry is grown loud before the Lord." [19]

The third sin is oppression of the poor, against which God spoke in Exodus: "Thou shalt not molest a stranger nor afflict him, for yourselves also were strangers in the

---

[12] Cf. Ps. 33:22.   [13] Isa. 28:15.   [14] Eph. 4:30.
[15] Ps. 94:8.   [16] Ecclus. 3:27.   [17] Gen. 4:10.
[18] Gen. 13:13.   [19] Gen. 19:13.

land of Egypt. You shall not hurt a widow or an orphan. If you hurt them they will cry out to Me and I will hear their cry, and My rage shall be enkindled and I will strike you with the sword, and your wives shall be widows and your children fatherless." [20] Pharao and the Egyptians were afflicted with many plagues and afterward were drowned in the sea because they oppressed the children of Israel. "I have seen the affliction of My people in Egypt," said the Lord, "and I have heard their cry because of the rigor of them that are over the works. And knowing their sorrow I am come down to deliver them out of the hands of the Egyptians." [21] Again, speaking through Isaias, the Lord warned us: "Woe to them that make wicked laws, and when they write, write in justice to oppress the poor in judgment and do violence to the cause of the humble of My people, that widows might be their prey and that they might rob the fatherless." [22]

The fourth sin that cries to heaven for vengeance is to defraud laborers of their wages. St. James says of this sin: "Behold the hire of the laborers who have reaped down your fields, which by fraud has been kept back by you, crieth, and the cry of them hath entered into the ears of the Lord of Sabaoth." [23] No less strong are the words of Ecclesiasticus: "The bread of the needy is the life of the poor; he that defraudeth them thereof is a man of blood. He that taketh away the bread gotten by sweat, is like him that killeth his neighbor." [24] In addition to this, the divine law commands us: "Thou shalt not refuse the hire of the needy and the poor, whether he be thy brother or a stranger that dwelleth with thee in the land and is within thy gates. But thou shalt pay him the price of his labor the same day,

[20] Exod. 22:21–24.   [21] Exod. 3:7–8.   [22] Isa. 1–2.
[23] Jas. 5:4.   [24] Ecclus. 34:25–26.

before the going down of the sun, because he is poor, and with it maintaineth his life, lest he cry against thee to the Lord and it be reputed to thee for a sin." [25]

These four sins are enumerated in Scripture so that we may know how grievous they are and how severely they will be punished by God, both in this life and in the next. The fruit that we gain from a consideration of this doctrine is that we learn the gravity of sins and we are urged to avoid grave sin with greater fear and to repent with greater sorrow of any fault we may have incurred in these matters. We also learn what a great difference there is between the wise man and the fool, the just man and the sinner, according to the words of Solomon: "A wise man feareth and declineth from evil; the fool leapeth over and is confident." [26] "The path of the just, as a shining light, goeth forward and increaseth even to perfect day. The way of the wicked is darksome; they know not where they fall." [27]

CHAPTER 8 ✍

The Slavery of Sin

"AMEN, amen I say to you, that whosoever committeth sin is the servant of sin. Now the servant abideth not in the house forever, but the Son abideth forever. If, therefore, the Son shall make you free, you shall be free indeed." [1] In these words the Lord gives us to understand that there are

[25] Deut. 24:14–15.   [26] Prov. 14:16.   [27] *Ibid.*, 4:18–19.
[1] John 8:34–36.

two types of liberty: one which has the appearance of liberty but in reality is false, and the other which is true liberty. That is a false liberty wherein the body is free but the soul is held captive by being subject to the tyranny of sin and passion. True liberty, on the other hand, is that in which the soul is free of all tyranny, whether the body be free or captive.

The reason why we call liberty of soul a true liberty is because the soul is incomparably more noble than the body. For that reason, he is truly free who enjoys liberty of soul, but he enjoys only apparent freedom whose soul is enslaved while his body has complete liberty of action. And if you ask me to whom such a man is enslaved, I shall answer that he is a slave of the most base and despicable tyrant that can be imagined—sin. The truth of this statement is borne out by the words of our Lord: "Whosoever committeth sin is the servant of sin." [2]

But the sinner is not only the slave of sin; he is also the slave of the principal instigators of sin: the world, the flesh, and the devil. For he who is a servant of the son is likewise a servant of the parents, and these three things are the parents of sin. For that reason they are called enemies of the soul, because once they gain dominion over the soul they subject it to the tyranny of sin. Yet there is this difference among them: the world and the devil cater to the flesh, in much the same way that Eve persuaded Adam and led him to sin. Hence, St. Paul designates the flesh as sin and theologians refer to the flesh as the *fomes peccati,* which signifies that the flesh is the fuel which sustains the fire of sin. However, we commonly refer to the flesh as sensuality or concupiscence, to signify the disordered sensitive appetites or passions which incline us to sin.

[2] John 8:34.

An excessive attraction for the things that we desire makes us strive to obtain them at any cost and to overcome every obstacle that lies in our path, even when the thing desired is forbidden by the law of God. For that reason St. Basil advises that the principal weapon against sin is holy desires. It is evident from this that the sensitive appetite is one of the principal tyrants to which evil men are enslaved when, as the Apostle says, they are "sold under sin." [3] St. Paul does not mean that the sinner loses his free will through sin, for he will never lose that, however many sins he may commit, but that the sinner's free will becomes so flaccid and his passions become so strong that the sinner is under the sway of his sensitive appetite.

If you wish to understand something of the power and tyranny of the passions, consider the evils they have caused and still cause in the world. Consider what an adulterous wife will do to satisfy her disordered passion. She knows full well that if her husband should catch her in the act he would possibly kill her and thus at one and the same time she would lose her life, her honor, her home, her children, and her soul. Nevertheless, so great is the power of passion that it makes the wife ignore all these evils and drink eagerly of the horrible cup of sin. What other tyrant has ever commanded that a slave obey him under the risk of losing so much? What slavery could be more demanding and rigorous than this? They who suffer under the tyranny of this vice can scarcely be called their own masters, and neither the fear of God, of death, of hell, nor the possible loss of life, honor, and heaven itself deter them from their evil way nor enable them to break the chains of their captivity.

And what shall I say of the jealousy, fear, suspicions,

[3] Cf. Rom. 7:14.

dread, and dangers in which such persons live day and night, risking life and soul for sensual pleasures? Does any tyrant in the whole world have such power over the body of his slaves as this appetite does over the human heart? No servant is so bound to his master that he does not have some moments in which he may rest from his duties, but this vice and others like it are such that once they have gained control of the heart, a man scarcely has time for anything else. Thus we read in Ecclesiasticus: "Wine and women make wise men fall." [4] A man may be so absorbed by this vice that however wise he may be, he becomes as useless and helpless in the affairs of human life as if he had drunk large quantities of wine. O pestilential vice, destroyer of nations, death of virtue, perverter of good intentions, intoxication of wise men, foolishness of old men, fury and flame of young men, and common scourge of the human race!

But tyranny is not found in this vice alone; it is common to many others as well. If you do not think so, consider the vainglorious and ambitious man. See how he lives, a slave to his ambition. Everything in his life is directed to this one end. Whatever he does, he does so that he will make the best appearance and be praised and admired. Whatever he does becomes a net or snare to capture the applause of men and gain popularity.

Who is more foolish than the wretched man who spends his whole life seeking the smoke and air of glory and praise? He cannot do as he pleases, cannot dress as he pleases, and cannot go where he pleases. Sometimes he does not even go to church or speak with good people, for fear of what the world will say. What is equally as bad, he is forced to spend

[4] Ecclus. 19:2.

much more than he wishes and even more than he can afford.

And what shall I say of the miser, who is not only a slave of money but an idolator, for he worships and obeys its every command. For the sake of money he will fast and even take the bread from his own mouth. He loves money more than he loves his God and as a result, he sins against God time and time again for the sake of money. Money is his rest, his glory, his hope. His heart and mind are so fixed on wealth that he is forgetful of self and everyone else. Is such a man the master of his own wealth and able to do with it as he wishes? Or is he not the slave and captive of money? The avaricious man does not use money; money uses him.

What greater slavery than slavery to our own passions? You call him a prisoner who is confined behind bars or whose hands and feet are bound; how is he not also a prisoner whose soul is shackled by the disorderly affection for some created good? When this happens, there is no faculty in a man that remains perfectly free. He is no longer master of himself, but a slave of that which he loves, for whatever he loves, holds his heart captive. And it matters not what kind of bonds hold him prisoner if the best part of a man is thus enslaved.

Neither does it lessen the slavery if a man freely chooses to be a prisoner or captive; indeed, it will be all the more dangerous as it is voluntary. And there is no greater slavery than for a man to be so captivated by the object of his passion as to close his eyes to God, truth, honesty, and the laws of justice. Thus the drunkard is not master of himself, but wine rules him; the avaricious man is not master of himself, but the servant of money. And if the slavery itself is a torment, consider the misery that these wretched men suffer when they cannot achieve that which they desire and yet cannot cease to desire it, so that they know not what to do or which way to turn. Such men must say to their ruling passion: "I love you and I hate you, because I cannot live with you nor can I live without you."

If these were the only shackles or bonds, the sinner's lot would not be so wretched, for if a man is attacked by only one enemy, he is less likely to despair of victory. But what of the many other bonds that hold the sinner a prisoner? Some men are so fearful that they cannot extricate themselves from any difficulty or evil. Others are melancholy and as a result, they also may become fearful or even vehement. Still others are timid and everything appears great to them and worthy of great esteem, because to the small heart everything appears great. Others are naturally vehement in all their desires, as is frequently the case with women, of whom the Philosopher says that they either love or they hate because they do not know how to moderate their affections.

All these persons suffer to some extent from the tyranny of their passions and if it is a lamentable state to be bound by one chain and to be the slave of one master, what must it be to be bound with so many chains and to be a slave of so many masters? If man's dignity rests on his reason and free will, what can be more contrary to these two faculties than the passions? For passion blinds reason and takes the will captive. From all this you can see the danger and harm of any disordered passion, for it drags a man down from the throne of his dignity, it obscures his reason and perverts his free will, so that a man is no longer a man but a beast. Such is the wretched slavery of those who are not ruled by God or reason but by their passions.

CHAPTER 9

Safeguards Against Sin

NOW that we have seen the various types of sin and the means by which we may purge ourselves of sin, let us consider the ways in which we can protect ourselves against sin. The first safeguard is to arouse in our hearts the firm resolution to die rather than commit a serious sin. Just as a virtuous wife is prepared to die rather than betray her husband, so the Christian should be so loyal to God that he would endure any hardship rather than betray his God. And in order to arouse in your heart this holy resolve, it will be of great help to recall what a man loses through mortal sin. When you see that the evil effects of sin are so numerous and so serious, you will be amazed that certain men can fall into serious sin so easily.

In the first place, mortal sin deprives a man of the grace of God, which is His greatest gift to us. For grace is a supernatural quality which enables man to participate in the divine nature and which makes him God, so to speak. Mortal sin also destroys man's friendship with God, and if it is a great loss to be deprived of the friendship of the great ones of this world, how much greater to lose that of the King of heaven and earth? Lastly, serious sin causes the loss of the infused virtues and the gifts of the Holy Ghost, which adorn and beautify the soul of the just and fortify it against the power of Satan.

Moreover, the sinner is deprived of the right to the kingdom of heaven, which is an effect of sanctifying grace, for

St. Paul tells us that grace gives life everlasting.[1] He loses the spirit of adoption which makes him a child of God and bestows on him the fatherly providence which God manifests to those whom He receives as His sons. The prophet rejoiced in this adoption when he said: "Because Thou hast been my helper and I will rejoice under the covert of Thy wings." [2] He loses the peace and serenity of a good conscience and the consolations of the Holy Ghost, which incomparably surpass all the riches and delights of this world. He loses the merit of all the good works he has ever performed, as well as his participation and communication in the goods of Christ, for the sinner is no longer united to Christ through grace.

The sinner's condition is like that of Samson after he had lost his hair, the source of his strength. In his weakened condition he was at the mercy of his captors, who bound him hand and foot, gouged out his eyes, tied him to the turnstile of a mill, and made him grind grain like an animal.[3] In like manner, the sinner who has lost sanctifying grace is too weak to resist evil inclinations; he is bound hand and foot so that he cannot perform good works; he is blinded to the knowledge of divine things; he is a captive of the devils and occupies himself with the things of an animal by seeking to satisfy the demands of his passions.

Is not this a condition greatly to be feared? Do you not think that these losses should be avoided at any cost? How can they be considered reasonable men who dare to commit such sins? Truly, mortal sin is so horrible a thing that the sight of it would cause more terror in us than the sight of hell itself. And it is even worse when we consider how much God hates it, the fearful punishment that He

[1] Cf. Rom. 6:22.   [2] Ps. 62:8.   [3] Cf. Judg. 16:21.

has prepared for it, and all that He did and suffered to destroy it.

Therefore, arouse in your heart the firm resolution never to sin and if at any time you are tempted to do so, place on one side of the balance all the losses we have mentioned and on the other side, the advantage and delight of sin. Then decide whether it is reasonable that you should surrender such precious treasures for some temporal pleasure or gain, as Esau did when he sold his birthright for a mess of pottage and surrendered the paternal blessing.[4]

Secondly, if you wish to avoid sin you must avoid the occasions of sin. He who does not avoid the occasions of sin can be lamented as one already dead. If a man should be so weak that he frequently falls to the ground, what assurance will he have that he will not fall if someone pulls him by the arm or gives him a blow? Likewise, if a man is so weakened as a result of his sins that he falls many times without provocation, what will he do when he is faced with temptations and occasions of sin?

The third protection against sin is to resist temptation at the very beginning. To do this, one should recall the figure of Christ crucified, covered with wounds and flowing rivers of blood, and realize that He was brought to that condition because of sin. Then the sinner will tremble at the thought of being partly responsible for placing God in such a state. Considering these things, he will call upon God from the depths of his heart, asking to be delivered from temptation so that His great sufferings will not have been in vain.

The fourth safeguard against sin is the reception of the sacraments, which were instituted by Christ to purge us of

[4] Cf. Gen. 25:34.

our past sins and to preserve us from future sins. And although the worthy reception of the sacraments is of great spiritual benefit at all times, this is especially true in times of temptation. Moreover, of all the sacraments, the sacrament of penance is the one principal remedy for ridding ourselves of sin. If you should fall into sin, on no account go to your bed that night with the sin on your soul, for you know not whether you will rise from that bed on the morrow. Endeavor to confess your sin on that very day and to repent of it, for St. Gregory says that if we do not rid ourselves of our sins, they will bring other sins in their wake.

The fifth remedy against sin is the practice of examining our conscience each night before retiring in order to account for the deeds done that day. Considering the various types of sin and the chief remedies against sin, you can discover whether you must accuse yourself before God of pride and vainglory; of envy, hatred, and enmities; of suspicions and rash judgments; of false vanity concerning the goods of this world; of disordered desires for worldly possessions or honors; of temptations against faith or chastity; of lies, idle speech, or unnecessary swearing; of ridicule and unkind words against your neighbor; of slothfulness and negligence in the works of virtue; of lukewarmness in the love of God, ingratitude to Him, and forgetfulness of the blessings received from Him; of aridity in prayer and lack of charity for the poor. Then repent of all your faults and ask forgiveness of the Lord, firmly resolving to amend your life. And after you have washed your couch with your tears, as David advises,[5] you will experience a great relief of conscience and will sleep peacefully.

They who are frequently tempted in regard to some particular vice should, in addition to this nightly examina-

[5] Cf. Ps. 67.

tion of conscience and act of contrition, arm themselves each morning with good resolutions and prayers against this vice, seeking special help from God. This practice will greatly aid the soul in conquering the enemy. It is also helpful to assign oneself to some special task, such as the destruction of a particular vice or the cultivation of some virtue, for in this way the soul gradually makes progress in the spiritual life.

Another remedy against sin is the practice of frequent prayer, wherein we ask God for strength and grace and receive the consolations of the Holy Ghost, which make us lose our taste for the delights of this world and foster the spirit of devotion to make us prompt in the performance of virtuous deeds. Closely connected with this is the reading of good books, whereby time is well spent, the understanding is enlightened with the knowledge of truth, and the will is aroused to devotion, with the result that we are better fortified against sin and more inclined to virtue.

The Christian who engages in pious works and holy exercises is also protected against sin, for the idle man is like a fallow field which produces nothing but thorns and weeds. For this reason it is said that idleness teaches a man many evils.[6] But among the holy exercises that serve as a safeguard against sin, fasting, abstinence, and corporal penances are of special value. If the body is weakened through fasting and mortification, its passions and evil inclinations are likewise weakened. Therefore, it is a salutary counsel that the Christian should strive, especially on Fridays, to do some form of penance, however small, for this will serve not only as a protection against sin, but also as satisfaction for sin and an imitation of the sufferings of Christ.

Yet another remedy against sin is silence and recollec-

[6] Cf. Ecclus. 37.

tion, for Solomon says that in a multitude of words, sin is not lacking.[7] We also read in the *Imitation of Christ:* "I never enter into the company of men that I do not depart less a man." Therefore, he who wishes to defend himself against sin should avoid useless conversations and frivolous association with others. Experience will soon teach him that if he does not do this, he will return home disconsolate and discontented, with his head filled with images that will make him wish he could recapture the time that has been wasted.

The last two safeguards against sin are to strive conscientiously to avoid venial sin and to detach oneself from the world and its vanities. We have already seen that venial sins frequently lead to mortal sins, but he who is accustomed to flee from even the smallest evil will be much better protected against the great evils. In regard to detachment from the world, St. James tells us that this is the first lesson that the Christian must learn if he wishes to be a friend of God: "Whosoever therefore will be a friend of this world becometh an enemy of God." [8] Moreover, Christ Himself has told us that we cannot serve two masters,[9] especially when they are so opposed to each other, for God is the sum of all good and this world is, as St. John says, "seated in wickedness." [10] You can be certain that he who does not break with this world, will commit many sins out of respect for the world or will neglect many obligations for the same reason. He will become a slave of the world and not a servant of God and rather than displease the world, he will choose to displease God.

In the battle against sin we do not so much need strong arms to fight nor feet to flee as we need eyes to see, for

[7] Cf. Prov. 10:19.   [8] Jam. 4:4.   [9] Cf. Matt. 6:24.
[10] Cf. I John 5:19.

they are the principal weapons in our spiritual struggle. The great concern of our adversary is so to disguise temptation that it does not appear as a temptation, but as something very reasonable. Thus, if he wishes to tempt us to pride or wrath or avarice he tries to make it appear reasonable for us to desire this honor, that wealth, or that vengeance. By making it appear that it would be contrary to reason to act otherwise, he hopes to deceive even those who are usually governed by reason. For that reason the Christian must have eyes to see the hook that is hidden beneath the bait. The Christian must also have eyes to see the evil, degradation, danger, and harm that follow in the wake of the vice to which he is tempted. This will greatly assist him to control his passions and to refuse to taste that which, once having been tasted, leads to death. Truly, the servant of God must be all eyes, that is, he must have the foresight to make prudent investigations and judgments if he wishes to overcome vice and safeguard virtue.

CHAPTER 10

The Law of God

TWO things are necessary for a good life: knowledge and power. In other words, we must know what we ought to do to live a good life and we must have the power to put this knowledge into practice through our works. The first thing pertains to the law and the second pertains to grace, for the law gives us a knowledge of good and evil, and grace gives us the power to do good and avoid evil. The law illumines the intellect and grace moves the will; the law teaches us the way to heaven, but grace gives us the power to travel toward heaven. The law is the body, but grace is the soul that gives life to the body. God gave us the law through the hands of Moses, but He gives us grace through His only-begotten Son. So St. John tells us: "For the law was given by Moses; grace and truth came by Jesus Christ." [1]

We hold it to be infallibly true, as declared and verified in Scripture, that God Himself is the Author of the Ten Commandments. We read in Exodus: "And the Lord, when He had ended these words in Mount Sinai, gave to Moses two stone tablets of testimony, written with the finger of God." [2] But if God is the Author of the law, it is only fitting that we should hold it in the greatest honor and reverence. For if the laws of a king, who is a mere man, are honored and fulfilled, how much more should one venerate and obey the law of God?

First of all, God's law teaches us what things are sins so that we shall always know when, in what manner, and how seriously we sin. Thus, St. Paul tells us: "By the law is the knowledge of sin," [3] and: "I do not know sin, but by the law." [4] This knowledge is a great incentive for us to seek the grace of God and to do penance for our sins.

Secondly, the law instructs us concerning good works and tells us what God wishes us to do in order to fulfill His holy will. St. Paul says: "The law indeed is holy, and the commandment holy and just and good." [5] The law enables us to know whether we are doing the will of the heavenly Father and whether we are moved by His Spirit in all that

[1] John 1:17.   [2] Exod. 31:18.   [3] Rom. 3:20.
[4] *Ibid.*, 7:7.   [5] *Ibid.*, 7:12.

we do, for St. Paul says: "They who are in the flesh cannot please God." [6] Thus, the law is a spiritual sanction that commands us not to do evil but to live virtuously. "Why then was the law?" asks St. Paul; and he answers: "It was set because of transgressions." [7]

However, it may be asked: "What do Christians have to do with the Ten Commandments which were given to the Jews? We are not Jews; we are Christians, redeemed by the grace of Christ, as St. Paul tells us: 'You are not under the law, but under grace.' " [8]

We may answer this objection by saying that while it is true that the doctrine of Christ pertains to Christians, it is likewise certain that His doctrine is the perfection and culmination of the Commandments of the law, as is stated in the fifth chapter of St. Matthew's Gospel. It follows, therefore, that the law of the Ten Commandments pertains no less to us Christians than to the Jews to whom it was first announced. Granted that Christ has freed us from the law, it does not follow that we are exempt from observing the Ten Commandments, for Christ freed us only from those laws that regulated the ceremonies, court procedures, and other affairs of the Jewish people. These statutes do not oblige us, because they were given only to the Jews and were to remain in force until the Messias should come. But Christ did not liberate us from the fulfillment of the Ten Commandments; rather, He declared explicitly: "Do not think that I am come to destroy the law or the prophets. I am not come to destroy, but to fulfill. For amen I say to you, till heaven and earth pass, one jot or one tittle shall not pass of the law, till all be fulfilled. He, therefore, that shall break one of these least commandments, and shall so

[6] *Ibid.*, 8:8.   [7] Gal. 3:19.   [8] Rom. 6:14.

teach men, shall be called the least in the kingdom of heaven. But he that shall do and teach, he shall be called great in the kingdom of heaven." [9]

The purpose of the commandments is that man should serve the Lord in all his actions, both internal and external. The will of God is declared through the Ten Commandments because these laws cover all the works in which a man may occupy himself in this life.

It is also to be noted that some of the Commandments are affirmative, while others are negative. The former command us to perform some specific work, such as to honor our father and mother; the latter forbid certain actions, such as murder or theft. The obligations that flow from these two types of laws are also different. The affirmative precepts, although they always oblige us, do not oblige us in every circumstance. Thus, the Commandment that obliges us to honor our parents, obliges us to actual fulfillment only when the occasion arises. But the negative precepts oblige always and in every circumstance, for at all times we are forbidden to kill, to steal, or to hold the possessions of another against his will. For that reason, one who has the goods of another does not fulfill the Commandment merely by having the intention of making restitution if he is actually able to make restitution here and now.

We should also understand that although some Commandments are affirmative and others negative, every negative Commandment implies a positive one, and vice versa. For example, the positive Commandment to honor one's parents implies the negative precept that forbids us to dishonor or injure them or to treat them with disrespect. On the other hand, the negative Commandment which forbids

[9] Matt. 5:17–18.

us to have strange gods, implies the affirmative precept to acknowledge the true God and to adore and serve Him as such. These various aspects of the Commandments should always be borne in mind so that we shall the better understand them, and through understanding them may more easily obey them.

CHAPTER 11

Divine Grace

OF the two elements necessary for a good life—law and grace—the second element is much more necessary and excellent, just as the spirit is more excellent and necessary than the body and the New Testament is more excellent than the Old. The reason for this is that if men sin, it is not because of lack of knowledge of what is good and what is evil, for the natural light of reason suffices for this, but because of the corruption of the appetites, which often reject the good and seek evil. Thus, the Apostle says: "For I do not that good which I will; but the evil which I hate, that I do." [1] In other words, man delights in the attraction and sweetness of vice but is repelled by the bitterness that he sees in virtue, although the latter is more salutary and profitable. Indeed, men have much greater need of the power to do good deeds than the ability to know good things, for all men to some degree know what is good, but not all men seek the good, due to the difficulties connected with it.

In this regard the sinner is in much the same state as a

[1] Rom. 7:15.

sick man, whose sense of taste is so vitiated that he has no desire for the foods that are beneficial for him. When food is placed before him and he is told to eat of it because it will do him good, he answers that he doesn't want to eat; not because he doesn't agree that the food is good for him, but because he has no appetite.

The sinner finds himself in a similar state because of his sin. He knows very well that his salvation depends on the observance of the Commandments of God, but he says that he does not feel drawn to these things. He realizes that charity, chastity, humility, patience, temperance, and the other virtues are the very health of his soul, but he despises these virtues and loves dishonesty, vanity, gluttony, licentiousness, and other vices.

But if virtue is so natural to man, why is it that he finds its practice so difficult? If man is a rational animal and virtue is in conformity with reason, why does the rational creature find it so tedious to live and act in conformity with reason? It is not difficult for the horse to run, the bird to fly, the fish to swim; rather, all these things are delightful, since they are so conformable to the natures of these various animals. If, therefore, it is so much in conformity with the nature of the rational animal to live according to reason, why is it so difficult to do so?

If human nature were in that state of integrity in which God first created it, it would not be difficult, but very easy, to practice virtue. But man has fallen from that happy state because of sin. He has become sick, and it is not to be wondered at that a sick man cannot do what a healthy man could do with ease. A healthy man can run and jump and do any number of things without any noticeable effort; but a sick man can do these things only with the greatest difficulty and sometimes not at all. Hence, it is not surprising that virtue should be difficult and insipid to a man in a weakened state, whereas if he were spiritually strong and healthy, virtue would seem easy and perfectly conformable to his nature.

It is evident from this that the curses that God placed on our first parents because of their sin have affected them both spiritually and bodily. God told Eve that henceforth she would bring forth her children in pain, whereas she had never previously known pain. So also, if it had not been for sin, man would have performed good works with the greatest facility and even with delight, but now the performance of good works is difficult because sin has vitiated his nature. Moreover, God said to Adam: "In the sweat of thy face shalt thou eat bread," [2] and this is likewise verified in the spiritual order, for we see with what sweat and labor man performs the works of the virtues, which are the true nourishment of our souls.

Again, we can apply to our flesh the curse that God placed upon the earth, of which He said that it would produce thorns and thistles. What land is there that produces as many thorns as our flesh? And if you want to know what these thorns are, listen to the words of St. Paul: "Now the works of the flesh are manifest, which are fornication, uncleanness, immodesty, luxury, idolatry, witchcrafts, enmities, contentions, emulations, wraths, quarrels, dissensions, sects, envies, murders, drunkenness, revelings, and such like." [3] The Apostle calls such things the works of the flesh because the root of all of them is our flesh corrupted by sin.

Such is the fruit that our flesh brings to harvest, and if it is to produce any other fruit, it must be done by efforts, labor, and the sweat of our brow. The land that lies fallow produces, without effort or the help of anyone, clumps of

[2] Gen. 3:19.   [3] Gal. 5:19–21.

thorns and thistles and other useless weeds, but if it is to produce fruitful plants and profitable things, the worker must plough the land, sow the seed, and cultivate the soil. So also, the land of our flesh will of itself produce the thorns of the vices and disordered appetites, and if it is to produce the flowers and fruits of the virtues, it requires much labor, industry, diligence, and the help of heaven. This, in addition to the effects of evil habits which intensify their natural depravity, is the reason men find it difficult to practice virtue.

Now you will ask: "If this is true, how are we to overcome such difficulties?" The same question was asked by the Apostle concerning the rebellion of the flesh: "Unhappy man that I am, who shall deliver me from the body of this death?" And he answered: "The grace of God, by Jesus Christ, our Lord." [4]

For this did Jesus come into the world: to reform our nature, to heal our wounds, and to be our Redeemer and Savior. What we have lost through the sin of the first Adam, we can regain through the grace of the second Adam. As the first Adam, by his pride and disobedience, has wounded our nature, the second Adam, by His humility and obedience, has given a remedy for these wounds: the grace of His passion. This grace reforms our nature, restores the image of God to our souls, makes the soul pleasing in the sight of God, and, by the virtues and holy habits that it produces, cures our evils, heals our wounds, enlightens our intellect, inflames our will, strengthens our weakness, pacifies our passions, rectifies our evil inclinations, restores our taste for spiritual things, gives us a distaste for carnal things, and makes the yoke of God's law sweet.

[4] Rom. 7:24–25.

Jesus merited for us the first grace of conversion and justification, so that we are justified and are accepted by God as His children and heirs of His kingdom. After this first grace, Jesus merited for us all the other graces necessary for our salvation and to such an extent that the Eternal Father has never given and never will give any degree of grace except through the merits of the passion of His only-begotten Son. Moreover, a diversity of graces is communicated through the seven sacraments of the New Law, and although they have diverse effects according to the various needs of our souls, they all concur in the one common effect of bestowing grace on him who places no obstacles to its reception.

One of the principal means for obtaining grace is to plead for it from Him who alone can give it, for the Apostle tells us that the Lord is rich for all those who call upon Him. And what other virtue is required for this but the practice of prayer? "Ask, and it shall be given you; seek, and you shall find; knock, and it shall be opened to you." [5] What could be more liberal on the part of God and of greater consolation to man? As St. John Chrysostom says, God will not deny assistance to those who ask for it because He Himself inspires us to ask.

And if you ask me what grace is, I shall tell you, in the language of theology, that grace is a participation in the divine nature. In other words, it is a sharing in the sanctity, goodness, purity, and nobility of God Himself, through which man casts off the baseness and villainy that is his by reason of his heritage from Adam and becomes a sharer in the divine perfection of Christ. To explain man's transformation through grace, the saints and holy writers are accustomed to use the example of iron cast into the fire.

[5] Matt. 7:7.

Without ceasing to be iron, it comes out of the fire entirely inflamed, possessing the brilliance, heat, and other characteristics of fire. In like manner, the heavenly quality of grace, when infused by God into the soul, has the marvelous power of transforming man into God, in such wise that without ceasing to be a man, he shares, according to his capacity, in the nature and life of God. As St. Paul says: "I live, now not I, but Christ liveth in me." [6]

Grace is a supernatural and divine form which makes man live a life that is likewise supernatural and divine. In this the providence of God shines forth in a remarkable manner, for since He has willed that man should live two lives, one natural and the other supernatural, He has provided two forms or principles which are like two souls, one for the natural life and the other for the supernatural life. And just as the faculties and powers of the soul proceed from the essence of the soul, so also from the essence of grace, the soul of the spiritual life, proceed the infused virtues and the gifts of the Holy Ghost which perfect the various powers of the soul and facilitate them for the performance of good works. This will be greater in some souls than in others, depending on the degree of grace that is communicated to each soul.

Grace is a spiritual adornment which makes the soul so pleasing and beautiful in God's sight that He accepts the soul as His daughter and bride. So the prophet gloried in the vesture of grace when he exclaimed: "I will greatly rejoice in the Lord and my soul shall be joyful in my God, for He hath clothed me with the ornaments of salvation, and with the robe of justice He hath covered me, as a bridegroom decked with a crown and as a bride adorned with her jewels." [7] Grace is the vesture of many colors in

6 Gal. 2:20.   7 Isa. 61:10.

which the daughter of the King is clothed as she sits at the right hand of her Spouse,[8] because from grace proceed the colors of all the virtues which beautify the just soul.

From what has been said, one can readily understand the effects that grace will produce in the soul. Its principal effect is that it makes the soul beautiful and pleasing in the sight of God so that He accepts it as His bride, His daughter, His temple, and His dwelling place. Here it is that He finds His delight among the children of men.

What picture could be more beautiful than this? If the beauty of the purely natural virtues is such that it captures the heart, what must be the beauty of a soul that is filled with grace and adorned with the riches of the supernatural virtues and the gifts of the Holy Ghost? There is no comparison whatever between the two kinds of beauty, because there is such a difference between God and man that there is no comparison between that which God effects and that which man accomplishes by his own efforts. God showed St. Catherine of Siena the vision of a soul in grace and when she was so overwhelmed by its beauty, He said to her: "See whether I was well employed in all that I suffered to beautify souls in this manner."

Another effect of grace is that it fortifies and strengthens the soul through the virtues that proceed from it. These virtues are comparable to the hairs in which Samson found his beauty and his strength. Thus, the beauty and strength of the just soul are praised in the Canticle of Canticles: "Who is she that cometh forth as the morning rising, fair as the moon, bright as the sun, terrible as an army set in array?"[9] So great is the strength of the just soul that St. Thomas says that the slightest degree of grace suffices to overcome all the temptations and devils in the world.

[8] Cf. Ps. 44:10.   [9] Cant. 6:9.

Grace also makes a man so pleasing in God's sight that all the deliberate good actions performed by the just soul for supernatural motives are pleasing to God and meritorious of an increase of grace. As a result, not only strictly virtuous acts, but even natural actions such as eating and drinking and resting can be pleasing to God and meritorious, because if the one who performs these actions is pleasing to God, all his good works are likewise pleasing to God.

Moreover, grace makes man a son of God by adoption and an heir of the kingdom of heaven. It places his name in the book of life, where the names of all the just are written. He thereby acquires a right to the heritage of heaven, and this is the great privilege that the Savior commended so highly to His disciples when, somewhat proud of the fact that even the devils obeyed their commands, He said to them: "Rejoice not in this, that spirits are subject unto you, but rejoice in this, that your names are written in heaven." [10]

To all these benefits we may add yet another marvelous effect of grace: the abiding presence of the Holy Ghost and of the entire Trinity in the souls of the just. The Savior tells us that a multitude of evil spirits makes the soul of the sinner their dwelling place,[11] but once those infernal monsters are cast out, the Holy Ghost and the entire Trinity enter in and make it Their temple and dwelling place. As Christ says: "If anyone love Me, he will keep My word, and My Father will love him, and We will come to him and will make Our abode with him." [12]

By virtue of these words, all the holy doctors and theologians teach that the Holy Ghost, by some special man-

[10] Luke 10:20. [11] Cf. Matt. 12:24. [12] John 14:23.

ner of appropriation, dwells in the souls of the just. They make a distinction between the Holy Ghost and the gifts of the Holy Ghost, saying that not only are the gifts of the Holy Ghost received, but that the Holy Ghost Himself enters the soul and makes it His temple and dwelling place. He sanctifies and purifies the soul and adorns it with His gifts so that it will be a fitting abode for such a Guest. But the works of the Holy Ghost do not stop here. Not content with assisting us to enter into the gate of justice, He also aids us after we have entered therein so that we may walk along its paths, until He has led us, safe and secure, to the portal of salvation. For once the Holy Ghost has entered the soul through grace, He does not remain idle. He is not satisfied merely to honor the soul with His presence; He sanctifies it with His power and, with the cooperation of the soul, He works in it all the good that is necessary for its salvation.

Thus, the Holy Ghost governs the soul as the father of a family rules his house; He instructs the soul like a master in the school; He cultivates the garden of the soul as a gardener works the soil; He reigns in the soul like a king in his realm; and He illumines the soul as the sun enlightens the world. He is, in a word, like the very soul in the body, which gives life and movement, although not as a substance informing matter. Like a fire, He illumines our intellect and inflames our will. Like a dove, He makes us simple, meek, compliant, and mutual friends. Like a cloud, He protects us against the heat of the flesh and tempers the violence of our passions. Like a soft breeze, He turns and inclines our will to good and removes it from evil. As a result, the just Christian abhors the vices which he previously loved and begins to love the virtues which he once hated, as we see in the case of David, who hated iniquity and loved and delighted in the ways of the Lord.[13]

Thus grace renders man capable of all good, smooths the path to heaven, makes God's yoke sweet, enables man to run along the way of the virtues, restores and heals his wounded nature and thereby makes that light which in his weakened condition seemed heavy. In an ineffable manner it arms him with the supernatural virtues that illumine the intellect, inflame and fortify the will, temper the concupiscible appetite, and rectify the irascible appetite.

Note carefully what the Lord promises to do for us if we turn to Him: "The Lord thy God will circumcise thy heart and the heart of thy seed, that thou mayest love the Lord thy God with all thy heart and with all thy soul, that thou mayest live." [14] But how is it that He promises to do this for us, when at another time He commanded that we ourselves must love God with our whole heart and soul? If God will do this for us, why does He command us to do it? And if we must do it, how can He promise to do it for us?

The difficulty is resolved by St. Augustine: "Lord, give me the grace to do what You command me to do and command me to do what You will." God commands us to do what we ought to do and He likewise gives us the grace to do it. Hence, at one and the same time there is a command and a promise. God and man perform the same action together, He as the first cause and man as a secondary cause. In this regard God is like the artist who guides the brush in the hand of a student in order to help him paint a picture. Both produce the work but each contributes to the effect in a different manner. God acts with us, always safeguarding our liberty, but after the work is finished, man

13 Cf. Ps. 118:14; 104.   14 Deut. 30:6.

has no reason to glory in himself, but should glorify God in the words of the prophet: "Lord, Thou wilt give us peace, for Thou hast wrought all our works for us." [15]

CHAPTER 12 ✍

Justification Through Grace

GREAT and numerous are the divine benefits and blessings, but what shall they profit me, Lord, if they do not awaken me from my sleep and call me to repentance? I have been such an unworthy vessel of the grace Thou didst give me at baptism that I have defiled the temple which Thou didst sanctify for Thyself. I have erected in it the idols of my delights and I have desecrated it with my evil deeds.

There was a time, my Savior, when I was so blind and lost that I lived as if there were no law and, indeed, as if there were no God. Never did I think of death, judgment, or the next life. The law that governed me was the law of my passions. I did whatever I pleased and I desired many other things that I could not attain. In this way many years of my life have passed, years in which I lived in such heavy darkness that I could almost feel it with my hands. How late have I known Thee, eternal Light! How late have I opened my eyes to gaze upon Thy beauty! Yet, during all those years Thou didst endure me and wait for me patiently, because Thou didst not desire that death should take me unprepared. O the loftiness of Thy judgments and

[15] Isa. 26:12.

the greatness of Thy mercy! How many others have been snatched from this life in the very midst of their sins, to suffer eternal torment, while I, who was also a sinner, have been spared by Thy mercy.

What would have become of me if Thou hadst called me to judgment at that time? What account could I have given Thee while I was in that sinful state? O my merciful and redeeming Lord, how grateful I am to Thee that I am not now numbered among the condemned, as I surely would have been if Thou hadst snatched me from life during sinful years. Blessed be Thy patience through which I live and blessed be Thy mercy which has endured me for so long.

Even more, Thou didst not merely wait for me while I lived in sin, but Thou didst visit me many times as if I were Thy friend, to call me back to Thee with sweet and secret inspirations. Frequently Thou didst remind me of the greatness of my sins, the brevity of this life, the eternity of the life to come, the rigor of Thy justice, and the clemency of Thy mercy. Thy presence would suddenly surprise me even in the midst of my sins, so that although I persisted in the pursuit of mundane pleasures and wished to eat of the onions of Egypt, Thou didst make the tears come to my eyes even as I ate. All my efforts were spent in offending Thee, but Thou wert equally desirous of converting me. In all the paths of my life I fled from Thee, as if it meant nothing to me to lose Thee, but Thou didst seek and pursue me, as if it were of great importance that Thou shouldst find me.

In this way didst Thou pursue me for many days, but I responded to Thy blessings with curses. All these things were so many voices by which Thou didst sweetly call me and seek to draw me to Thyself. But when these voices did not suffice, Thou didst utter a loud cry in the ears of my soul, commanding me to rise from my sin and return from death to life. It was a voice filled with power and mercy, for if it is the greatest mercy to pardon sinners, it is the greatest power to make them just.

No one, Lord, can have certitude in this life that he is justified, for no man knows whether he is worthy of hatred or love. But a man can have a greater or less degree of moral certainty, according to the signs of justification and the manifestations of Thy grace. And not the least of these signs is the fact that a man has abandoned his evil ways and has persevered for a long time without being conscious of mortal sin or any attachment to mortal sin. Any Christian who recognizes this or any of the other signs of justification in himself should give Thee thanks for so singular a blessing and speak to Thee as follows:

"May Thou be blessed forever, dearest Lord, and most liberal Benefactor. In spite of what I am and have been, Thou, in Thy great mercy hast given me the Spirit of Thy grace as the sign of adoption and the pledge of eternal life. Through Him my soul receives Thee as Spouse and is clothed in beauty and strength, so that it may be pleasing in Thy sight and terrible to the demons.

"Blessed be the day that such a Guest entered into my house and blessed be the hour in which the doors of my soul were thrown open to receive Him. Truly that was the day of my birth and my own Christmas, for then the Son of God was born in my soul. It was also my Easter, because on that day I rose from death to life. And it was the day of my Pentecost, because then I received the Holy Ghost. Let Job curse the day of his conception and birth because he was born a slave of sin and son of wrath; I shall praise and sing with joy for this second day, and I shall pray that the memory of it will always remain with me, because on that day the Lord freed me from sin.

"This is the day on which the angels sing for the conversion of the sinner, the pious mother rejoices over the talent that has been found, the Good Shepherd rejoices over the finding of the lost sheep, and the devils weep because of the prize that has been snatched from them. This is the day on which the heavenly Father receives the Christian as his son, the Son receives him as a brother, the Holy Ghost accepts him as His dwelling place, and the whole court of heaven welcomes him as a future fellow-citizen.

"But if the angels sing for joy on this day, how can my mouth be silent, my tongue be mute, and my lips not sing with praise? All those canticles, rejoicings, and thanksgivings that the prophets prescribe at the coming of the Messias should now be offered by the true penitent for the blessing of his conversion, for now the Son of God has truly come to him.

"To what other blessings, Lord, shall I compare this great benefit? Great was the blessing of creation, wherein Thou didst draw me from non-being to being, but still greater is the blessing of justification wherein Thou didst draw me from the state of sin to the state of grace. In the first instance Thou didst produce a human being, a son of man; in the second, a divine being, a son of God. And not only is it a greater thing to justify a man than to create him, but it is even greater than to create the heavens and the earth, because all these things are limited and finite goods, while the grace of justification is a participation in an infinite good.

"Great is the blessing that we expect in glory, but in its own way justification is no less a bessing, for it is no less remarkable to make a just man out of a sinner than to make a just man blessed. Indeed, there is a greater distance between sin and grace than between grace and glory. Moreover, redemption is also a great blessing, but what would it profit a man to be redeemed if he were not also justified? Justification is the key to all other blessings; without it, not only are all the others of no profit to us, but they would become the basis of a greater condemnation.

"But if this blessing of justification is so great and if, as I piously hope, I am among those who are justified, I beseech Thee, Lord, to tell me why Thou didst confer so great a blessing on me? What dost Thou see in me, in whom there is naught but sin? I did not truly know Thee; I did not truly love Thee; I did not serve Thee or think of Thee. I cannot cease to be astonished, for I find no other reason for my justification than Thy goodness. And when, in addition to this, I recall the many companions of my sins, of whom I was the worst, I see that Thou didst reject some of them and didst choose me instead. When I consider this, I am so deeply moved that I know not how to praise Thee nor how to thank Thee. I could spend my whole life asking: Lord, what didst Thou see in me that was better than the others? Thou hast called me and gazed on me with love, but Thou hast left others to their sins, although they were much less evil than I. I know not what to say or do, except to thank Thee in the words of the Psalmist: 'Thou hast broken my bonds. I will sacrifice to Thee the sacrifice of praise and I will call upon the name of the Lord.' [1]

"Thou alone, O Lord, didst create us from nothing and Thou alone dost conserve us in being. So also, through Thy Spirit, Thou dost enable us to be reborn through grace

[1] Ps. 115:16.

and dost preserve the grace that Thou hast given us. As the prophet says: 'Unless the Lord build the house, they labor in vain that build it. Unless the Lord keep the city, he watcheth in vain that keepeth it.' [2] Thou hast raised us up from sin and Thou dost keep us from falling back into sin. Therefore, if I have risen from my evil ways, Thou hast given me Thy hand, and if now I am standing upright, Thou dost support me lest I fall.

"All my good resolutions and inspirations have been blessings from Thee. As often as I have conquered the enemy or my evil inclinations, it has been through Thy help. For if it is true that no one can worthily say 'Jesus' without the special favor of the Holy Ghost and that one can no more perform a meritorious act without Thy help than a branch can bear fruit when separated from the vine, it is clear that if this poor branch has produced any fruit of good works, it is because of the vine to which it is joined. If at any time I have fasted, it is through Thee that I have fasted; if at any time I have suffered, Thou hast enabled me to suffer; if at any time I have denied my own will, Thou hast assisted me to do so; if I have shed a single tear or said a single prayer that was pleasing to Thee, I have done it through Thee. All my works Thou hast worked in me, and for all of them I give Thee thanks and acknowledge that I am Thy debtor.

"And what shall I say of the numerous opportunities Thou hast given me so that I might live well? How many preachers Thou hast sent to instruct me, how many good confessors, holy friends, and good companions! How many good examples and pious books to awaken me to a better life! Who can count the dangers and evils into which I could have fallen, but from which Thou hast protected me?

[2] Ps. 126:1–2.

There is no sin committed by one man that another man could not commit just as easily. Accordingly, the sins of all men could just as easily have been my sins, for I could have committed those sins if Thou in Thy infinite mercy had not saved me from them. And although these blessings are not so evident, they are nevertheless deserving of many thanks, for it is no less a blessing to protect a man from evil than to do him good. How often, O good Jesus, Thou hast bound the hands of my enemy so that he could not tempt me or, if he tempted me, so that he could not overpower me! How often I could say with the prophet: 'The Lord is my helper. I will not fear what man can do unto me. . . . Being pushed, I was overturned that I might fall, but the Lord supported me. The Lord is my strength and my praise and He is become my salvation.' [3]

"In addition, sweetest Lord, it is a source of admiration at Thy goodness when I pause to consider how often, through my grave sins, I have deserved that Thou shouldst remove Thy hand from me, as Thou hast done to others. Surely, there are many reasons why men deserve to be abandoned by Thee. The proud man deserves to lose Thy grace because he uses it only for his own pride and vainglory. The ungrateful man deserves to lose Thy grace because he does not give thanks to Thee for this great gift. The slothful man deserves to be deprived of grace because it is only proper to take it away from him who does not know how to profit from it. And he who does not keep himself from the occasions of sin, deserves to fall into sin.

"But how can I think that I am free of such faults? Many times I have been vain and proud because of Thy gifts to me and have thus stolen the glory that belongs to Thee alone. I have been ungrateful for Thy blessings and sloth-

[3] Ps. 117:6–14, *passim.*

ful and lazy in making use of them. I have been so daring and imprudent as to place myself in great danger of sin. Consequently, many times in my life I have deserved to be abandoned by Thee and my fall would have been a just recompense for my folly. But so great is Thy patience that Thou hast overlooked my negligence and hast closed Thy eyes to my weakness. Until now Thou hast endured me with great patience and hast not willed that any help should be denied me, even when I have repayed Thee with so many offences. The sorrow and remorse of conscience that would be mine if Thou wert ever to abandon me, I now convert into thanks and words of praise, saying with the prophet: 'Turn, O my soul, into thy rest, for the Lord hath been bountiful to thee. For He hath delivered my soul from death, my eyes from tears, my feet from falling.' " [4]

[4] Ps. 114:7–8.

BOOK FOUR

The Theological Virtues

CHAPTER 13 🖋

The Necessity of Faith

FAITH signifies a belief in things we have not seen and for which we do not know the reason of their being. It is impossible to live without some kind of faith, and St. Augustine testifies to this in his *Confessions* [1] when he describes the wretched state of his soul before he received supernatural faith:

"But as sometimes it happens that he who has fallen into the hands of an unskilled physician is afterward unwilling to commit himself even to a good one, so my soul, for fear of believing false things, refused to be cured, although it could not be healed except by believing. . . . Then little by little, O Lord, with Thy sweet and merciful hand, Thou didst compose and rectify my heart. I began to consider the countless things that I believed and which I had never seen or experienced, such as the facts that are recorded in history, the descriptions of cities and places that I have never seen, and the things told me by friends, doctors, this man or that man. If such things were not believed, nothing could be accomplished in life. But most of all I was struck by my certainty concerning the parents who had begotten me, and yet I could not know this except on the testimony of others. And thus Thou didst persuade me that they were not to be censured who believed in Scripture, which Thou hast established with such authority in all nations, but that they were deserving of blame who did not believe in Scripture. . . . Realizing that we are too weak

[1] Cf. Book VI, chaps. IV, V, *passim*.

and limited to find the truth by the use of reason alone and that we therefore need the authority and testimony of Scripture, I began to believe that Thou wouldst not have given such eminent authority to Scripture unless it was Thy will that men should believe in Thee through the Scriptures and seek Thee therein."

Granting that man cannot live without some kind of faith, let us now proceed to treat in particular of Christian faith. In the first place, we should observe that there are two kinds of faith: acquired and infused. Acquired faith is that which is obtained through the repetition of many acts of belief. Such is the faith possessed by heretics, who are so accustomed to give credence to the truths proposed to them that it is almost impossible to separate them from the erroneous doctrine that they embrace.

Infused faith is that which is bestowed on the soul of the Christian by the Holy Ghost. It is infused into the soul at the moment of baptism, together with sanctifying grace and all the other virtues that flow from grace. It is a special supernatural light which illumines the intellect of the Christian and efficaciously inclines him to believe all that God has revealed and the Church teaches, without seeing the reasons for the truths proposed for belief. Indeed, whatever the intellect is able to accomplish in regard to divine truth, the light of faith is able to accomplish in a more eminent manner. This is manifested in the constancy of the martyrs, especially the women and children who were so firm in their belief that they willingly suffered death for their faith.

However, although faith is firm and infallibly certain, since it is founded on the authority of God Himself, it does not have the clarity and evidence of reason, for it treats of matters that surpass the powers of reason, such as the mysteries of the Trinity and the Incarnation. For that reason the Apostle says that faith is of those things that are not seen,[2] that is, of those things which reason cannot comprehend but are known only through the revelation of God. But it is precisely the merit of faith that it commands reason to believe those things which reason itself cannot attain. The Apostle cites the example of Abraham who, although he was nearly a hundred years old and his wife Sara was sterile, "was not weak in faith, neither did he consider his own body now dead. . . . In the promise of God also he staggered not by distrust, but was strengthened in faith, giving glory to God, most fully knowing that whatsoever He has promised, He is able to perform. And therefore it was reputed to him unto justice."[3]

St. John Chrysostom says that the servant of God must be so constant that even if there appear to be a contradiction in the things that God reveals, he must not on that account refuse to believe them. He gives as an example the faith of Abraham, who had been promised by God that he would be the father of many nations, and yet he did not hesitate to prepare to sacrifice his son Isaac as a holocaust before Isaac himself had any children.[4]

The authority of God is a sufficient basis for our faith and we need not seek elsewhere for other reasons for believing. Thus, we read in Scripture that it was forbidden to look upon the things in the sanctuary out of curiosity[5] and that thousands of the men of Bethsames were slain by God for having looked upon the ark of the Lord.[6] This should serve as a warning to us not to try to probe the mysteries that are above our power of understanding. When God speaks, we must humble ourselves and let down the

[2] Cf. Heb. 11:1. [3] Cf. Rom. 4:16-22. [4] Cf. Gen. 22:2.
[5] Cf. Num. 4:20. [6] Cf. I Kings 6:19.

wings of our intellects, as did those holy animals described by Ezechiel.[7]

But no one should think that because the truths of faith surpass reason, we should on that account believe in them for any light or baseless motives. The divine truths which surpass our understanding are nevertheless compatible with reason. Moreover, there is all the more reason for believing when miracles have been performed to demonstrate the truth of the revelation. Thus, they who believed in Christ when they saw Him raise Lazarus from the dead considered it altogether fitting that they should believe in Him. The same is true of Nicodemus when he witnessed the miracles worked by Christ. For only God can work miracles and when they are performed as proof of some truth, God Himself is witness to that truth and His testimony is infallible.

But the Christian faith and religion are confirmed by a flood of miracles and also by the fulfillment of clear and evident prophecies and by the testimony of countless martyrs and learned men. In this regard Richard of St. Victor states: "It pleased God that the Jews and pagans should witness with what confidence we Christians can look forward to the final judgment. For we can confidently say: 'Lord, if what we believe is error, Thou art the cause of the error, because these things have been confirmed by so many signs and prodigies that it is impossible that they could have been performed by anyone but Thee.' "

Hence, it cannot be said that we believe in the truths of our faith for any light reasons, but our faith is based on the most solid foundation. For that reason theologians wisely state that the truth of the mysteries of faith is not clear and evident to us, for faith is of things unseen, but that it is

[7] Cf. Ezech. 1:25.

clear and evident that such things are worthy of belief.

We should also observe that infused faith is not lost by any mortal sin except that which is directly opposed to faith itself, such as heresy or apostasy. For faith is the foundation of the entire spiritual edifice and although the superstructure of the other infused virtues may fall as a result of mortal sin, the foundations of faith and hope still remain, although they lack the perfection that charity gives to them. We should also remember that the best and surest safeguard of faith is purity of life and a good conscience. For faith teaches men to live well, but if we are slothful and do not utilize this gift, God will let us fall into blindness and lose this divine gift. Therefore the Apostle advises that we should join a good conscience with faith or run the risk of shipwreck in the faith.[8]

CHAPTER 14

The Perfection of Faith

SOMETIMES the virtue of faith is accompanied by charity and in that case it is called formed faith or living faith, because it receives life from charity, which is the soul of faith. At other times it is found to exist in a soul without charity and then it is called unformed or dead faith, not because it is not true faith, but because it lacks the vitality, perfection, and beauty which come to it when it is vivified by charity. Moreover, charity is a much more excellent virtue than faith, as the Apostle teaches.[1]

[8] Cf. I Tim. 1:19.   [1] Cf. I Cor. 13:13.

When faith is accompanied by charity it carries with it obedience to the divine commandments, for it is proper to a vital and formed faith to incline the Christian to live in accordance with the truths which faith proposes. Thus, when faith considers the words of the Savior: "Unless you shall do penance, you shall all likewise perish," [2] it inspires us to do penance. When faith reminds us of the words of Christ: "Not every one that saith to Me, 'Lord, Lord,' shall enter into the kingdom of heaven, but he that doth the will of My Father who is in heaven," [3] it strives with all its power to fulfill the divine precepts. And when the Lord says: "Unless you be converted and become as little children, you shall not enter into the kingdom of heaven," [4] the living faith of the Christian strives to imitate the humility and simplicity of the little ones. Such was the faith of those who heard the preaching of St. Peter, for they renounced all that they possessed and placed the price of the things they had sold at the feet of the apostles.[5] Such also was the faith of the Ninivites, who believed so strongly in the preaching of Jonas that they were converted to God and abandoned their evil ways.[6]

Thus, faith is a master and tutor that teaches us how to live. It is a candle that enlightens our understanding and gives us a knowledge of the truth. It is a physician that shows us the remedies by which we can cure the illness of our soul; a legislator that gives us laws of good living and guides our life by salutary precepts; an architect of the spiritual edifice that declares to the other laborers what each one must do in his particular capacity. Faith is the sun of our lives, brightening the darkness and showing us where and by what paths we should travel. It is the eyes by

[2] Luke 13:3. [3] Matt. 7:21. [4] Matt. 18:3.
[5] Cf. Acts 4:32–35. [6] Cf. Jonas 3:5.

which the wise man directs the steps of his life.[7] It is the commander-in-chief that marches in advance to point out the ambushes of the enemy and guide us by a safe path. It is the wings of prayer by which we soar to the presence of God and obtain from Him that which we ask, as our Lord has told us: "All things whatsoever you ask when you pray, believe that you shall receive, and they shall come to you." [8]

In addition to all these titles and excellent qualities, St. Bernard states that there is nothing hidden to faith. For what is there to which faith does not reach? Faith does not know what falsity is; it grasps that which reason itself cannot understand; it embraces obscure things and immense things; it understands the future and passes beyond the limits of human reason and the boundaries of experience; in its narrow breast it contains all eternity.

Faith is, as St. John says, the victory that overcomes the world.[9] It is faith, says St. Paul, that justifies souls, because it is the root and foundation of all the virtues that are required for our justification. In another place he says that faith conquers kingdoms, effects justice, obtains promises, stops the mouths of lions, quenches the violence of fire, escapes the edge of the sword, recovers strength from weakness, makes men valiant in battle, puts the enemy to flight, and restores to mothers their dead children.[10]

Such is the faith, as St. Paul reminds us, that the patriarchs had from the beginning of the world. By faith they regulated the steps of their life, trusting in the words and promises of God, believing in that which they could not see and hoping for that which they did not yet possess, going beyond the testimony of their human faculties and being governed by the light of the divine revelation. This

[7] Cf. Eccles. 2:14.   [8] Mark 11:24.   [9] Cf. I John 5:4.
[10] Cf. Heb. 11:33–34.

is what Habacuc meant when he said that the just man shall live in his faith.[11] Thus, faith raises a man to a state far above that which is his by nature, for in receiving the enlightenment of the Holy Ghost, the Christian possesses something that is more than human and enters into the region of divine things.

Since the blessings of faith are so great and numerous, it follows that one of the principal efforts of the good Christian should be to strive as much as possible to perfect and intensify his faith. Faith, like hope and charity and all the other infused virtues, grows by meritorious acts. Moreover, charity and the gift of understanding greatly perfect the virtue of faith, and as a Christian is moved more and more by the gift of understanding, the clarity of his faith is proportionately increased. Sometimes this clarity reaches such a point that the soul feels that it no longer sees by faith but by some light that is much brighter than faith. Such is not the case in reality, however, but faith itself has been greatly illumined by the gift of understanding.

Conversely, the gift of understanding is greatly aided by the truths of faith, and as the Christian humbly studies the truths of faith, he disposes himself for an increase in the light of faith and the gift of understanding. The more he penetrates these mysteries, the more firmly he believes them and the more he is moved to live a life that is conformable to the truths he believes. And since the mysteries of the Incarnation and the Passion as well as the punishment or glory that are decreed by God for the good and the evil are most efficacious motives for arousing the love and fear of God and the observance of His commandments, it follows that the more firmly and palpably a man believes these things, the greater the efficacy with which they will move

[11] Hab. 2:4.

him to lead a good life. In this sense the prophet Habacuc refers to the just man who lives in faith, because by faith and consideration of these motives for a good life we are better able to direct our lives. Therefore, the stronger the faith, the greater the incentives we have to travel along the road to heaven.

We can conclude this chapter by observing that just as the gardener exerts all his energy and diligence in cultivating the roots of the trees so that nourishment can be diffused to all the branches, so also one of the principal tasks of the good Christian is to cultivate faith, the root of the other virtues, because if faith is strong and well nourished, the branches of the virtues will grow and bear abundant fruit.

CHAPTER 15 🖋

Faith Confirmed by Miracles

DIVINE providence, which orders all things sweetly, has not obliged man to believe things that are above his reason without sufficient motives of credibility. And since the revealed truths themselves surpass the powers of nature, the testimony to their credibility must likewise be supernatural. Such are the miracles and prophecies, of which we shall now treat.

Miracles are the work of God alone, who imposed certain laws on His creatures which cannot be dispensed or lifted except by Him who imposed them. To do so is to work a miracle, such as to command fire that it should not burn, as in the case of the three boys in the fiery furnace, or to command water not to flow, as when the Jordan was held back so that God's people could pass over.

Miracles are such adequate proof of the credibility of faith that no mathematical demonstration could ever compare with them. When a miracle is worked in proof of a doctrine, it signifies that God Himself is a witness to the truth of that doctrine, because no one can work a miracle but God. Even when the saints worked miracles, they did so only through the power of God and not through their own. And since the testimony of God surpasses every other testimony, it is the best argument that could be offered in defense of any truth.

Through the working of miracles many received the faith and knowledge of the true God, as is evident from many passages in Scripture. Thus, we read in the Book of Kings how Naaman the Syrian was cleansed of his leprosy by Eliseus and as a result of this miracle he confessed that the God of Israel was the only true God. Nabuchodonosor commanded three young men to worship an idol and when they refused, he had them bound and cast into a fiery furnace. But when he saw that the fire did not even singe their garments but that the young men stood in the midst of the flames praising God, he blessed God and freed the young men. At another time, when Daniel had interpreted a dream for him, this same king replied: "Verily your God is the God of gods and Lord of kings and revealer of hidden things." [1] The same thing is true of Darius, who succeeded Nabuchodonosor and who was prevailed upon by wicked men to cast Daniel into a den of lions, from which the prophet was miraculously delivered. When he heard

[1] Cf. Dan. 2:47; 3:95.

of the event, Darius decreed that all his subjects should fear the God of Daniel, the living and eternal God, whose kingdom shall never be destroyed and whose power shall endure forever, for He is the Deliverer and Savior who delivered Daniel out of the lion's den.[2]

In the New Testament we read of those who believed in Christ when they saw Him raise Lazarus from the dead, after he had been in the tomb for several days. Nicodemus also believed in Christ and confessed that He was the Master come from heaven, after witnessing the miracles of Christ. Likewise the ruler believed in the Savior when he discovered that his son had been healed at the precise moment when Jesus had said: "Go thy way; thy son liveth." [3]

These examples (and there are many others in Scripture) prove that miracles are sufficient proof of the truths of faith and are efficacious means for leading men to believe in those truths. And for those who already believe, miracles serve to strengthen the faith they possess. For that reason wise men consider a true miracle to be something of great importance.

Even if the truth that is confirmed by miracles far surpasses human understanding, it should not on that account cease to be believed, for the authority of Him who has worked the miracle is infallible. When the Magi came from the East to adore the King of the Jews, they did not find any palace or servants or any of the appurtenances of a king. Instead, they were led to the extreme poverty and lowliness of a stable. Nevertheless, they did not hesitate to prostrate themselves on the ground and reverently adore the Infant wrapped in swaddling clothes and offer Him the

[2] Cf. Dan. 6:21–27.   [3] John 4:50.

gifts they had brought Him.[4] How could men so wise bring themselves to believe in something that was so contrary to human reason and prudence? Because they had the miraculous testimony of the star that had guided them.

However, I would remind the Christian reader that although miracles are sufficient proof and testimony for convincing the intellect and inclining a person to believe, he also needs the favor of God in order to embrace the faith. For faith is a gift of God, as the Apostle tells us,[5] and therefore it is necessary that He touch the intellect so that it will humbly submit and assent to the truths of faith. Many of the persons who witnessed the miracles of Christ did not believe in Him, because they were blinded by their malice and were not disposed to receive the gift of God. Therefore, he who reads about the miracles that we have recounted should not read with curiosity, but with humility and devotion, so that he may merit that God will use this means to increase and perfect his faith.

It is well to observe at this point that there are two kinds of faith: supernatural faith, which the Holy Ghost infuses into souls, and human faith, which is the belief we give to human witnesses. In infused faith there is no measure or mean, as there is in the moral virtues, for just as there is no limit or measure to the love of God, neither is there any limit or measure to our belief in God. The more we love Him and the more we believe in Him, the more perfect will be our charity and our faith. But there is a measure or medium in human faith, as in all other acquired virtues, and it is discovered by the virtue of prudence which is the queen of the moral virtues. The two extremes of credulity and incredulity are both vices because it is a vice to believe anything too readily and on light grounds and it is a vice

---

[4] Cf. Matt. 2:11.   [5] Cf. Eph. 2:8.

to refuse to believe when prudence dictates that a thing is worthy of credence.

The vice of incredulity was severely censured by Christ, the model of meekness, who became indignant and cried out: "O unbelieving and perverse generation! How long shall I be with you? How long shall I suffer you?" [6] St. Mark tells us that Christ also upbraided those who refused to believe in His resurrection.[7] When writing to the Hebrews, St. Paul warned them to take care not to foster the vice of incredulity because God had sworn that the incredulous would not enter the kingdom of heaven. In order to strengthen our faith, God permitted Thomas to fall into the sin of incredulity, although Thomas should have believed the other apostles because they were worthy witnesses and Thomas himself had known about the resurrection of Lazarus from the dead through the power of Christ.

The reason why the vice of incredulity is so severely reprimanded is because it usually proceeds from great malice and little faith. It is malicious to believe that most men are liars or that they fabricate miracles; it is a lack of faith to be unwilling to give credence to the proofs that confirm our faith. If we are prone to believe every good thing that is said about a man who is known by us to be virtuous, then we who are certain of the mysteries of faith and the miracles that were worked in proof of the credibility of faith should not hesitate to believe other miracles that are similar to those we already believe. Of course, we should follow the judgment of prudence and not believe too readily or without any reason, for this would be the vice of credulity, but we should believe those things that have clear and certain proofs that make them credible. For even if a man may

[6] Matt. 17:16. [7] Cf. Mark 16:14.

make a mistake in believing, he does not do wrong in believing that for which sufficiently good arguments have been proposed.

CHAPTER 16 🖎

The Joy of Faith

IN order to understand the cause of the joy of faith, we must presuppose first of all a knowledge of certain religious truths and especially of the first truth, which is God, of whom we can also obtain some knowledge through the structure of this universe and the order of created things. Although such knowledge of God is relatively weak in its certitude, it carries with it a great sweetness. Thus, for Aristotle the knowledge of God was most savory, because he believed that the ultimate end and happiness of human life consisted in the contemplation of this first truth.

But if the natural and acquired knowledge of God brings with it the great sweetness and joy of which Aristotle speaks, how much more joy will follow the knowledge of the truths which faith teaches? For this knowledge surpasses every human intellect and reaches a lofty height which reason of itself can never attain. And although the knowledge of faith is sometimes accompanied by doubts and uncertainty, as is that of the philosophers, it carries with it the infallible certitude of God's own truth.

We should also consider, as the same philosopher teaches, that the sign of the truth of a thing is its harmony and consonance with other things that are related to it. In other words, everything has a cause from which it proceeds, while other causes either accompany it or follow after it. The cause of a thing precedes the thing itself, its accidents and properties accompany it, and its effects follow after as a testimony of that which has produced them. Now, Aristotle says that the sign of the truth of a statement is that all these qualities should be in harmony with the statement, and if there is anything contradictory or repugnant, the statement is not true but erroneous.

Such harmony is perfectly illustrated in all the mysteries of the Christian faith and religion. I shall not speak of the harmony of the prophecies and symbols in the Old Testament with the facts related in the New Testament, but I shall discuss the remarkable harmony that is to be found in the Christian faith and religion. We shall discover that all the Christian truths are in perfect accord and that each in its own way perfectly blends with all the others.

What religion in the whole history of the world has had a more lofty experience of God? What religion has proposed better laws, imposed more salutary precepts, or possessed greater sacraments? What religion has offered such efficacious means for the practice of the virtues, has been the source of such great blessings, has so forcefully condemned vice, and threatened sinners with such terrible punishments? What church possesses such salutary teaching, filled as it is with the mysteries of Holy Scripture, which offer most efficacious stimuli for moving men to the love and fear of God, to the detestation of sin, and detachment from this world?

If we know the causes of things through the excellence of the effects they produce, then what religion has produced so many martyrs, confessors, holy pontiffs and doctors, monks and virgins? In what religion can one find the fortitude, the purity, the fasting, the mercy, the detachment from the world, and the practice of prayer and contemplation that are found in the lives of the Christian saints? The consolations and spiritual joys which the friends of God enjoy even in this life and the peace and confidence which mark their daily life, who can explain them? And yet all these blessings are effects of this holy religion.

But even in regard to the general effects which the Christian religion has produced in the world, who could ever praise them sufficiently? It was Christianity that manifested such admirable courage in resisting the kings and emperors who promoted idolatry, that transformed the temples of the pagans into Christian churches, that brought men to a knowledge of the true God, and changed the fierceness of proud men to the meekness of lambs and the craftiness of serpents to the simplicity of doves. And for all these great benefits we are indebted to the Christian religion. Indeed it would have been impossible that so great a light given by God should be hidden away and not cast its rays to the very ends of the earth in order to enlighten those who live in darkness and in the shadow of death.

Moreover, since men place such value on witnesses, what religion has ever had better witnesses than the Christian religion? Consider the holy and most learned doctors who were experts in philosophy, theology, and Scripture and who have taught and defended this holy religion against all the calumnies and falsehoods which heretics have brought against her. Consider also the countless martyrs whom neither prisons nor fire nor the rack nor the jaws of wild beasts could keep from the confession of their faith. Thus they signed their testimony, not with ink, but with their own blood. Indeed, the testimony of the martyrs is not really human at all, but divine, for it would have been impossible for those early Christians, especially women and young children, to suffer so many cruel torments if they had not been strengthened and aided by God.

Returning now to our main theme, when the devout soul considers all these excellent testimonies and realizes that they are all in perfect harmony and that they greatly confirm our faith and dispel many of the clouds that surround it, a great peace and joy results at finding himself so firmly established in the faith. For the truths of faith are the loftiest and most excellent, and most salutary, because they give us a knowledge of God and teach us the path to eternal happiness. Therefore, the soul should greatly rejoice in the possession of such a precious treasure, and the soul itself experiences no difficulty in believing, because it sees that it would be little better than a brute animal not to believe in something that has been manifested by so many excellent testimonies.

The Christian who wishes to foster this peace and joy in his own soul should humbly and attentively consider all the benefits that we have described above. He should realize that all these things testify to the truth of his faith and that they are all in perfect harmony with it. And when he sees the remarkable harmony of all these elements, his soul will be strengthened, consoled, and animated. Moreover, the virtue of faith becomes more perfect and more deeply rooted in the soul, as we read in the Book of Proverbs: "The path of the just, as a shining light, goeth forward and increaseth even to perfect day." [1]

[1] Prov. 4:18.

CHAPTER 17

The Articles of Faith

THE rational soul has two faculties, the intellect and will, and God desires that both of them should be used in His service. In this way the whole man can become reformed and perfect. In the first place, God desires that man's intellect should be truly enlightened and instructed so that it will have a clear knowledge of who God is. Then it will gradually grow in the knowledge of God's being, power, goodness, justice, mercy, and knowledge. It will likewise understand all that God has done and still does for man. And when he has attained the knowledge of these things, the Christian will know how to adore God as he ought, how to recommend himself to God, how to trust in God, how to follow God's instructions, and how to thank God for everything.

God does not want man to construct a false god in his heart, nor to conceive of God other than He really is. For if a man were to have an erroneous concept of God, he would not be able to adore the true God, but he would adore the false notion of God that he has in his intellect. Neither would he be able to attribute the works of creation to the true God, but to the false notion of God by which he has been deceived. Therefore, he who lacks a true knowledge of God is in great danger of going astray and missing the path that leads to salvation.

If you were to ask me what are the principal articles that serve as a summary of this necessary knowledge of God, I would tell you that the Church has already taken care of this matter for us. The reason why the Church has done so is to prevent the possibility of each Christian's following his own opinion or presuming to make his own judgment in this important matter. Therefore, the Apostles' Creed was drawn up as a brief and compact formula which Christians can understand and commit to memory. The Church has done this under the inspiration of the Holy Ghost, selecting the most important doctrines of our faith from Sacred Scripture. Twelve articles of faith are enumerated in the Creed:

"I believe in God, the Father almighty, Creator of heaven and earth; and in Jesus Christ, His only Son, our Lord; who was conceived by the Holy Ghost, born of the Virgin Mary, suffered under Pontius Pilate, was crucified, died, and was buried. He descended into hell; the third day He arose again from the dead. He ascended into heaven, sitteth at the right hand of God the Father almighty; from thence He shall come to judge the living and the dead. I believe in the Holy Ghost, the holy Catholic Church, the communion of saints, the forgiveness of sins, the resurrection of the body, and life everlasting."

The Creed itself is divided into three parts. The first part treats of God the Father and that which pertains to Him; the second part treats of the Son and whatever is proper to Him; the third part treats of the Holy Ghost and that which is attributed to Him. To the Father is attributed creation and power, not in the sense that these activities are not works of the entire Trinity, but because the Father does not proceed from any other Person but is the principle from which the others proceed. To the Son is attributed redemption and wisdom because He is the eternal Word of the Father, who preached the will of His Father and died for the redemption of men. To the Holy Ghost is attributed grace and the sanctification of souls because He is substantial Love.

Let us now turn to a consideration of the first articles of the Creed, not merely to enlighten our intellect but more especially to arouse our will. For there are two types of faith: the cold and dead faith that lacks charity and good works, and the faith that is warmed and vitalized by charity, a faith that is not content merely with believing, but which puts into effect that which is believed. Accordingly, we shall treat of the first article of the Creed in the hope of arousing the will in regard to those things that are accepted and believed by the intellect.

The first article of the Creed is stated as follows: "I believe in God." This is a short phrase, but the words are of such efficacy that anyone who experiences in his heart that which his lips utter, will undoubtedly attain to eternal life. We should note that there are three ways of believing. We may say "I believe in God," "I believe God," or "I believe that there is a God." The last type of belief is the first step by which one approaches salvation, for it is first necessary to believe that there is a God and that whatever He has revealed is the truth. This faith is called historical faith and is common to us and to the demons, for they also believe in God in this manner.

When we say "I believe God," which is the second step to salvation, we mean that God is truthful and we give credence to His promises and warnings. This type of faith is had by all Christians, both the good and the bad, the just and the unjust.

When we say "I believe in God," which is the third step to salvation, we mean that we place all our hope and trust in God, we love Him as the highest good, and in loving

Him we advance toward Him as our ultimate end. This type of faith is proper to the just Christian, who possesses what the theologians call a living and formed faith and what St. Paul calls the "faith that worketh by charity." [1] This is the faith that saves us and justifies us. It is a virtue infused by God into our souls, by which we know for certain that there is only one true God, Father, Son, and Holy Ghost, and we believe whatever is written in the sacred books of Scripture. Thus, we believe most firmly in the things that God has promised, we fear with a holy fear those things against which He has warned us, we dedicate our whole lives to the fulfillment of His holy will, and, out of reverence and obedience to Him, we do and suffer whatever is conducive to His greater glory. Such is the true and living faith, of which we read in Ecclesiasticus: "In every work of thine regard thy soul in faith, for this is the keeping of the Commandments. He that believeth God taketh heed to the Commandments, and he that trusteth in Him shall fare never the worse." [2]

Therefore, let no one think that any kind of faith at all will suffice, nor let him consider faith merely a useless and empty name. On the other hand, faith that is not accompanied by charity and good works and not fortified by obedience to the Commandments is a dead faith and can justify no one, as St. James tells us. [3] But to believe in God with a true and vital faith, our human energies and powers do not suffice. We receive faith from God, for faith is His gift to us, and therefore we must ask it of Him and once He has given it to us, we must petition Him to preserve it in us. For that reason when Peter confessed that Christ was the Son of the living God, the Lord said to him: "Flesh

[1] Cf. Gal. 5:6.   [2] Ecclus. 32:27–28.   [3] Cf. Jas. 2:26.

and blood hath not revealed it to thee, but My Father who is in heaven." [4] And to the Jews He said: "This is the work of God, that you believe in Him whom He hath sent. . . . No man can come to Me, except the Father, who hath sent Me, draw him. And I will raise him up in the last day." [5] Moreover, it is written in Scripture that man will be taught by God.[6]

St. Augustine refers to many other passages of Scripture in his treatise on predestination in order to prove this same point, but he especially emphasizes the statement of St. Paul: "And such confidence we have through Christ toward God. Not that we are sufficient to think anything of ourselves, as of ourselves, but our sufficiency is from God." [7] He then proceeds to say that these words should be well considered by all those who believe that faith has its beginnings in us and that God merely supplies what is lacking to us. For no man believes anything unless he first thinks about that which he is supposed to believe. Hence, if we are not sufficient to think anything of ourselves in regard to Christian faith, but all our sufficiency comes from God, neither are we sufficient unto ourselves to believe, for we must think before we can believe.

But someone may say to this: "If that be true, then it is of no use to listen to the word of God nor is there any point in preaching God's word." In spite of what we have said above, I do not wish to exclude the means through which God gives us faith. For we know that the reception of faith requires the free consent of our will and that the hearing of the word of God engenders faith in us, and for this, we must listen to the preachers.

Nevertheless, we say with St. Augustine and with Scrip-

---

[4] Matt. 16:17.   [5] John 6:29, 44.
[6] Cf. Isa. 54:13; Jer. 31:4.   [7] Cf. II Cor. 3:4–5.

ture itself, that if our will is disposed to listen and believe, it is because it is prepared by God and we cannot desire these things if God does not call us. As we read in the Book of Proverbs: "The hearing ear and the seeing eye, the Lord hath made them both." [8] For that reason, St. Paul says: "By grace you are saved through faith; and that not of yourselves, for it is the gift of God." [9] And St. Augustine says: "In vain labors the tongue that preaches if the Lord does not work in the soul with His grace." Therefore, however necessary it is to hear the word of God and however important the office of the preacher, we must nevertheless attribute the gift of faith to God alone. Consequently, in Him alone should we glory and not in our own efforts nor in the assistance of any other human being.

CHAPTER 18

Temptations Against Faith

AT the very outset I wish to point out a great consolation and remedy for uneducated persons who are seriously tempted against faith and for whom these temptations are a great trial. For people such as these I would like to construct a place of refuge where they can find assistance in times of temptation. I would build a kind of oratory and establish it on the firm columns of those four truths that are so certain that no human intellect can deny them. And in the midst of this refuge I would place a crucifix.

The four basic truths are the following: first, God exists

[8] Prov. 20:12. [9] Eph. 2:8.

(a truth which is preached to us by this visible universe and is acknowledged by all nations, however barbarous); secondly, God is the most perfect of all beings that are or could be imagined, the Author and Giver of all the fruits and blessings of nature, and through Him we live and move and have our being; thirdly, nothing in the whole world is of greater obligation than to love, honor, and serve God; fourthly, there is no church that gives more honor to God and a greater appreciation of Him, none that possesses better laws, is more favorable to virtue and more intolerant of vice, has worked greater good both in individuals and in the whole world, possesses a more holy doctrine, has been approved by the testimonies of so many doctors and martyrs as well as miracles and prophecies, as the Catholic Church. Let him who is tempted against faith enter this oratory and embrace these four columns of truth which all the power of the devil can never destroy.

Once a man has been firmly established in Catholic doctrine and the devil begins to molest him with temptations against faith, he should not attempt to dispute with the devil, because the devil is a great deceiver and can easily win the argument. Rather, as soon as the Christian is aware of the temptation, he should hasten with all possible speed to this oratory, prostrate himself in spirit at the foot of the crucifix, and promise to live and die in the Catholic faith. Then let him cling to the four columns of divine truth, saying in his heart: "I know that there is a God and that He is the Father, King, and Lord of the entire universe. I know that there is nothing of greater obligation nor more fitting than that I should honor and serve Him. I likewise know that no honor or service could be more perfect and fitting than that which is prescribed by the Christian religion. I shall content myself with this and I shall be consoled, for I am sure that if I live in accordance with the precepts of this holy religion, I shall be traveling by a road that is most certain and most secure."

When a man clings confidently to these truths of Christianity, all the power of the devil cannot prevail against him. And in order that the Christian may have a clearer knowledge of the first three truths, let him recall the doctrine that has been treated in the first volume of this work, where we discussed the creation of the world, the divine perfections, the care that God has for all his creatures, and how he deserves to be adored and served by each and every one.

A knowledge of these things is very useful for all Christians, but especially so for those who have a pure love of God, loving Him not for what they expect from Him, although this is good and holy, but loving Him for what He is—infinite goodness. St. Bernard says of this love that it takes no account of hope and it does not suffer the evils of despair, meaning that such Christians do not serve God because of that which they expect from Him nor would they cease to serve Him if they could expect nothing from Him. The Christian who has such a disinterested love easily wards off all the arrows of the enemy because he sees that there is no manner of life more pleasing to God than the Christian life.

It also seems well at this point to reply briefly to the anxiety that some persons feel when they look upon the universe and see the great number of heathens and infidels that are in it. I would answer first of all that we have a most clear and sufficient proof of the truth of our faith because, although the mysteries of faith are not evident, since they treat of things that we cannot see, nevertheless there is nothing more evident than the fact that these truths should be believed, because of the miracles and prophecies and other proofs by which they have been confirmed. This being so, it should not be a cause of anxiety to Christians that so many men are blinded by their sins and vices that they do not want to believe. For if I see clearly that I have five fingers on my hand, should I cease to believe the truth of this fact even if all the rest of the world says the contrary? Of all the people during the first epoch of the world's history, only Noe was found to be just. Nevertheless, the holy man did not on that account cease to be holy and to keep his faith intact. In the time of Abraham there were still very few just men, but they did not lose or deny their faith in spite of the fact that they lived among so many infidels. Therefore, the modern Christian should be reassured and find consolation in his faith, considering in all humility the lowliness of his intellect which is admitted to a knowledge of the mysteries of God Himself. Let him exclaim with St. Paul: "O the depth of the riches of the wisdom and of the knowledge of God! How incomprehensible are his judgments and how unsearchable his ways!" [1]

We know that our Lord appeared among men in order to help souls be converted and that he will not deny to anyone sufficient help for conversion. We also know that God has impressed upon all human intellects the natural law, that is to say, a knowledge of good and evil, and has given man a free will whereby he can choose the one or the other. When we sin, we do so out of our own malice and evil will, without anyone forcing us to do so. But if the judges of this world have the power to punish evil doers, much more does the supreme Judge have the power to do so.

Perhaps you will say: "But His punishment is eternal!"

[1] Rom. 11:33.

This is true, but it is also true that punishment is meted out by a God who is not only just, but is justice itself. He rewards good works more than they deserve and He punishes sinners less than they deserve. If His punishments last forever, it is because divine wisdom has decreed that the present life should be a state of merit or condemnation and that eternity should be a state for receiving a reward or punishment according to our just deserts. Evil men have been given a period of time and God has waited for them to amend their lives, but they do not want to take advantage of the opportunity that God gave them. Therefore, it is only just that they should suffer the punishment for their ingratitude and rejection of God. St. Gregory says that those wicked men who have been condemned never wanted to put an end to their evil deeds. Consequently, if they were to live on this earth forever, they would sin forever. Therefore, divine justice decrees that there should be no end to their sufferings, since they themselves would never have put an end to their sins.

But what shall we say of those to whom the true faith has never been preached? They shall not suffer for any sin of infidelity because this sin cannot be imputed to those who have never heard of the true faith. But they can be punished for any sins that they have committed against that natural law which God has impressed on the hearts of all men and for the evil deeds of any kind that they have committed out of malice and evil will.

Nor should we be disturbed if the number of those who are lost is greater than the number of those who will be saved, for St. John tells us that countless souls will be saved and will take with them to heaven those who have followed their example and done penance for their sins. Hence, it is a source of greater glory to those who are saved if the

number of the condemned is greater, because it was the
fortunate lot of the former to win heaven in spite of the
fact that they lived in the midst of so many evil men. Moreover, the very condemnation of sinners will redound to the
glory of divine justice, which leaves no sin unpunished, and
it will redound likewise to the greater consolation and happiness of the blessed who have escaped such a terrible fate.

Therefore, let the humble Christian be tranquil and consoled and not try to scrutinize the secrets of the divine judgment. As the philosopher says, what difference would there
be between God and man if man wished by his own efforts
to attain and understand the counsels and decrees of the
ineffable majesty of God? Through his humility, by which
the Christian gives glory to God and confines himself to
his own proper place by recognizing the lowliness of his intellect, he will merit that the Lord should give him that
peace and quiet and joy which God gives to His faithful
friends in the knowledge of the mysteries of faith.

CHAPTER 19

The Faith of Nations

IN ancient times God promised the holy patriarchs a countless number of children and as time went on He fulfilled
this promise. But once the promise had been fulfilled, the
sins of men were also countless and God punished the
human race by sending the Deluge. In like manner, God
has promised through the mouth of His prophets the ex-
tension of the kingdom of Christ throughout the entire

world. This also has been accomplished, and even in the time of the apostles, Christ's kingdom had spread to all the parts of the civilized world.[1] But after the time of the apostles, when the persecution of the Church raged fiercely, the number of the faithful increased accordingly, and when the persecutions ended and Christian emperors such as Constantine and Theodosius came to power, the gospel was preached to all the nations of the world. Pagan temples and altars and idols of the devil were torn down and cast to the ground and the prophecy of Zacharias was fulfilled: "I will destroy the names of idols out of the earth, and they shall be remembered no more." [2]

After the Church had been extended throughout the whole world and the number of the faithful had increased, it amassed great wealth and enjoyed the favor of kings and emperors. As a result, there was an increase in pomp, avarice, vanity, ambition, and all the sins that accompany such worldliness. Thus was fulfilled the prophecy made by Moses to the children of Israel: "The beloved grew fat, and kicked: he grew fat and thick and gross. He forsook God who made him, and departed from God his Savior." [3]

When certain causes or conditions prevail, certain effects will follow inevitably unless God prevents them by a special privilege of his grace. And so it has happened in religion as with almost every nation in the history of the world— material prosperity has been the occasion of moral weakness and an abundance of sins. And what can the divine Judge do but permit such nations to lose the precious jewel of faith? Thus, God warned certain churches that if they did not do penance, He would move their candlestick out of its place,[4] meaning that He would deprive them of the

---

[1] Cf. Col. 1:6.   [2] Zach. 13:2.   [3] Deut. 32:15.
[4] Apoc. 2:5.

light of faith and give it to some other community. This is the greatest calamity that could have befallen them, for to lose the faith is to close the door to salvation.

Christ also has said that to him who has, more will be given, but from him who has not shall be taken away even that which he has.[5] This means that he who uses the gifts received will be given an increase, but he who does not make use of the gifts of God will lose even that which he has. Therefore, such a man will even lose faith and hope, the only virtues that can remain in a soul that has lost grace through sin.

This doctrine enables us to understand the meaning of the parable of the slothful servant who kept his talent hidden away in a napkin and did not invest it profitably. As a result, the master commanded that he should be cast out and that his money should be given to that servant who had increased his talent tenfold.[6] And what does this talent signify but the goods of grace which the Christian ought to increase? For the light of faith and all the gifts of grace are given to us to be used and increased and they will be taken from him who does not use them.

St. Paul teaches the same doctrine when he says that the anger of God is manifested against the impiety of those men "that detain the truth of God in injustice." [7] In other words, faith is a great gift of God which teaches us the royal road to eternal life, but he who does not practice what the faith teaches has actually imprisoned his faith or has bound it hand and foot, so to speak, so that it cannot work those good deeds which it could effect if it were not impeded. For that reason, evil men deserve to be deprived of this precious gift, because not only does it not serve to their advantage, but it will be the basis of their greater con-

[5] Luke 8:18.   [6] Luke 19:24.   [7] Rom. 1:18.

demnation. Our Savior says that the servant who knows the will of his master and does not obey it, shall be more severely punished than the servant who does not know his master's will.[8] If evil men do not love the truth and do not wish to be saved by it, God will let them be deceived by many errors and, once they have abandoned God's own truth, He will even let them believe the lies of the devil.

You see, therefore, how the loss of faith among many nations has largely resulted from the fact that these nations did not appreciate or utilize the faith. Sacred theology is both a speculative and a practical science because it teaches us what we ought to believe and what we ought to do. The virtue of faith has this same double function. Whence, if we do not use and perform the works of faith, we shall ultimately reject it and even, perhaps, believe things contrary to the faith. Therefore, it should not surprise us if God permits one to lose the faith who has not made use of it according to his capacity and has not made it the guide and rule of his life.

Moreover, some men are so inclined to sensual pleasures and vices and are so habituated to these things, that they think it impossible to live without such pleasures. The perversity of their evil inclinations is strengthened by a long-standing custom of sin. As a result, they firmly believe the lie which states that they cannot cease sinning and they consider themselves so hardened in sin that there is no way for them to escape from their evil habits. Men such as these are very greatly disposed to lose their faith. The reason for this is that the faith is constantly casting bitterness in the midst of their delights, for it reminds them of the last judgment and fills them with a fear of the pains of hell. Consequently, if any heretic should come to them and

8 Luke 12:47–48.

deny the immortality of the soul or the existence of divine providence, they are in great danger of accepting this false teaching, if only to rid themselves of the thorn in their heart and to sleep more easily in the midst of their vices.

The intellect and will are so closely related that a strong love or vehement desire easily blinds human reason. Hence, if our will is greatly attracted or attached to some object which it would be very painful for us to lose, the intellect, in order to protect the will against such suffering, finds reasons to approve or justify what the will desires, even if it be something contrary to the faith. This is all too evident from the many examples in the lives of persons who believe that faith without good works is sufficient for salvation. Therefore, we should not be surprised at the weakening of faith in our day when sins have multiplied so greatly. Many Christians live as if there were no God or as if they did not believe in God, the final judgment, heaven or hell, or any life after this one. So widespread is vice and so great are the excesses in eating and drinking, in clothing and entertainment, and in all kinds of sensuality, that one would think we were living among pagans. And who can describe the ambition, the lust, the avarice, the deceit, the injustice, and the oppression of the poor, which serve to add to the excesses of men?

But God's providence and His judgment do not sleep. As the evils increase, so will the punishments increase. Look at the Church as it stands today, and you shall see how the Christian people are afflicted with heresies and misfortunes and calamities of every kind. See the various punishments that divine wrath has inflicted on many nations. In all these things the rigorous justice of God is evident. Wherever He finds sin, He inflicts punishment, without respect of persons, and He will not hesitate to destroy entire nations. Indeed, the sins of men are increasing so greatly that if we did not have the divine assurance that the gates of hell will never prevail against the Church, we should have reason to fear that the fire that has enveloped the Church, would completely consume and destroy it.

CHAPTER 20

Christian Hope

THE Christian needs the virtue of hope because sin has left him poor and naked and there is no other remedy but to lift his eyes to God and hope for divine assistance in the midst of so many evils, many of which cannot be cured except by God. In this tempestuous sea of life, where new storms arise every hour, hope is the anchor [1] by which we must be safely secured. God said through the mouth of Isaias that the strength of His people should be in their silence and hope.[2] This is one of the greatest treasures in the Christian life, for it is the common remedy for all the miseries of this life.

But lest we deceive ourselves, it should be noted that just as there are two kinds of faith, the living faith informed by charity and possessed by just Christians and the dead faith of the sinner, so there are two kinds of hope: the dead hope of the sinner, which does not strengthen the soul in good works or console it in its labors, and the living hope which animates, consoles, and strengthens the just

[1] Heb. 6:19. [2] Isa. 30:15.

Christian in the midst of his labors. Such was the hope of David when he said: "Be thou mindful of Thy word to Thy servant, in which Thou hast given me hope. This hath comforted me in my humiliation." [3] Hope works many remarkable effects in the soul in which it dwells and these effects are so much the greater as they participate more in the love of God which gives life to the virtue of hope.

There are four principal matters about which hope is concerned. The first is the happiness of the life to come; the second is the pardon of sins, which are impediments to the fruit of hope; the third is the granting of our petitions; and the fourth is the assistance of God in the midst of our labors and temptations. The virtue of hope pertains to all these matters and to those things that are related to them, and all these objects of our hope have their foundation in the tree of the Holy Cross.

But the principal object of our hope is the eternal happiness of the beatific vision. This vision of the divine essence requires that God elevate and strengthen the human intellect by the light of glory and that the divine essence itself, without any other medium, be immediately joined to our intellect, which is thereby deified and made like unto God. In other words, the human intellect is rendered sufficiently strong to be able to see God as He is in his divine beauty and as He is seen by the angels. It is one of the most ineffable of all unions imaginable and from a human point of view it would seem incredible, because of the infinite distance between the divine and the human natures and by reason of the weakness of our human intellect, which cannot understand spiritual things except through images taken from bodily things.

St. Thomas teaches that it is only with the greatest diffi-

[3] Ps. 118:49–50.

culty that man can hope for so lofty and remarkable a union. Yet God has effected another union that is even more remarkable—the union of the divine Word with human nature. As a result, the Christian need never doubt that he can become one with God through grace, for he sees that God Himself has become man. St. John Chrysostom says that it was a much greater thing that God should become man than that man should become God through sanctifying grace. Therefore, if we see that the former has actually taken place, there is reason to believe and hope in the latter, especially since the first is the cause of the second, for through the mystery of the Incarnation man receives grace and, ultimately, the beatific vision.

Nor are the difficulties any less in regard to the virtue of hope than in regard to the virtue of faith. For just as a man must exert a kind of violence on his intellect in order to believe what he does not see, he must do the same to his will in order to hope for that which he does not yet possess, especially when all human powers are insufficient. It is difficult to do what Abraham did,[4] that is, to hope against hope, but that is what we must do when we are unable to gain any help from reason or human prudence.

To accomplish this, what greater help could be given us than the mystery of the Cross? For if all the motives which we have enumerated as incentives to the love of God likewise move us to hope in Him, in whom shall we hope with greater confidence than in so good a God and so powerful a Father? If a son has the greatest confidence in his father, why should I not hope in Him who is much more than a father to me? This is the argument which the Christ Himself uses in the gospel: "If you then, being evil, know how to give good gifts to your children, how much more will

[4] Cf. Rom. 4:18; Gen. 15:6.

your Father from heaven give the good Spirit to them that ask him?" [5] Indeed, is there anything we could not expect from a Father who has loved us so much that He gave us His only Son?

St. Paul gives us another proof when he says: "He that spared not even His own Son, but delivered Him up for us all, how hath He not also, with Him, given us all things?" [6] It is as if St. Paul had said: "He who has given so much, why shall He not give that which is less? For whatever else God could give us, however great it may be, it is little in comparison with that tremendous gift of His only Son."

But if God has been so merciful to us and at such a price, how can we expect that He will now punish us severely or that He will ignore us? This is the principal foundation of our hope. Who, then, will consider himself so dejected and so afflicted in the midst of his tribulations that he will not be encouraged at the thought of the generous promises of God's mercy and paternal care? And if he is not animated by this thought, is there anything at all that can give him encouragement?

It should be evident, therefore, how great is the benefit of hope and in how many ways it profits us. It is a safe port where all just Christians can find refuge in the time of storm. It is a strong shield with which we defend ourselves against the attacks of the world. It is a supply of bread for the poor in time of hunger. It is that tent and shade which God promised His chosen people, wherein they might take refuge from the heat of day and the whirlwind and the rain. [7] It is a common remedy for all our evils.

But we now come to the consideration of a point that is very lamentable, namely, the perversity of the human heart

[5] Luke 11:13.   [6] Rom. 8:32.   [7] Cf. Isa. 4:6.

which, even as it relies on this great virtue of hope, nevertheless perseveres in its sin. If you were to ask any of these shameless people how they can hope to be saved, they will reply that they will be saved through faith in Christ and hope in His sacred passion. Christ's passion is truly the greatest stimulus to hope and the greatest motive for fear of God, but these wicked persons pervert it and make it an excuse for continuing their sin, when in reality it is supposed to make souls love and serve God. This has been and continues to be one of the greatest deceptions of the devil, who strives to compete by his evil ways against the greatness of God's goodness. God manifests His great goodness by drawing good out of evil, but the devil endeavors to make even good things serve an evil purpose. Thus, he makes Scripture, which was given to us for the enlightenment and government of our life, a source of error and perversion for heretics, distorting the divine words in order to use them as a basis for his lies. So also, he has craftily used the divine mystery of the Cross as an excuse for sin. All men, however evil they may be, desire to be saved, even when they refuse to enter upon the path of virtue. But these evil men have looked upon the Cross for consolation and sometimes have used it as an excuse for their evil deeds, saying that Christ has already atoned for them. It is as if one were to say that the Son of God came down to earth and suffered in order that men might become evil and slothful and enemies of every virtuous work.

All the teaching of Scripture militates against this error. How often we are urged to perform good works and how frequently Scripture associates fear of God with the virtue of hope so that the one will serve as a corrective to the other. Christ has told us that we must rid our hearts of all anxiety and that we must not rely on temporal help: "Seek ye first the kingdom of God and His justice, and all these things shall be added unto you." [8] In other words, if our confidence and trust are to be well placed, they must be accompanied by justice. And when speaking of those who on the day of judgment will have recourse to the miracles that they worked, Christ says that He will answer: "I never knew you. Depart from Me, you that work iniquity." [9] On what other basis will the evil be condemned and the good saved, but the works of mercy that they performed and those that they neglected? And when the Lord said: "If any man will follow Me, let him deny himself and take up his cross and follow Me," was he telling us to be slothful or to perform good works? [10]

God takes no account of the sacrifices of evil men, nor of their prayers and hymns. What is it that He asks? What is it that pleases him? He answers through the mouth of Isaias: "Wash yourselves; be clean. Take away the evil of your devices from My eyes. Cease to do perversely. Learn to do well. Seek judgment. Relieve the oppressed. Judge for the fatherless. Defend the widow. And then come and accuse Me." [11] And the prophet Micheas, in teaching men how they should please God, says: "I will show thee, O man, what is good and what the Lord requires of thee. Verily, to do judgment and to love mercy and to walk solicitous with thy God." [12] By the phrase "to do judgment" the prophet means that we should not live according to the inclinations of our flesh but according to the judgment of reason and the divine law.

Since Scripture declares that the remedy for our spiritual

---

[8] Matt. 6:33.   [9] Matt. 7:23.   [10] Mark 8:34.

[11] Isa. 1:16–18. Tr. note: The phrase "then come and accuse me" means "then come let us reason together." In other words, one cannot be a true friend of God until he repents of his sins and is converted.

[12] Mich. 6:8.

health consists in the performance of good works and that our perdition lies in the performance of evil deeds, how is it possible that the devil can blind the intellects of so many men so that they believe that merely by trusting in the passion of Christ and without putting their hand to the plough, they can hope to be saved? If man has become so poor and naked as a result of sin, and if hope in divine mercy is such a necessary remedy, what will happen to him if he is deprived of this support? To live without hope, what is it but to live without God? A man may not know the cause of his weakness, but he does know that he is weak, and for that reason he naturally turns to God to seek a remedy for his weakness. This being so, what must life be like for those who live without any hope of assistance from God? Who will console such men in their labors? To whom shall they go in time of danger?

If the body cannot live without the soul, how can the soul live without God, for God is no less necessary for the life of the soul than is the soul for the life of the body. And if a living hope is the anchor of our life, who will dare to enter upon the stormy sea of this world without the assurance of such an anchor? If hope is the shield by which we defend ourselves against the enemy, how can we walk in the midst of so many enemies without this protection? If hope is the staff by which human nature is sustained in its weakness, what will happen to weakened man if he lacks the support of this staff?

This should suffice to point out the necessity and blessings of the virtue of hope. And although hope may seem to be nothing more than a special providence by which God cares for His own, it actually differs from divine providence as the effect differs from its cause. For while there are many causes and foundations for hope, such as the divine goodness, divine veracity, and the merits of Christ, the principal cause of hope is God's paternal providence. The knowledge that God has a special care for us is sufficient to arouse our trust in him. Therefore, in all our works and trials and anxieties we should go to God and commend ourselves to Him with the greatest confidence, for He is our Father who has made us out of nothing and will never be deficient in those things that are necessary for us. In His goodness and paternal love He will grant us whatever is helpful to us in soul or in body. For that reason, we should not fear that anything can ever hurt us—neither the devil nor evil men nor wild beasts, neither cold nor hunger, neither sickness nor death nor the terrors of hell.

If God is with us, who can be against us? If He places us in His abundant pastures, what hunger or cold can ever afflict us? If He is the defender of our life, whom shall we fear? If He covers us in the shadow of His wings, who can harm us in any way? Therefore, we may rightly say with David: "Though I should walk in the midst of the shadow of death, I will fear no evils, for Thou art with me. If armies in camp should stand together against me, my heart shall not fear. If a battle should rise up against me, in this I will be confident. For He hath hidden me in His tabernacle. In the day of evils He hath protected me in the secret place of His tabernacle. He hath exalted me upon a rock and now He hath lifted up my head above my enemies." [13]

[13] Cf. Ps. 22:4; 26:3–6. *passim.*

CHAPTER 21 ✔

The Excellence of Charity

BEFORE we treat of the practices and methods by which we may grow in the love of God, it will be well to consider the excellence of this love, for we are eager to undertake labors when the reward is great. And once we have gained this precious jewel of charity, I do not doubt that we shall say with the spouse in the Canticle: "If a man should give all the substance of his house for love, he shall despise it as nothing." [1] Like the valiant woman of whom Solomon speaks,[2] we should first taste something of the excellence of charity and then we shall consider it good traffic to give all that is asked for this virtue.

But one should not think that we can properly evaluate the true worth of this virtue in a short chapter. Indeed, I do not know whether it would not be better to honor charity in silence, since it cannot be adequately praised with words. Charity is the goal of all the divine commandments, as the Apostle tells us,[3] and all that is written in Scripture or in the works of the saints and mystics is either about charity or something that pertains to charity. Nevertheless, I shall point out very briefly the outstanding qualities which place charity above all the other virtues.

In the first place, charity is the queen of all the virtues. To understand this, we should recall that the theological virtues of faith, hope, and charity far surpass all the other

[1] Cf. Cant. 8:7.
[2] Prov. 31:10–28. The valiant woman "hath tasted and seen that her traffic is good."
[3] Cf. I Tim. 1:5.

virtues because they are concerned with God as the supernatural end and they direct man to Him, although in different ways. Faith sees God as the First Truth and enables man to believe firmly in all the truths that God has revealed. Hope looks upon God as our sovereign Good, whom we strive to attain through the help of His grace and our own good works. But charity embraces God as the supreme Good who is worthy of being loved for what He is and with the greatest possible love.

Faith sees God obscurely and, as it were, beneath a veil. Hope looks to God as an arduous good not yet possessed but capable of being possessed, and thus it implies a note of self-interest and a desire for our own perfection, which theologians call the love of concupiscence. But charity tends to love God with the love of true friendship, which is a pure and disinterested love and, as St. Bernard says, does not seek its own interests. The just soul possesses God through charity because it is the nature of love to fix all one's affections on the beloved, even to the point of becoming transformed into the beloved. Thus, St. John says that "God is charity, and he that abideth in charity abideth in God, and God in him." [4] For that reason St. Augustine says that there is nothing greater than a soul that has charity, except God Himself, who gives charity.

But if charity is the most excellent of all the virtues, it follows that the exercise of charity will be the most excellent of all the practices in the spiritual life, for the most excellent activity proceeds from the most excellent principle or habit. Therefore, if the habit of charity is the best of all spiritual habits, the actual love of God is the best and the most meritorious act that a man can perform. Nor is this contrary to the doctrine on the excellence of martyrdom, for if martyrdom is pleasing to God, it is because of

[4] Cf. I John 4:16.

the charity which imperates it. Without charity, martyrdom would be no martyrdom at all, but merely a fruitless torment, as the Apostle tells us.

The second excellence of charity is that it is not only the most noble of all the virtues, but is the very goal and end of all the divine commandments and counsels. They are all ordained to charity in one way or another. Indeed, not only the law of God and all the counsels of Scripture, but all created things in heaven and on earth are in some way ordained to the love of God. It is for this purpose that man has been fashioned by the hands of God; for this he lives and for this do all the creatures of the heavens and the earth serve him. The universe and all things in it would be fruitless and vain if they did not in some way lead man to a greater love of God.

The third excellence of charity is that it is not only the end and goal of all the other virtues but it is the very soul and perfection of all the virtues. The body without the soul is still a body, but it does not have life; so also, without charity the virtues are still good habits but they do not have any life or merit before God. They can do nothing to satisfy for sin or to merit an increase of grace or glory, although they may serve many other good purposes. As long as a man is not pleasing to God, neither are the works that he performs. God has no obligation to be pleased with any work, however excellent, if it has not been done for love of Him. If a man fasts, gives alms, preserves chastity, or endures suffering, but does none of these things for the love of God (as is actually the case with many persons), what has God to do with such works or why should He be pleased by them? Charity alone is profitable and pleasing in the sight of God and without charity nothing is pleasing to God. For that reason it can be compared to the Son of God, for just as no creature in heaven or on earth is pleasing to God except through the Son of God, so no virtue or good work is pleasing to God unless it proceeds in some way from the virtue of charity.

Charity is the root and principle of all merit, because if anything has any value in God's eyes, it is because of the virtue of charity. What the root is to the tree and the soul is to the body, charity is to the spiritual life of the Christian. The branches of a tree will have no leaves unless they receive life from the roots and the members of the body will have no life unless they are informed by the soul. So also, our works will have no life or value if they are not permeated with charity. St. Paul testifies to this when he says: "If I speak with the tongues of men and of angels and have not charity, I am become as sounding brass or a tinkling cymbal. And if I should have prophecy and should know all mysteries and all knowledge, and if I should have all faith, so that I could remove mountains, and have not charity, I am nothing. And if I should distribute all my goods to feed the poor, and if I should deliver my body to be burned, and have not charity, it profiteth me nothing." [5]

However, if the Christian acts for the love of God, not only are his good deeds acceptable to God and meritorious, but also those works which are indifferent or purely natural. Without charity the gold of the virtues becomes dross, but through the mysterious alchemy of charity the dross of purely natural or indifferent works, however lowly, become pure gold. For that reason St. Augustine says: "Love and do what you will. If you are silent, you will be silent out of love; if you forgive, you will forgive out of love; if you punish, you will punish out of love; and whatever you do out of love is meritorious before God." And if we have said that charity is gold, we can now say that charity has the power to transform into gold whatever it touches. How

[5] Cf. I Cor. 13:1-3.

greatly we should esteem that virtue which can make even the humblest and lowliest work meritorious of eternal life! One of our greatest cares should be to fulfill what the Apostle advises when he tells us to do all things in charity,[6] or, as he says in another place, "whether you eat or drink or whatever else you do, do all to the glory of God." [7]

The fourth excellence of charity is that it is not only the life of all the other virtues, but it also stimulates the other virtues, for it arouses them to perform their various offices and functions. When the love of God is intense it produces a fervent desire of pleasing Him and of doing His holy will, and since the Christian realizes that nothing pleases God more than obedience, he strives to obey the commandments and perform the works of virtue.

"It seems to me," says St. Augustine, "that the briefest and most concise definition of virtue is to call it the order of love, for that is truly virtuous which gives all things their rightful share of love, loving them in the measure with which each one deserves to be loved, and no more." Hence, charity observes the proper measure in all things. St. Augustine continues: "Charity is patient in adversity, temperate in prosperity, strong in times of passion, cheerful in the performance of good works, confident in times of temptation, liberal in hospitality, joyful among true brothers, and patient among false brethren."

Even more inspiring are the words in which St. Paul praises charity: "Charity is patient, is kind. Charity envieth not, dealeth not perversely, is not puffed up, is not ambitious, seeketh not her own, is not provoked to anger, thinketh no evil, rejoiceth not in iniquity, but rejoiceth with the truth; beareth all things, believeth all things, endureth all things. Charity never falleth away." [8]

Although charity is a great stimulus for all the virtues,

[6] Cf. I Cor. 16:14.　　[7] Cf. I Cor. 10:31.　　[8] Cf. I Cor. 13:4-8.

it is especially so in regard to the virtue of fortitude, which enables us to bear the burden of all the other virtues. That is why charity undertakes great things, does not refuse labors, faces great dangers, stimulates vacillating hearts, gives spurs to our efforts, and makes cowards courageous. For charity does not measure the difficulties by a rule of reason, but by the strength of its desires. The reason for this is that effects naturally follow the condition of their causes, and when the causes are more powerful, so also are the effects that they produce. But the end or goal is the first and principal cause, since it moves all other causes to operate. Therefore, the greater the love of the end, the greater force it has to move all other causes into motion and to direct them toward that end. Thus, the greater a man's love of money or honor or the study of letters, the greater the efforts he expends to attain what he loves.

In all the affairs of our life our fortitude will be in direct proportion to our love. This is true even among animals, which frequently fall into the snare of the trapper or become the victims of the hunter because they have rushed to the defense of their young. Love gives them the courage that they do not have by nature, for love takes little account of danger when it is a question of the well-being of the beloved. For that reason, love readily risks the one for the other and the fear of danger to self is submerged in the fear of danger to the beloved. So also, the greater our love of God, the greater will be our fortitude in the performance of works done for Him, and that is why we read in the Canticle that "love is strong as death." [9]

What is stronger than death? What weapons have ever prevailed against death? Yet even death itself is conquered by the love of God, because the true lover of God may

[9] Cant. 8:6.

suffer death but he will never be conquered. Who would say that St. Lawrence did not conquer death and the flames over which he suffered? His persecutors exerted every effort to break his faith and his constancy, but both remained unshaken in the midst of his torments, like a fine diamond which no hammer could ever shatter.

Hear the inspired words of that great lover of Christ as he describes the strength of charity: "Who then shall separate us from the love of Christ? Shall tribulation, or distress, or famine, or nakedness, or danger, or persecution, or the sword? As it is written, 'For Thy sake, we are put to death all the day long. We are accounted as sheep for the slaughter.' But in all these things we overcome because of Him that loved us. For I am sure that neither death, nor life, nor angels, nor principalities, nor powers, nor things present, nor things to come, nor might, nor height, nor depth, nor any other creature, shall be able to separate us from the love of God which is in Christ Jesus, our Lord." [10]

O charity, how great is thy power! If you have prevailed over God Himself, will you not also prevail over men? O sweet tyrant, with what tenderness do you fortify the hearts of men and enable them to accomplish great things! This is the heavenly fortitude that the Lord promised His disciples at the descent of the Holy Ghost at Pentecost.[11]

The sixth excellence of the virtue of charity is that it brings spiritual happiness and joy. Spiritual joy is one of the fruits of the Holy Ghost, who is called the Paraclete or Consoler because He consoles and strengthens souls who work for the love of God. These consolations and delights far exceed all sensible pleasure. In the first place, they are more proper to the nature of man, who is a rational creature and for that reason finds his greatest delight in spir-

[10] Rom. 8:35–39.   [11] Cf. Luke 24:49.

itual joys. Moreover, they proceed from the operations of man's most noble faculties, his intellect and will. Secondly, the delights that proceed from charity are not natural delights at all, but delights of grace and the supernatural order. They are not the delights that we find in creatures, which are finite and limited, but the delights that we find in God, our universal and infinite good.

St. Thomas says that desire is a movement of the heart toward the desired good. When this movement has reached its goal, the lover rests in the good and delights in it. But we should note that the joy which results from possession of a good will be in accordance with the type of good that is attained, and since all the goods of this life are limited and particular, so also is our enjoyment of those goods. On the other hand, God is the universal good in whom all other goods are to be found and for that reason the happiness that will be ours when we possess God will be greater beyond compare than any happiness in created goods. Nor should we marvel at this, for if the sun is better able to enlighten the world than all the stars together, and if the light of the stars is lost in the brilliance of the sun, why should it seem remarkable that the Creator alone should be sufficient to satisfy the human heart and that He gives greater happiness than all created goods together? Rather, it is the greatest foolishness for men to seek perfect happiness outside of God. For one thing is certain, and it is that no creature can have complete contentment apart from its ultimate end and as long as the creature remains separated from its true end, it will always be yearning for it. Therefore, what greater absurdity than to seek perfect happiness and contentment outside of God? And although the plenitude of this happiness will not be enjoyed until the next life, nevertheless, He communicates to His intimate friends in this life some small portion or foretaste of the heavenly banquet as a consolation for those who endure great trials for him.

When the Lord finds a soul that seeks Him and loves Him truly, He enlightens the understanding with a great light and inflames the will with a tremendous love and the joy of the Holy Ghost, so that it can exclaim in the words of David: "My heart and my flesh have rejoiced in the living God." [12] This is clearly manifested in the lives of the saints, to whom the things of God were so sweet and who were so detached from the world that they joyfully renounced all things, sometimes even going into the desert to live among wild beasts and live on roots and herbs in the caves in the mountain sides. They could never have endured such a life if they had not received greater consolation from God than the sorrow they may have felt in abandoning the world. But this is not surprising, for if many philosophers and men of science have left the world in order to give themselves to the study of these natural things, how much more should we expect that the great friends of God should do the same in order to contemplate supernatural and divine things?

Another excellency of charity is that it is not only sweet in itself, but it sweetens and makes lighter the yoke of God's commandments. It is characteristic of love that when one understands what means are necessary to attain the good that is loved, he also loves those very means because he does not consider them as works or labors, but as helps for attaining the object that is loved. Consequently, he experiences greater joy on this account than he does sorrow at the difficulty of his labors. For that reason St. Augustine says that labors are not difficult or tedious for those who

[12] Ps. 83:3.

love, but are a source of delight. And St. Bernard says that when a soul is filled with the love of God, it is prompt and joyful in any kind of good work. It labors but does not tire; if it becomes fatigued, it does not notice it; if others mock it, it takes no account. The same Saint says in another place: "Yoke of holy love, how sweetly you seize us, how tenderly you exhaust us, and how pleasantly you weigh us down with your burdens."

From what has been said, one can readily understand the truth of Christ's words when He said that His yoke is sweet and His burden light.[13] His burden is the law, and the fulfillment of His law is love, and love is sweet and makes all other things sweet. And although Jesus speaks of a yoke and a burden, these things are no more of a burden than are the feathers which enable a bird to fly.

Yet another excellence of charity is that it unites man to God and transforms the soul into God. St. Augustine says that love joins the lover to the beloved and of the two makes but one thing. The philosophers stress this difference between the intellect and the will, namely, that the intellect in understanding makes things like itself, as when it spiritualizes material things and thereby adapts them to the human intellect. But the will becomes like that which it loves, because love transforms the lover into the beloved. The intellect is like a stamp which impresses itself on everything that comes into contact with it, but the will is like soft wax which takes on the shape of that to which it is joined. Hence, if a man loves earthly things, he will become earthly; if he loves God, he will become godly. And what greater excellence could be found in charity than that it has the power to transform a man into God? But in order to understand this correctly we must realize that this

[13] Matt. 11:30.

is not a substantial transformation, but a spiritual or moral one, for the nature of one thing is not changed through love into the nature of another.

This will be more evident if we consider the dominion of the will over the other powers and faculties. When the will inclines to anything, it draws with it all the other powers of soul and body: memory, intellect, passions, and even the external members. And since the will has this rule over the whole man and love exercises its dominion over the will (for where love inclines, there also does the will incline), it follows that wherever love rests, there also rests the will and the one who loves becomes that which he loves. Hence, if a man loves vice, then he becomes vicious; if he loves the world, he becomes worldly; if he loves the flesh, he becomes carnal; if he loves the things of the spirit, he becomes spiritual. Therefore did the prophet say that sinners "became abominable, as those things were which they loved." [14]

The soul that loves God becomes transformed into God so that what God wishes, the soul wishes, and what is pleasing to Him is pleasing to the soul, or what He abhors, the soul abhors. The soul takes little account of its own profit or contentment but is more concerned with the honor of God. Thus the soul and God eventually come to have but one desire and one will, and once the desire and will of the soul are changed, so also are its life and works. If a piece of iron is cast into the furnace, it soon takes on all the properties and characteristics of fire, yet it does not cease to be iron. So also, the soul that is inflamed with the love of God, without ceasing to be human, shares in the sanctity of God Himself. Thus St. Dionysius says that love has the power to unite things and that the lover is no longer master

[14] Os. 9:10.

of himself but is subject to the beloved. That is why St. Paul could say: "I live, now not I, but Christ liveth in me." [15]

To come to an end in this matter, let us observe that since charity is the greatest of all the virtues and the goal of all the others, the perfection of the Christian life must consist essentially in charity. Consequently, the measure of the perfection of just souls, both in this life and in glory, is taken from the degree of their charity. St. Bernard says that he who possesses great charity is great, but he who possesses little charity is little, and he who possesses no charity is nothing. St. Paul states that if he has not charity, he is nothing." [16]

Thus, if a woman finds herself at the moment of death with greater charity than that possessed by another who has worked miracles and converted many souls, undoubtedly the woman will receive a much higher degree of glory in heaven, because she possessed greater charity here on earth. Accordingly, St. Thomas points out that the fact of having done more work or converted more souls does not pertain to one's essential glory, but to accidental glory, but he who has greater charity will receive a greater essential glory. Likewise, St. Augustine says that it is not the multitude of good works nor the long years of service but the greater charity that gives greater merit and a greater reward. Nor should we marvel that this is so, for although whatever a man may do of himself is little in comparison with that which he receives from God, he can still do much if he loves much, because in loving he gives himself and thus performs the greatest service of which he is capable. He who gives his love, gives his will and all that he is and has. But this offering is due only to God, and in making

---

[15] Gal. 2:20.   [16] Cf. I Cor. 13:2.

this offering, a man gives all that he can. Then God responds to this generosity of the Christian soul by giving Himself completely.

This doctrine offers much consolation and encouragement to those who have little to give; those who, because of lack of education or ingenuity or because of sickness or old age, cannot offer great services and labors to the glory of God. For even without doing these things, they can love God greatly. Moreover, he who loves much can do much; he who gives himself through love, already gives much; and he who desires to do much, has the credit of doing much, for God sees the heart of man and in God's sight a good intention is of no less value than the good work itself.

If, therefore, you cannot do great deeds, then desire to do much and love as much as you can. In so doing, you will be doing great things for God. If you are poor in worldly wealth and cannot give alms, then be rich in love and have the desire to give alms, and know that thereby you will have the merit of doing so. Perhaps no one is actually persecuting you, but if you desire with all your heart to be so treated for God's glory, you will be a martyr in God's sight.

You can judge from this, Christian reader, how great is the excellence of charity and how numerous its benefits. Theologians say that the inordinate love of self is the beginning of all sins. But since the love of God is contrary to the love of self, it follows that charity is the knife that cuts away all sin. Who, then, will not strive with all diligence to obtain a medicine that is so efficacious for curing the sickness of sin? Who will not strive to possess a virtue that is so helpful to us in acquiring all the other virtues?

O marvelous virtue, root of all the virtues, fairest daughter of grace, mistress of sanctity, mirror of religion, source of merit, gown of the mystical marriage, heritage of the children of God, key to heaven, support of the soul, and sweetness of the heart! Thou art the fortitude of those who struggle, the crown of those who conquer, the sister of truth, the mother of wisdom, the companion of the saints, the joy of the angels, the dread of the devils, and the sum of all perfection! Without thee, all human efforts fail, the intellect is obscured, faith remains lifeless, hope becomes a vain presumption, the merit of all good works is lost, and the bond of fraternal love is destroyed. But with thee, man is strong in all temptations, humble in all his afflictions, and confident in the face of adversity.

CHAPTER 22 ✍

The Perfection of Charity

IT is the common teaching of all the saints that the perfection of the Christian life consists in the perfection of charity. St. Paul calls charity the bond of perfection [1] and the end of the law.[2] The reason for this is, as St. Thomas teaches, that a thing is said to reach its full perfection when it has attained the ultimate end for which it was created, beyond which there is nothing else that it can attain. But man's ultimate end is God, in whom the human intellect finds all that it is able to understand and the human will embraces all that it is capable of loving, since God is all-perfect. It follows from this that the perfection of the rational creature will consist especially in that virtue which

[1] Col. 3:14.   [2] Cf. I Tim. 1:5.

unites man to his supreme good and transforms him into God, and this is proper to the virtue of charity, which unites man to God through love, as St. John tells us: "God is charity, and he that abideth in charity abideth in God and God in him." [3] It is evident, therefore, that charity is the virtue that unites the soul with God and enables it to reach its ultimate end and that the perfection of the Christian life consists in charity.

But perhaps you will ask in what the perfection of charity consists. St. Thomas answers this question by saying that there are three grades of perfection in charity. The first and highest grade of perfection is to love God as much as He deserves to be loved, but only God can do this, for just as He alone perfectly comprehends Himself, so also He alone perfectly loves Himself. The second perfection of charity is the perfection of those blessed souls in heaven who see God in all His beauty so that they always actually love Him without ceasing, for just as a person who has his eyes open cannot help but see the objects in his line of vision, so when the will is in direct contact with Supreme Goodness it is always actually loving this Goodness. The third perfection of charity is that of the Christian who loves God in this life and although he cannot reach the high degree of the blessed, he strives with all his power to love God to the best of his ability. For that reason, perfect charity not only strives to avoid all sin, but to overcome all the obstacles that may prevent it from actually loving God or may weaken its affection for God. And since all these obstacles arise from self-love, charity wages a constant warfare against self-love, with the result that its perfection can be measured by the degree of its victory in the battle against self.

[3] Cf. I John 4:16.

St. Augustine says that self-love is the poison of the love of God and that the perfection of the love of God is mortification of self-love. He also says that self-love may be lessened in this life, but it can never be completely destroyed, and he concludes that perfect charity in this life is that which strongly resists and rejects anything that may weaken or prevent the actual love of God, namely, anything that fosters self-love and diverts the Christian from the love of God. Moreover, man's charity on earth will be more perfect as it more closely approaches the charity of the blessed in heaven, who are always actually loving God with all the ardor of their being.

This is the model that is given to us for the perfect love of God and we are commanded to strive for this perfection by the precept which states that we must love God with all our heart, and soul, and strength. This does not mean that this precept can be perfectly fulfilled in this life, but St. Thomas teaches that the perfection of charity that is possible in this life is that a man employ all his efforts and diligence in loving God and renounce any earthly concern or interest that is not of obligation to his state in life or is not of personal necessity.

This is a great truth which even the pagan philosophers were able to discover by reason alone. As one of them has said, the principle and end of perfect happiness is the continual gazing upon God and the profound affection of our will toward him. Therefore, the soul should strive for the perfection for which God has created it. But if the soul departs from God, it will wither away like a branch that has been cut from the tree. Accordingly, when the Christian has reached such a degree of love in this life that he is detached from all perishable things and has no inordinate affection for any of them, but places all his love on God in such a way that his heart is almost always fixed on God and when, dead now to all created things, he lives only for God, he will have entered into the wine cellar of the Lord where, as we read in the Canticle,[4] he will be inebriated with the wine of love and will forget all other things and even himself out of love for God.

I realize that few souls arrive at this degree of perfection and that the necessities and various obligations of justice and even of charity frequently demand that we leave God for God. Nevertheless, we speak of this degree of perfection so that we may know the goal toward which we should travel as best we can, for although many never attain it, they will approach it more closely if they direct their desires and intentions to greater things rather than to lesser things.

In conformity with this teaching, a certain wise man has said that we should desire the best and greatest of all good things and perhaps we shall attain at least half of what we desire. A strong and intense desire takes no account of one's strength, it recognizes no limitations, it does not submit to the restrictions of reason, because strong desires do not consider so much what one can do, but what one wishes to do.

But not every degree of charity suffices to give the internal peace and tranquillity of which we have spoken. Only perfect charity can give perfect peace and joy. When God so ordains, charity brings an experimental knowledge of the goodness and sweetness of God and then passes through the eight steps of charity until the soul ultimately reaches a state of perfect repose in God. These eight grades of the perfection of charity are so closely linked together that one leads directly to the other, so that the preceding grade disposes for the one that follows. The first grade is

[4] Cant. Cf. 5:1.

an experimental knowledge of God and it is the gate through which the gifts and blessings of God enter the soul and greatly enrich it. From this experimental knowledge proceeds a great impulse by which the will bursts forth in love for the immense goodness that is revealed to it. This is followed by a most sweet delight which is like a hidden manna that nobody knows except him who has tasted it. It is a normal effect of love and one of the principal means that God uses to draw men from the world and detach them from all sensual delights. It so far surpasses every earthly pleasure or delight that men readily renounce all lesser things for it.

Since spiritual things are so excellent, the more they are tasted, the more they are desired, and the taste of them produces a vehement desire to possess them, for by this time the soul can find rest and satisfaction in nothing else. Moreover, the soul knows that it can attain spiritual goods only at the cost of the labor of the virtues and a mortified life, as the Savior has told us: "I am the Way, and the Truth, and the Light. No man cometh to the Father but by Me." Consequently, the soul experiences a strong desire not only to meditate on spiritual truths but to imitate Christ and to walk in His footsteps of humility, patience, obedience, poverty, abnegation, meekness, mercy, and the other Christian virtues.

This desire is followed by an intense satisfaction, for God does not arouse desires in us in order to torment us, but to perfect us and prepare us for even greater things. He it is who gives life and takes it away; He it is who arouses holy desires and satisfies those desires. In this way He arouses in souls a great distaste for the things of the world so that they can trample these things under their feet and be content with the spiritual manna in which the soul finds all pleasures and delights together.

Then follows the spiritual inebriation, which far surpasses the delights previously described, for here the soul completely forgets all perishable goods and even forgets itself, because it is submerged in the abyss of the infinite goodness and sweetness of God. Next the soul reaches the seventh step, which is the assurance of attaining glory. This assurance is not yet perfect, but it is far greater than most persons imagine. Indeed, the prophet says: "Blessed be the man that trusteth in the Lord, and the Lord shall be his confidence" [5] and: "The Lord is our refuge and our strength. We shall not fear although the world be shaken and the mountains shall be moved and shall fall into the sea." [6]

Lastly, this great confidence produces a spiritual tranquillity which is like a sweet sleep on the breast of the Lord. It is a peace which surpasses all understanding. "And My people shall sit in the beauty of peace and in the tabernacles of confidence and in wealthy rest." [7] This is the kingdom of heaven on earth and the paradise of delights that we are able to enjoy in this exile.

Certain souls, after having practiced prayer, mortification, and works of charity, and after having walked along the paths of the Lord with fervor of spirit and perseverance in the practice of virtue, ultimately reach that type of love which mystical theologians call unitive love. Reaching this state is like reaching the promised land after traveling through the desert. One of the characteristics of this love is that it brings a sweetness and joy that never cease by day or by night. No matter what the activity, the soul can-

[5] Jer. 17:7.   [6] Ps. 4:2.   [7] Isa. 32:18.

not be separated from God. The sweetness of this love seizes the devout heart and holds it captive, giving it a distaste for the things of this world. God alone is its desire, its treasure, and its joy. This is characteristic of the love of union.

He who has reached the union of this divinc love already enjoys in this life a happiness that is similar to that of glory, for it brings a kind of plenitude, an interior repose and satisfaction, so that the soul can repeat with St. Francis: "O my God and my all! O my God and my all!" Nor is this a cause for surprise, for our souls were created for God and when they attain Him, they are at rest. The clamor of all other desires ceases, for the soul has no hunger for anything apart from God. Such is the happiness with which God rewards the works of His faithful servants even in this life.

After he had tasted the sweetness of this love, St. Augustine said: "The just man rejoices in Thee because Thy love is sweet and calm and because Thou dost fill the hearts wherein Thou dwellest with sweetness, peace, and tranquillity. Such things are not given by the love of the world or the flesh, which are distressing and filled with tribulation and therefore bring no peace to the souls they enter. Rather, worldly love brings suspicion, passion, and many fears. But Thou, O Lord, art true delight for the good, for in Thee are found a tremendous and overwhelming tranquillity and a life that is alien to all anxiety." In another place he says: "What is this that I experience? What fire is this that inflames my heart? What light illumines it? O fire that ever burns and never dies, may I be consumed by thee! O light that always shines and is never eclipsed, illumine my soul. . . . O holy fire, how sweetly thou dost burn, how secretly thou dost illumine, and how tenderly thou dost inflame the soul!"

Moreover, charity not only makes a man enjoy peace with his neighbor and with God, but also to be at peace with himself. It quiets the passions and suppresses the struggle that the inferior powers wage against the spirit. The internal warfare that we suffer is born of the struggle between the flesh and the spirit and of the restlessness caused in us by our inordinate desires. When the lower appetites are quieted, a man remains at peace and desires nothing from this world and even looks upon it with disdain.

Together with this internal peace, the Christian receives a true liberty of spirit which is given to those who are no longer slaves of their flesh. They reach a point when they enjoy the true liberty of the sons of God, through which they easily obtain the mastery over all the passions which formerly ruled their lives. This liberty raises them above all the anxieties and fears of this life and of the next. Freed from all impediments, they are so united with God that neither the company of men nor external occupations can separate them from the presence of God. Amidst a multitude of activities they preserve their simplicity of spirit and they use all things as occasions for raising their minds to God, for they can find God in all things. In Him is all their love and they remain so absorbed in Him that seeing, they do not see, and hearing, they do not hear.

What words can describe the virtues of these souls, their firmness of faith, their peaceful hope, their joy in that which they love, their delight in the attainment of their desires, their peace in the midst of sufferings and their great courage in all their undertakings? They find delight in all their labors, wealth in their poverty, contentment in their hunger, glory in their persecution, honor in injuries, rest in their night vigils, and paradise in their practice of prayer.

The delights and consolations of the love of God, who shall expound them? He who wishes to know something of these things should meditate on the beautiful words of the Bridegroom: "Arise, make haste, My love, My dove, My beautiful one, come. For winter is now past; the rain is over and gone. The flowers have appeared in our land; the time of pruning is come; the voice of the turtle is heard in our land; the fig tree hath put forth her green figs; the vines in flower yield their sweet smell. Arise, My love, My beautiful one, and come. My dove in the clefts of the rock, in the hollow places of the wall, show Me thy face. Let thy voice sound in My ears, for thy voice is sweet and thy face comely." [8]

"O my soul," says St. Augustine, "you have a Spouse but you do not know Him. He is the most beautiful of all beings, but you have not seen His beauty. But He has seen your beauty, else He would not love you. But what shall you do? Now in this time you cannot see Him because He is absent and for that reason you do not fear to injure and offend Him by disdaining His love and giving yourself to other alien loves. Do not desire to commit so great an evil, and if for the time being you cannot know what this Spouse is like, at least consider the pledge that He has given you so that you will understand with how much affection you ought to love Him and with how much care you ought to be vigilant over yourself for His sake.

"Much has He given you but even more has He loved you. What, my soul, has your Spouse given you? Cast your eyes over this entire universe and see whether there is any-

[8] Cf. Cant. 2:10-14.

thing in it that is not for your service. All created nature was made for this purpose: to serve for your benefit and to do that which perfects you. And who has arranged all this? To be sure, it was God Himself. And how is it that you can accept all these benefits and not know the Giver? O what a geat folly it is not to desire the love of the omnipotent Lord and what great ignorance it is not to love Him who loves you so! Love Him for what He is and love yourself out of love of Him. Love Him for yourself and love yourself for Him."

But perhaps you will say, Christian reader, that while it is true that the Lord is the Spouse of souls, He has many brides and therefore He gives but a little love to each one. This may be true of men, who are defective in love as they are in all virtues, but the Lord is omnipotent in virtue and also in love. Consequently, He is infinite in His love. No matter how many receive His love, He will never reach a limit or terminus. Just as no one man receives less of the sun's rays than another, although the sun enlightens all, so the Lord expends no less love on the souls of holy men than if there were only one holy soul in the universe. God is not like Jacob, who loved Lia less because of his greater love for Rachel, for He is infinite and His love is not lessened by being divided among many. Therefore, let others go in pursuit of their loves and let them love what they wish, but I know for certain that He is the eternal Father and Spouse of souls, for love of whom all is well spent, even to death itself, if one ultimately attains His love.

CHAPTER 23 ✒

The Gift of Wisdom

THE function of grace is to make a man holy, and this cannot be achieved unless he be aroused to the actual love of God, sorrow for the sins of his past life, and a disdain for the things of the world. But the human will cannot perform these acts unless the intellect possesses the knowledge proportionate to this end. For the will of itself is a blind faculty and cannot take a step unless the intellect first show the way by declaring to the will what is good or evil. For that reason St. Thomas says that as the just soul grows in the love of God, it also grows in the knowledge of His goodness and beauty. Hence, if a man's actual love of God grows by one hundred degrees, his spiritual knowledge grows in like proportion, for he who loves much knows many reasons for loving, while he who loves but little knows of few reasons for loving.

Moreover, if grace causes God Himself to dwell in the soul of the just, and if God, as St. John points out,[1] is the Light that illumines every man who comes into the world, it is clear that as He finds the soul more pure and cleansed of sin, the rays of His divine light are more resplendent in the soul. In like manner, the rays of the sun are more brightly reflected in a mirror that is clean and well polished. For that reason St. Augustine calls God the wisdom of the purified soul, for God wondrously illumines this soul with the rays of His light and thereby teaches it all that it needs to know in reference to its salvation.

[1] John 1:9.

But why should it seem so remarkable that God should do this for man, when He does something similar for all His creatures? The brute creatures know by an instinct implanted in them by their Creator whatever is necessary for their conservation. Who teaches the sheep which plants in the pasture are harmful and which ones are beneficial, so that the sheep instinctively eats one thing and avoids the other? Who informs the animals which creatures are their friends and which are their enemies, so that the sheep will follow the mastiff but flee from the wolf? It is the Creator who does these things, and if He gives animals the knowledge to preserve their life, how much more readily will he provide man with the knowledge necessary to preserve his spiritual life, especially since man has no less need of these things that are above his nature than the brute does for the things that are in conformity with its nature? If God has been so solicitous in providing for the works of nature, how much more will He provide for those of grace, which are so much more excellent and so much more above man's powers?

These examples not only demonstrate that there is such a knowledge as that of which we have spoken, but they also declare something of the type of this knowledge. It is not merely a speculative knowledge, but a practical knowledge, for it is not given that man may know, but that he may work; not to make learned disputants about divine truth, but to make virtuous Christians. For that reason this knowledge does not remain dormant in the intellect, as that which is learned in the schools, but it communicates its power to the will and inclines the will to perform all those acts which such knowledge awakens and arouses in the will.

These things are proper to the instincts or movements of the Holy Ghost, who is the perfect Master who teaches His own that which it is necessary for them to know. Accordingly, we read in the Canticle of Canticles: "My soul melted when He spoke." [2] These words show the great difference between this knowledge and other types of knowledge, for the others do no more than enlighten the intellect, but this knowledge moves the will to do all that is necessary for the soul's conversion and reformation. Thus the Apostle says: "The word of God is living and effectual and more piercing than any two-edged sword, and reaching unto the division of the soul and the spirit, of the joints also and the marrow." [3] In other words, this inspiring knowledge makes a division between the animal and the spiritual parts of man and separates one from the other, thus destroying that evil union wherein the spirit is attached to the things of the flesh. And lest you think that this doctrine is an arbitrary one, listen to the words of David: "I have understood more than all my teachers, because Thy testimonies are my meditation. I have had understanding above ancients, because I have sought Thy commandments." [4] Hear also the promises made by God through the mouth of Isaias: "The Lord will give thee rest and He will fill your soul with splendor and He will be to you a fountain that always runs and never lacks water."

What are those splendors with which God fills the souls of the just but the knowledge that He gives them concerning the things that pertain to salvation? He will teach them how great is the beauty of virtue, the ugliness of vice, the vanity of the world, the dignity of grace, the greatness of glory, the sweetness of the consolation of the Holy Ghost, the goodness of God, the malice of the devil, the shortness of this life, and the almost universal errors of all who live in it. Isaias tells us that by means of this knowledge, God

[2] Cant. 5:6.   [3] Heb. 4:12.   [4] Ps. 118:99.

frequently raises souls high above the mountains where they contemplate the King in all his beauty while their eyes see this world as something remote and far away. Such blessings are similar to the joys of heaven, for heaven itself seems very near while the things of earth seem very unimportant. The contrary happens in the case of evil men, for they see the things of heaven as something far away but the things of this earth they look upon as being very close to them.

This is the reason why those who share in the heavenly gift of wisdom are neither puffed up in the days of their prosperity nor dejected in the time of adversity. For by means of the light of wisdom they realize how insignificant are all the things that the world can give or take away in comparison with that which God gives to the soul. Therefore, Solomon says that a holy man perseveres in wisdom like the sun, but the fool is as changeable as the moon.[5] St. Ambrose, commenting on these words, writes: "The wise man is not broken by fear; he does not change by gaining power; he does not become proud in times of prosperity; and he is not smothered in time of adversity. For where there is wisdom, there is also virtue, constancy, and fortitude." As a result, the just man is always the same; he does not fluctuate with the changes that occur in his life nor does he follow every new doctrine, but he perseveres in Christ, established in charity and firmly rooted in faith.

We should not marvel that this wisdom should have such great power. We have already said that it is not a wisdom of this world, but a heavenly wisdom; not a wisdom to make one proud, but one that edifies. It is not a wisdom that merely enlightens the intellect in a speculative way, but one that moves the will as it moved that of St. Augustine, of whom it is written that he wept when he heard

[5] Cf. Ecclus. 27:12.

the psalms chanted in church. The voices of the singers penetrated the very depth of his heart and aroused so intense a devotion that the tears flowed from his eyes.

O blessed tears and blessed wisdom that has produced such fruits! What can be compared to such wisdom? We should not trade it for all the gold or silver in the world. The most precious stones can never equal it in value. Consider how this wisdom should arouse in you a fear of the Lord so that you will depart from your sins.

Although everything that has been said about this heavenly wisdom of the Holy Ghost is very true, no man, however holy, should neglect to subject himself in all humility to the directions and judgments of his superiors, especially to those who have offices of dignity and authority in the Church. For who was more filled with light than St. Paul, who had, as it were, spoken to God face to face? Yet he went to Jerusalem to communicate to the other apostles that which he had learned in his remarkable vision. Again, Moses did not hesitate to confer with Jethro, although he was a Gentile.[6] It is evident from this that the internal help of grace does not exclude the external guidance of the Church. Divine providence makes use of both to supply for our weakness, but he is not deserving of the interior inspirations and movements of grace who does not humbly follow the doctrine and guidance of the Church.

[6] Cf. Gal. 2:2; Exod. 2:1.

CHAPTER 24 ✒

The Path to Holiness

HAVING spoken of the excellence of charity and the gift of wisdom that perfects this virtue, we must now point out the path to the perfect love of God. First, we must understand the nature of the goal that is sought. We have already explained that charity unites the just man to God in such a way that he has the same desires and aversions as God Himself, so that the just soul imitates God's own holiness as much as is possible. The Lord Himself asks this of us when he says: "Be ye holy, because I, the Lord your God, am holy." [1]

One can readily understand from this what means are necessary to reach the goal of holiness. Holiness implies the most perfect imitation of God that is possible, but if a thing cannot become what it is not unless it first ceases to be what it is, then the first requirement for holiness is that we rid ourselves of all the characteristics of the old man and put on those of the new man, who is fashioned to the image and likeness of God. Even in the natural order, there can be no generation of a new substance without the corruption of the old. So also, man cannot become divine unless he first cease to be human, that is, unless he put aside as much as is possible the imperfections and weaknesses of his human nature. A person cannot become wise if he does not cease to be ignorant and he cannot become healthy unless he first rids himself of sickness. In like manner, the Christian cannot become just if he does not depart from

[1] Lev. 19:2.

his sinful life; much less can he become divine if he does not cease to be human.

There are two terms in every movement: that from which the mover departs and that toward which the mover travels, and it is not possible to arrive at the one without departing from the other. Likewise, in this spiritual movement the Christian must travel from self to God and he will never reach God if he does not first depart from self. Fire cannot ignite a piece of wood until the dampness has been ejected from the wood, for dampness is opposed to the heat of the fire. Neither can man, conceived in original sin and clothed in flesh and blood, succeed in transforming himself into the sanctity of God unless he first lose all those characteristics and qualities that are contrary or repugnant to this divine holiness. This transformation is effected principally by the grace of God, which is called in Scripture a consuming fire,[2] because it consumes all the depravity and imperfections of man and purifies him of all his sins. As St. Dionysius says, the nature of grace is to draw all things to itself and to make them share in itself.

But since God, who has created man without man's help, will not sanctify man without man's help, that is, unless man cooperates with God and does that which falls to his share, it follows that man must also work for the goal of holiness by mortifying himself and destroying in himself whatever is an obstacle to his transformation in God.

In order to plant a garden on a rocky mountain side, it is first necessary to clear the land of trees and shrubbery. Once this is done, the profitable and useful trees and vines can be planted. The same thing is true of the Christian life. One must first exert himself energetically to root out the thorns and weeds of vice and evil inclinations, and once

[2] Deut. 4:24.

this has been done, he can plant the virtues and especially the virtue of charity, which is the tree of life in the Christian's garden of Eden.

Accordingly, Cassian and other theologians teach that purity of heart is the principal means for attaining the love of God, for purity of heart uproots from our souls anything that would impede the love of God. Therefore, the first thing required is the purification and mortification of self-love. Then the Christian must proceed to the mortification of his own will, the avoidance of all sin, control of the passions, freedom from excessive anxiety, avoidance of too much attention to worldly affairs, mortification of one's evil inclinations, and purity of intention in both the spiritual and temporal interests of one's life.

Once the Christian is totally mortified, that is, when he holds the flesh in perfect subjection, the spirit will rule in him to such an extent that he will be always disposed to approach God in love, while God Himself will be ever ready to come to the Christian through His grace. Just as a stone that is held in the air seeks its natural position by falling to the ground when all impediments or restraints are removed, so the human soul, which is a spiritual substance, once it is released from the prison of the sensual appetite which oppresses it with an affection for worldly things, advances with the help of divine grace to spiritual things and embraces them as proper to the dignity of the human soul.

It is also well to observe that the principal difficulty in this matter of the love of God does not lie in the practice of love itself, because this is a work of great sweetness. Rather, the principal difficulty lies in ridding our souls of the impediments to this love. In other words, the resistance we encounter to igniting our hearts with the fire of charity lies in the dampness and coldness of our hearts. Once these obstacles are overcome, the fire of charity will burst into flame and will burn brightly. The difficulty is not in love, but in getting rid of the obstacles to love.

A very important conclusion follows from this doctrine and it should serve to make us understand and avoid a great part of the error that one may meet in this matter. We must not measure our progress in holiness by the sweetness or consolations that we may sometimes experience, although these things may be praiseworthy and holy, but we should measure our progress by our mortification and our victory over the obstacles to holiness, especially our victory over self-love and self-will and all the passions that flow from them. Some Christians are so tender of heart that any thought of the passion of Christ or some similar truth immediately reduces them to tears and they feel a great sympathy and compassion. But this often proceeds from a natural tenderness of heart rather than from the pure love of God. Therefore, such persons should not judge from that fact alone that they are making great progress, unless this tenderness is accompanied by a greater victory over their own will and passions and evil inclinations.

CHAPTER 25 ✍

Growth in Charity

BEFORE we begin to treat of this matter it is well to recall that in the blessed state of innocence in which God placed man at creation, nothing was more natural or more pleasant for man than to love his Creator. For what is more natural than for the creature to love its maker, the effect to love its cause, or the part to love the whole from which it proceeds? Unfortunately, original sin not only wounded the integrated human nature but it so corrupted man that he could no longer proceed as before nor could he accomplish those virtuous acts which had previously been so easy and pleasant. Instead, man was beset with great obstacles and impediments because of his sin. As a result, he who before his sin had loved God more than himself, afterwards loved himself more than God, and we have already seen that inordinate self-love is the principal obstacle to the love of God. It draws us into ourselves and separates us from God. It calls us to the love of earthly goods and makes us turn our backs on heavenly things.

Accordingly, he who truly desires to grow in the love of God must wage continual war against inordinate self-love. I say inordinate because if the love of self is regulated and controlled, it is not evil but good and necessary for the preservation of life. A thing may be good and necessary in itself but may become dangerous and evil if it is inordinate. The same thing is true of the natural heat of the body, which is good for life, but if it becomes excessive it is a dangerous fever. Likewise, the swift-flowing rivers cause no harm as long as they remain within their banks but if they become swollen and overflow their banks, they flood the entire surrounding area. So also, self-love and other affections such as honor are salutary and virtuous as long as they are kept within the rule of reason and the law of God, but if they exceed these limits they become vicious and sinful.

Inordinate self-love desires the various created goods in an excessive and unlawful manner. Although there are countless created goods that man may seek inordinately, St. John reduces them to three: wealth, honor, and bodily pleasure. Under honor are included such things as offices, dignities, titles, privileges, authority, exemptions, and all other things that are related to worldly honor. Under wealth are included the various kinds of temporal gain such as patrimonies, inheritances, rents, and the countless ways in which people can accumulate wealth. By bodily pleasure is understood all those things in which the senses of the body may take pleasure. Thus, the eyes naturally delight in the beautiful colors in paintings, tapestries, clothing, or the beauties of nature as well as the beauty of the dance or theatrical spectacles, or any kind of visible beauty. The ear delights in musical sounds; the sense of smell, in the various perfumes and ointments and aromatic spices or the natural scent of the flowers; the sense of taste, in the different kinds of savors in various foods; and the sense of touch, in comfortable furniture, soft clothing, and all other articles that contribute to bodily comfort and relaxation. In addition to these, there are other pleasures that satisfy the more spiritual faculties. Man's natural curiosity to know and to see all things is satisfied by many books, much visiting and conversation, and other such things. And since to love means nothing more than to wish well to that which is loved, it is evident that anyone who loves himself to excess, likewise inordinately desires all good things for himself.

It should be evident from the foregoing that he who wishes to grow in the love of God must wage constant war against self-love. The reasons for this are numerous and it is necessary to understand them so that we may see clearly those which pertain to us personally. One of the philosophers has said that he who truly loves cannot love more than one thing because the capacity of the human heart is so small that if a man's whole love is given to one thing there is no love left for anything else. Now, what is more contrary to the love of God than love of self? Self-love desires everything for the individual, directing all things to himself and making himself his own ultimate end. The love of God, on the contrary, directs all things to God and denies self and even crucifies self for love of Him. Since these two loves are so contrary, so also are the affections and works that proceed from them and for that reason it is impossible that both these loves should be contained in the one heart. For how can we possess at one and the same time the love of God and love of the world, love of the earth and love of heaven, love of the flesh and love of the spirit, selfish love and divine love? How can truth and vanity, temporal things and eternal things, lofty things and base things, the sweet and the bitter, the peaceful and the turbulent, the spiritual and the carnal be joined together?

Self-love not only impedes divine love because it proposes contrary ends and means, but it likewise impedes the love of God because it is always occupied in seeking those things that pertain to the profit or pleasure of the body. Brute animals are not interested in anything else except the preservation of their own life because they are not capable of anything greater than that, so those men who love themselves, since they are not at all concerned with the next life, are concerned only with goods of the present life and never have time for the practices or exercises that pertain to the love of God, such as prayer, meditation, confession, and the reception of Communion.

The love of God is likewise impeded by the restlessness and anxiety that accompany the occupations of self-love. A person never succeeds in worldly affairs except at the cost of much care which disturbs the soul, makes it restless, and causes it to lose its peace and liberty. Consequently, just as weeds choke out the good plants in a garden, as Christ said in his parable of the sower, so also the anxietics of worldly affairs and interests suffocate the love of God and cause one to think excessively of self.

The love of God is also impeded by excessive love of pleasure or luxury. Those persons who are filled with self-love are also great lovers of recreation and various kinds of pastimes. Although they would not openly admit the doctrine of Epicurus, which states that man's happiness consists in pleasure, they do profess this doctrine by their actions because they spend their whole life in the search for pleasure. They are ever seeking some new delight or recreation in music or entertainment, in hunting or feasting, in social gatherings and other such things. They hate to be alone; they avoid any kind of recollection; they are friends of the palate and enemies of the cross. Any kind of silence is unbearable to them and the practice of prayer is even more intolerable.

How could such persons be properly disposed for the practice of the love of God? The things that pertain to divine love are not to be undertaken by those who are effeminate or lovers of luxury. They demand strong men and courageous hearts. The valiant woman who was so highly praised in the Book of Proverbs opened her hand to great things and girded herself with fortitude and strengthened her arms to do great work. But these luxury lovers refuse to take up arms, to carry the shield, and to face their labors. Nothing is more contrary than the love of pleasure and the love of work, and since the love of God is attained only at the cost of great effort, how shall he ever attain it whose whole life is spent in seeking pleasure?

The servant of God who understands this truth will take up his weapons and shield and will gird himself for battle against himself, fighting under the royal banner of Him who said: "If any man will come after Me, let him deny himself and take up his cross and follow Me." [1] And if you wish to know what this cross is, I tell you that it is nothing other than that described by St. Paul: "They that are Christ's have crucified their flesh with the vices and concupiscences." [2] Self-denial is nothing other than the contradiction of all one's evil inclinations and self-will so far as they are contrary to the will of God. To deny oneself means not to be a law unto oneself but to follow the law of God.

Besides the mortification of self-love, mortification of one's own will is also necessary. Perhaps you will ask whether there is any difference between self-love and one's own will. To this I would answer that self-love signifies an inordinate love of those things that cater to the pleasure and convenience of the body, but self-will signifies the desires, appetites, and vehement inclinations for created things. Some men, for example, are inclined to play, to hunt, to fish, to spend much time in conversations and social affairs; others are inclined to murmur, to give exces-

[1] Matt. 16:24.　　　　　[2] Gal. 5:24.

sive attention to their appearance, to vanities; others, to travel, to curiosity, and so forth. Some men are very apprehensive and vehement in all that they pursue, for just as men differ in their facial appearance, so also they differ in their inclinations and appetites. All this is what we mean when we speak of self-will.

Self-will is no less dangerous than self-love; it is no less difficult to conquer and its victory is no less necessary. The core of the Christian religion is the love of God and perfect obedience to His laws and His will, which is an effect of the love of God. True friendship signifies that one has the same likes and dislikes as his friend. Therefore, since charity and obedience are so closely related, Christ has said: "If you love Me, keep My commandments." [3] Again, He says: "He that hath My commandments and keepeth them, he it is that loveth Me." [4]

Perfect obedience and perfect conformity of wills make a man a servant of God. Promptness of obedience should characterize the servant of God in regard to all that God commands or that which is commanded by those who stand in the place of God, and it is not only a question of obeying what God has commanded in so many words, but also in those things that He signifies by His inspirations, as long as we understand these inspirations in conformity with Scripture and the teaching of the Church.

Let us suppose that a man feels that all is well with him in regard to his prayer and recollection and yet he feels himself more inclined to some other virtuous practice in which, however, his soul is not as recollected or as free from imperfections as it would be in the practice of prayer, to which he is not so strongly inclined. This is a strong sign that God calls the man to the practice of prayer rather than

[3] John 14:15.   [4] *Ibid.*, 14:21.

the performance of the virtuous actions to which he is more inclined and that he should conquer his own inclinations as long as duties of his state in life or other obligations do not demand otherwise. This would seem to be the will of God, which, as the Apostle says, desires our sanctification.[5] The same thing is true in regard to all adversities, trials, afflictions, and aridities of spirit. We should in all things conform to the divine will, always placing ourselves in God's hands and always ready to accept the chalice that He offers us.

Accordingly, it is impossible for the divine will to reign in us perfectly if we do not first kill our own self-will. We have said that in order to attain divine love it is necessary to mortify and renounce self-love; so also, if the will of God is to rule us, we must destroy our self-will. Both wills cannot reign in us nor live together, but what is more fitting than that the will of God should live and not the will of man, that God should reign and not man? To achieve this, there is nothing more suitable than to strive always to dispossess ourselves of our own will so that the will of God may more sweetly be done in all things.

This holy practice is commended to us by the saints under various names. Sometimes it is called resignation; at other times, mortification or self-abnegation, but they all signify the same thing. It is called abnegation because we deny our own will and liberty and place them in the hands of God. We despoil ourselves of our own will, so to speak, and this is the greatest sacrifice we can offer to God. It is called mortification because we kill our own inclinations and desires, and this is not done without pain and a struggle. It is called resignation, which is the most significant description, because it places man in the hands of God

---

[5] Cf. I Thess. 4:3.

and makes him subject to God, despoiling him of self, as one does who resigns from some office or honor and places himself at the disposal of his superior. In this way the saints and saintly Christians have rid themselves of self and their own wills and subjected themselves to God so that they seemed always to be saying with the Apostle: "Lord, what wilt Thou have me do?" [6]

The Lord Himself invites us to this holy practice under the name of mortification when He says: "Amen, amen, I say to you, unless the grain of wheat falling into the ground die, itself remaineth alone; but if it die, it bringeth forth much fruit." [7] From this it is evident that the fruit of true life is hidden in perfect mortification, because he who is constantly dying to self is always living in a new manner to God. The resigned and mortified soul is like a cluster of ripe, sweet grapes, but the unmortified soul is a cluster of green grapes, bitter and filled with acid.

There is nothing we can offer to God that is more pleasing to Him than the resignation of our will because there is nothing that a man treasures more than this. Hence, when a man denies his own will, even in the smaller things, he can be assured that he has rendered to God a most agreeable service. If, while seated at table, a man is offered a tasty dish which he could eat without sinning, and yet he denies his appetite for the love of God, he does a service to God, as David did when he refused to drink the water at the well of Bethlehem. [8]

If God gives such great rewards for these little sacrifices, what will He not give to those who for love of Him deny themselves in all things? To practice this exercise successfully, the Christian should frequently say: "For the love of Thee, my God, I do not desire to see that, to hear that,

[6] Acts 9:6.   [7] John 12:24.   [8] Cf. II Kings 23:17.

to taste this mouthful, to take this period of recreation and entertainment." In doing these things, the Christian will gain merit and will also habituate himself to the practice of self-denial. As we have said, it is a great help to the conquering of self-love if we sometimes deny our appetites even in regard to those things that are lawful. So here it is helpful for mortification of the will if we sometimes resist the desires for things that are lawful, for self-love and self-will are closely related and so are the remedies that prevent their excesses.

Self-love is a most vehement passion and very difficult to conquer, for it enters into almost all the works that we do. Likewise, self-will, even when we do not fully realize it, may assume the guise of prudence, charity, necessity, mercy, or justice, or may advance some apparently honest reason such as the example of others or unwillingness to bother others, so that a man may do what he wants to do rather than that which is repugnant to him. It is merely a ruse by which the man seeks to do his own will rather than God's will, but sometimes the man is not only unaware of this fact, but he believes quite the contrary. And although a man is not guilty of sin in each and every instance that he is deceived by his own self-will, nevertheless he has been tricked into doing his own will under the guise of doing the will of God.

Consequently, we must cultivate a holy hatred of our own self-will and we must deny it whenever possible, being governed rather by the will of another than by our own will, finding pleasure in the humble subjection of obedience than in the liberty of our own will, and being very suspicious of anything that we esteem very highly if we have not first examined it very carefully. Moreover, we should accept all things as coming from the hand of God,

however difficult and painful they may be. The hairs of
our head are numbered and known to Him and not a leaf
from a tree falls to the ground without His will. Let us,
then, say with Christ: "The chalice which My Father hath
given Me, shall I not drink it?" [9] This is the way the Christian arrives at the mortification of his own will and once
he has attained to this, he will understand the words of the
Apostle: "For you are dead, and your life is hid with Christ
in God." [10] And if you want to know when a Christian
shall have arrived at this state of being dead to all that is
not Christ, I tell you that it is when he has abandoned his
own will for that of God, when he has rid himself of self-
love, when he has renounced the delights of the world,
when he has mortified the inordinate desires of the flesh,
when he considers himself the lowliest of all, when he
promptly obeys men for the love of God, when he does not
become involved in useless cares, when he does not judge
the words or deeds of his neighbor, when he is not gladdened by praise or afflicted by insults, when he suffers all
injuries and adversities patiently, when he complains about
no one and sees all his neighbors as the temple of God.
The Christian who can do all these things is truly dead to
self and lives only for God.

The third means for growing in the love of God is the
practice of prayer and recollection. The necessity of this
exercise can be seen from the following example. If a
woman wishes to preserve fruit that is somewhat bitter
and has a high acid content, she first cooks it until all
the bitterness and acidity have been taken out. Once this
has been done, she adds sugar or syrup to the fruit so
that it will absorb the sweetness of these condiments. In
like manner, if a man is to be transformed through the

[9] John 18:11.   [10] Col. 3:3.

love of God, he must first rid himself of all that is contrary to God, and once this has been done, he must unite himself to God through the practice of prayer so that he may become one spirit with God.

The servant of God must exert every effort so that his soul will always proceed under God's assistance through prayer and love. If the Christian perseveres in the practice of prayer, the Sun of justice will make the soul like unto Himself, so that it will be as beautiful as a cloud at sunset that is bathed in the rays of the setting sun.

This doctrine is based on two principles of philosophy, one of which states that causes have a natural tendency to make things similar to themselves, as happens when cold causes other things to be cold or heat radiates itself to make other things warm. The more powerful the cause, the more it is able to reproduce itself in its effects. The second principle states that the causes in the natural order cannot operate unless they are brought into contact with the matter upon which they are to work. Fire cannot ignite wood unless it is brought into contact with the wood. But God is the first and most noble and most powerful of all causes, and therefore He is the most communicative and He gives of Himself by way of the divine likeness to the soul of man. But in order that this be done, man must be united with God. This union with God is not effected by man's approach to God by bodily steps, but by a journeying of the spirit, that is to say, by uniting man's intellect and will to God through love and the practice of prayer.

St. Bernard speaks of four principal steps or grades of prayer: spiritual reading, meditation, vocal prayer, and contemplation. Spiritual reading walks, meditation runs, vocal prayer flies, but contemplation reaches the end of the journey and rests in God. That spiritual reading is most beneficial which is most affective and which treats of the love of God, as we see in the works of St. Augustine and St. Bonaventure. That meditation is the best which treats of the divine benefits and perfections and of those things that are designed for arousing the love of God. Those vocal prayers are best in which we ask for the divine love, especially if the prayers themselves flow from an intense desire for the love of God.

Referring to those who are constantly occupied in recollection and the practice of prayer, St. Augustine writes: "Blessed are they, O Lord, of whom Thou alone art their hope and whose life is a perpetual prayer." It is indeed a great thing to be constantly recollected, and it is not so difficult as some people imagine. For we do not mean by recollection and prayer that one must always be on his knees or that he must always be speaking with God. It suffices for constant prayer if the Christian always preserves a recollected and vigilant heart, a holy fear and reverence for God, and the constant desire to please God and to walk in His presence. Indeed, this is very common among those souls who are dedicated to the service of God.

But of all the things that help us to be recollected in God and live in His presence, the best method is the actual practice of the love of God. The virtue of charity grows best by the exercise of love rather than by the performance of the external works of charity, for the very act of loving is a function of the virtue of charity and it is most excellent and meritorious because it proceeds immediately from charity, which is the most excellent of all the virtues. Whence, just as habits acquired by the repeated performance of some action increase and become more perfect with each repeated act, so also do the infused virtues increase. Hence, the Christian merits an increase of charity with each repeated act, and he who is most continually occupied in loving God grows more and more in that love. Therefore this is the most fitting practice for growth in charity, for although there are many paths we may follow in order to reach the perfection of charity, the most efficacious, as St. Dionysius says, is to raise our hearts to God and to speak and converse with Him, walking always recollected in His presence.

This practice is proper to true wisdom and mystical theology, which is not learned by reading and disputing, but by praying and raising our affections to God in order to know Him through our experience of His goodness and to appreciate Him through receiving His blessings. Thus we can understand the difference between Scholastic theology and spiritual theology, for the one is learned through acts of the intellect and the other is attained by loving movements of the will which enable the intellect to understand anew how sweet is the Lord.

Accordingly, the path which leads to this wisdom is to speak always with God and to converse with Him day and night. For this reason, Scripture calls just and holy men heavenly men because, freed from all the affections and passions of this life and of all passing interests, their thoughts and desires, their hopes and joys are in heaven. Although the affairs of this life sometimes involve them in the things of this world, the spirit of God who dwells in them turns their minds back to the things of heaven. In like manner, if a piece of wood is held under water by force, it will immediately rise to the surface when it is freed.

In conformity with this doctrine, if the servant of God wishes to be a disciple of heavenly wisdom, he should construct an oratory in his heart wherein he can always be recollected. I mean by this that he should walk always in the presence of God and conduct himself in all his affairs as if God were always before him. Then he will never lose entirely the spirit of recollection and the devotion that flows from it. Thus David says: "I set the Lord always in my sight, for He is at my right hand, that I be not moved." [11] This is what the servant of God should do, not with violence and force, however, but with tranquillity and peace, lovingly inclining his spirit to the sovereign deity. And the soul should not be distressed when it sees that it loses much by the instability of its heart, but should return as soon as possible to the state of recollection. As the Christian becomes accustomed to this manner of acting, he will not find great difficulty in this practice nor will he be unduly anxious when it is absent. But it is important to remember that man can do nothing by himself alone, but his help is from God, and God never fails him who in all humility does all that he can.

Let the Christian, therefore, dwell within himself because there he will find God. For although God is in all things, he is especially present in the human soul and dwells there as in His own likeness. For that reason, let the Christian work with holy fear and reverence and humility in the eyes of God, as Elias did, as we read in Scripture: "As the Lord of hosts liveth, in whose sight I stand." [12] Let the Christian frequently repeat these words: "The Lord is present within me; the Lord sees me." By words such as these the Christian will more easily return to the presence of God when he has been distracted from the awareness of God's presence. Let him bury himself in God and rejoice that he is able to find God in his own soul. And if sometimes the affairs of human life prevent the Christian from being as recollected as he would wish, let him not on that

[11] Ps. 15:8.   [12] Cf. IV Kings 3:14.

account fail in his good resolutions nor abandon his good intentions. Rather, let him strive to keep a small part of his heart free to gaze upon God and this will make it easier for him later, when his affairs are finished, to return to the fullness of recollection. Blessed is the man whom neither the association of other men nor any other distraction or impediment can separate from the divine presence. This state will be reached when the soul is so hidden in God and so united with Him in love, that it is always more intimately united to God than with any other created thing.

Having shown that the principal means for growth in the love of God are the practice of constant prayer and the exercise of love, we shall now say something about those things that especially help us to achieve these virtuous exercises. The first is to assign for ourselves at least two periods during the day when we can be recollected in God and can continue in silence the prayers and meditations we have already proposed for arousing the love of God in our hearts. By means of this daily practice we can more easily keep our hearts recollected and, as often happens, this practice produces such a sweet affection in the soul that it forgets all other things and perseveres in this holy practice. But it is to be noted that one should always have control over the intellect in this practice, lest it become too speculative and talkative, even with God, and the affections and movements of the will are impeded. For we should not here be so concerned with knowledge and speculation about God as with the love of God. Therefore, we should relax our reins on the will and apply them to the intellect, not giving it too much freedom to theorize, except for whatever speculative knowledge is necessary to guide the will, so that the will may humbly extend the arms of its affections and embrace God. This warning is of great importance and it is because of not heeding this advice that many souls use this holy exercise as a preparation for preaching or teaching instead of arousing themselves to become lovers of God. The intellect is the door through which truths enter and reach the will, but sometimes truths are so long detained at the doorway of knowledge that they never reach the will, with the result that the intellect is fully satisfied but the will is empty and dry and the entire man remains empty and fruitless.

In order to understand how much better it is to love God than to know Him, consider the words of Mirandola, taken from a letter to a friend: "Observe, my friend, what great foolishness is ours. When we consider the various faculties that we have for uniting ourselves to God and enjoying His presence, we discover that we are able to love a great deal more than we are able to know. Therefore, by loving God we gain much more profit and with much less effort, and at the same time whatever works we perform are thereby more acceptable to Him. In spite of this, we are so foolish that we exert great labors in study, preferring to seek God through knowledge, without ever being able really to find Him, rather than seek Him through love. Indeed, if we do not love Him, we shall not find Him, and it will be through our own fault."

If against this doctrine you state that St. Thomas teaches that the happiness of the blessed in heaven consists essentially in the knowledge of God and that therefore it would seem better to know God than to love Him, I answer that in heaven we shall see God as He is in Himself and this will suffice to make us perfectly happy. In this life, however, we cannot see God as He really is, in all His glory and divine beauty, but we see Him only according to the measure of our capacity and according to the human mode of understanding, which is very small indeed. The Atlantic Ocean does not enter the straits of Gibraltar in all its width and immensity, but only in the measure that the straits can receive the ocean. In like manner, we understand and know God while we are in this life, making Him fit, so to speak, into the mode of our human understanding, which sees spiritual and divine things in a very imperfect manner.

But the love of God does not work in this way, because love transforms the lover into the object that is loved, so that the lover becomes one thing with the beloved. Here again we can see the vast difference between knowing God and loving Him. In this life we know God as best we can but we love Him as He is in Himself. In knowing Him, we make Him fit the capacity of our human understanding, but in loving Him we are made to His measure by being transformed into Him through love.

For the same reason the philosophers tell us that it is better to love lofty and divine things than to know them, but it is better to know lower and inferior things than to love them, because in knowing inferior things we spiritualize them, so to speak, by making them intellectual and proportionate to our human intellects, but in loving them we lower ourselves because love inclines us to those inferior things. On the other hand, the knowledge of lofty and divine things does not make them more excellent; it belittles them and lessens them by adapting them to our human intellect so that we may know them. But when we love lofty things, this does not happen, for in loving them we do not change those things into ourselves, but we are changed into them. If we love good things, we ourselves become good, and if we love evil things, we become evil, for a man becomes the things he loves. Again we see how important it is that the Christian should be very careful in this life to love God and even to strive much more energetically to love Him than to know Him.

In order that the holy practice of loving God may be most fruitful, we must have a vehement desire for this heavenly fire of love. Such a desire is born from the fact that God has showered many blessings upon man and has given him a taste of His sweetness. And in order that we may better appreciate the nature of this desire, let us consider a few examples. See how one acts who has lost a jewel of great value. He neither eats nor sleeps and if he does eat, he pays no attention to what he is eating. He no longer cares to converse and associate with others nor does he give any heed to what he is actually saying, for he is so absorbed in his search for that which he has lost that he has no mind for anything else. But if a man searches so anxiously for some temporal jewel or good, with what greater anxiety and effort should he not search for that precious pearl of the gospel? [13] He who has this ardent desire carries within his heart not only a constant preacher but a perpetual mover that inclines him always to seek God in everything, for everything in his life becomes another motive for loving God.

A man who has a colored glass before his eyes, sees all things in that color. So also, the Christian whose heart is seized with the love of God sees all things as in some way pertaining to the object of his love and all things likewise serve as motives or impulses to that love. It is like a raging fire that inflames all things that it touches and even the water that is contrary to fire sometimes serves to make the fire burn more brightly.

This effort to be continually loving God and ever desiring and asking for this love, importuning with faith,

[13] Cf. Matt. 13:45.

humility, and devotion, and begging God for a spark of this divine fire, is the proper study of mystical theology, which is the loving knowledge of God, and is attained not so much by discursus of the intellect as with affections and desires of the will. God will not fail to respond to such longings and desires, seeing the soul so sad and afflicted, like another Magdalen in its search for Him, especially when He Himself calls the soul and draws it after Him in the odor of His ointments.[14] For how is it possible that He will deny those who seek Him, when He Himself has moved them to seek Him and desires nothing more than to communicate Himself to souls?

CHAPTER 26 ✑

Obstacles to the Love of God

ONE of the greatest obstacles to the love of God is slothfulness, which is a laziness or languor of spirit in regard to the performance of good works and a repugnance for spiritual things. It is the source of many other vices such as malice, rancor, pusillanimity, lack of confidence, displeasure at obeying the Commandments, and attachment to vain and useless things. The great danger and harm of the vice of slothfulness can be learned from the words of Christ: "Every tree, therefore, that doth not yield good fruit shall be cut down and cast into the fire." [1] At another time, when admonishing His disciples to be vigilant, He said: "Watch ye, therefore, because you know not what

[14] Cf. Cant. 1:3.   [1] Matt. 3:10.

hour your Lord will come." [2] In order that you may know how to arm yourself against this vice, we offer the following considerations.

In the first place, consider how many labors Christ endured for you from the beginning until the end of His life. Consider how He passed many nights without sleep, praying for you; how He traveled throughout Galilee preaching and healing men; how He was always occupied with the things that pertain to your salvation; and how He carried the heavy weight of the cross upon His holy shoulders, already weary from His past labors. If the Lord of such great majesty labored so strenuously for your salvation, how much reason you have to work for it also. In order to free you from sin, the Lamb of God endured many sufferings and labors. Are you not willing to suffer a little for your own past sins?

Consider also the trials endured by the apostles when they traveled throughout the world preaching the gospel, the torments endured by the martyrs, the labors of the confessors and virgins and those holy people who withdrew to the desert to live in closer union with God. Consider all the saints now reigning in heaven, who have extended the Church throughout the world by their preaching and the example of their holy lives.

The choirs of angels sing the praises of God without ceasing; the sun and moon and stars are a silent testimony to the glory of God and a constant source of benefit to us; the various plants and trees are constantly growing to maturity; the ants and other insects are busily engaged in the summer to fill their storehouses with food for the winter; the bees work at making honey and kill the lazy drones. Shall you not then be ashamed to be slothful and lazy?

Moreover, if merchants and business men expend so

[2] Matt. 24:42.

much effort in accumulating perishable riches which must be safeguarded with much danger, with what greater reason should you, who are concerned with the affairs of eternity, seek to acquire those heavenly treasures which will last forever? And realize that if you do not wish to work now while you have strength and time, it may happen that later you will have neither the strength nor the time. Life is short and filled with many anxieties; therefore, while you have the opportunity to work, do not neglect it through slothfulness, because the night will come when you cannot work.

Realize that satisfaction for your numerous sins requires great penance and intense devotion. St. Peter denied Christ three times and for the rest of his life he wept over his sin, although he had already been pardoned. Mary Magdalen lamented her sins until the end of her life, although she had heard the sweet words from the lips of Christ: "Thy sins are forgiven thee." [3] For the sake of brevity I shall not refer to the countless other Christians who have spent their lives doing penance for their sins, many of whose sins were much less serious than yours.

But you, who daily increase your sins, how seriously do you consider your obligation to make satisfaction through good works? Now, in the time of grace and mercy, strive to perform acts of penance so that by means of good works in this life you may merit the blessings of the life to come. And although our works and efforts may seem small indeed, if they proceed from grace they are of great merit. The works are merely temporal, but the rewards are eternal; the time spent in running the race is brief, but the crown is everlasting. Therefore, we should not let the time allotted us as a time of merit pass by without bearing fruit.

If at times we find that we are overwhelmed by many

[3] Luke 7:47–48.

labors, let us remember that it is through many tribulations that we must enter the kingdom of God,[4] and that only he is crowned who strives manfully.[5] And if it seems to you that you have already worked and struggled enough, remember the words of Scripture: "He that shall persevere unto the end, he shall be saved." [6] Without perseverance, efforts will not bear fruit; there will be no reward for labors; the runner in the race will not achieve victory; and he who serves will not receive the final grace from the Lord. For that reason our Savior did not come down from the cross when the Jews demanded; He did not wish to leave the work of redemption incomplete. Therefore, if we wish to follow Christ we must work diligently until death. Let us never cease to do penance and to carry our cross in imitation of Christ. Otherwise, what shall it avail us if we have navigated the ocean of life and at the end we do not reach the port?

Nor should we be dismayed at the difficulties involved in our struggles and labors. God has told us that if we struggle He will help us conquer. God sees our combats; He will come to our aid when we are weakened and will crown us when we are victorious. Therefore, when you are fatigued with your labors, do not compare the difficulty in the practice of virtue with the pleasure that would come from the contrary vice, but compare the sadness that you may now feel in the practice of virtue with the sorrow that follows sin, or compare the joy that you have at the time of sinning with the joy that will be yours in heaven. Then you will see how much better it is to choose virtue than to choose vice.

If you are conquered in a battle, do not lose heart, because many times negligence follows victory and success.

---

[4] Acts 14:21.   [5] Cf. II Tim. 2:5.   [6] Matt. 10:22.

Rather, defeat should make you more vigilant and alert in case the trumpet should sound again for another battle. Remember also that there is no ocean without waves and there is no human life without its temptations. Moreover, he who begins to lead a good life is usually more strongly tempted by the devil, for the devil does not trouble to tempt those over whom he already has dominion, but only those who are as yet free from his power. Therefore you must be as alert and prepared as if you were on the front line of battle. And if at any time you feel that you have suffered a wound, do not cast down your shield and weapons and surrender yourself as a prisoner to the enemy. Rather, imitate those brave knights who often suffered the shame of being overwhelmed and who endured the pain of many wounds, but they did not flee and they never surrendered. On the contrary, such things incited them to fight more strenuously.

In like manner you can also gain greater strength from your own falls and weakness because through them you can learn how to avoid those who pursue you and fight against those who attack you. But if, as frequently happens in battle, you are again wounded, even then you must not be discouraged but you must remember that this is the lot of those who fight bravely. The brave soldier is not he who has never been wounded but he who has never submitted to his enemy. Likewise, a soldier is not conquered through being wounded frequently, but only if he loses his courage. Therefore, if you have been wounded in the struggle, heal your wound, because it is much easier to cure one wound than many, and it is much easier to cure a fresh wound than one that is already infected.

If you are tempted, do not give in to the temptations, but draw from the temptations themselves motives for the practice of virtue. In this way, with the help of divine grace, you will not be worse because of your temptations, but better, because you have made those temptations serve for your good. Thus, if you are tempted to gluttony or lust, put aside your usual comforts for a time, even those that are lawful, and increase your fasts and pious practices. If you are tempted to avarice, increase your alms and good works. If you are tempted to vanity, humble yourself in all things. If you do these things, the devil will be afraid to tempt you because he does not want to give you the occasion to improve yourself and to perform good works. He desires you to do evil. Avoid slothfulness as much as possible. Never be so idle that even in your leisure you do not find something profitable, and do not be so busy that you cannot in the midst of your duties raise your heart and mind to God.

Prostrate in spirit and with all the reverence of which I am capable, I present myself before Thee, O my God, as one of the poorest and lowliest of thy creatures. I place myself before the torrents of Thy mercy, the inspiration of Thy grace, and the splendors of the sun of Thy justice, which are liberally communicated to all who do not close the door of their souls to it. I place myself in Thy hands as a lump of clay; make of it, most merciful Father, that for which Thou hast created it.

Make me love Thee, Lord. It is the greatest audacity for me, a lowly creature, to ask for such a noble love. Since I am so base, I should perhaps beg of Thee something much more humble, but what shall I do, since Thou hast commanded me to love Thee, hast created me to love Thee, and hast threatened me if I do not love Thee? Thou didst die to make me love Thee, and Thou desirest that I should ask nothing of Thee with greater insistence than love. So much dost Thou wish me to love Thee that Thou didst institute the marvelous Sacrament of Thy love to transform my heart into love.

O my Savior, what am I that Thou shouldst command me to love Thee and shouldst have invented so many wonderful means to procure this end? What am I to Thee but labors and suffering and the Cross? And what art Thou to me but salvation and rest and all blessings? But Thou dost love me in spite of all that I am. Why, then, shall I not love Thee for all that Thou art to me?

Trusting in all the pledges of Thy love and in that gracious precept by which at the end of Thy life Thou didst sweetly command me to love Thee, I ask still another grace, which is that Thou givest me what Thou hast commanded me to give to Thee, for I cannot give it without Thee. I do not deserve to love Thee, but Thou dost deserve to be loved, and for that reason I do not dare to ask that Thou shouldst love me, but that Thou givest me permission to dare to love Thee.

O God, Thou who art love by essence, uncreated and infinite love, from which proceeds the love of all the angels and all Thy creatures, why do I not love Thee? Why do I not burn in that fire of love which inflames the whole universe?

O God, who art essential goodness, through whom is good whatever is good and from whom proceed all the goods of all creatures, as all the waters proceed from the sea, why do I not love Thee, since the object of love is goodness? Thou who art beauty by essence and in whom are concentrated all the degrees of created beauty, why do I not love Thee, when beauty has such a power to captivate the heart? If I do not love Thee for what Thou art in Thyself, why do I not love Thee for what Thou art to me?

The son loves his father because he has received from him his very being; the members of the body love the head and will sacrifice themselves for it because they are preserved in life through the head; all effects love their causes because they receive from them whatever they have. But which of these titles does not apply to Thee, my God, that I should think that I need not give Thee all the rights of love?

Thou hast given me the being that I have and in a much more perfect way than my own parents. Thou dost preserve me in the being that Thou hast given me much better than the head preserves the members of the body. Thou hast supplied whatever has been wanting once this work was begun, until Thou hast brought it to perfection. Thou art the Father who made me, the Head that governs me, and the Spouse that gives perfect happiness to my soul. Whatever I have, I have received from Thee; whatever I lack, I hope to receive from Thee.

As no one but Thee could give me that which I have, so also no one but Thee can supply for the things that I lack. Consequently, all that I have and all that I am and all that I hope to be is Thine. To whom else, then, shall I look but to Thee? To whom else shall I render an account but to Thee? With whom shall I be concerned but with Thee? In whose eyes shall I strive to live but in Thine? To whom shall I give all my love but to Thee?

But if Thou art the ornament and beauty of my soul, how is it possible that I can forget Thee? "For what have I in heaven and besides Thee what do I desire upon earth? For Thee my flesh and my heart hath fainted away. Thou art the God of my heart and the God that is my portion forever." [7] Drive from me all those things that rob me of

[7] Ps. 72:25–26.

my God and rid me of those things that prevent me from being Thine and keep Thee from being mine.

O uncreated Love that always burns and is never extinguished! O eternal heartbeat of the Father, that never ceases to shine forth from the face of Thy Son with rays of infinite love! May I be inflamed with this divine fire of love. May I follow Thee, my Beloved, and may I sing Thy canticle of love. May my soul swoon with jubilation and the praises of this ineffable love.

O most holy Father! O most merciful Son! O most loving Holy Spirit! When, heavenly Father, shalt Thou possess the very core of my soul and dwell therein so intimately as to possess me completely? When shall I be all Thine and Thou all mine? When, my King, shall this come to pass? How great the delay and how painful the waiting! Hasten, good Jesus, and do not tarry.

O my God, repose of my life, consolation in my labors, port of my desires, pledge of my glory, joy in my exile, guide in my journey, and most precious treasure of my heart, if Thou art all these things, how is it possible for me to be unmindful of Thee? If I should forget Thee, let all Thy protection be taken from me. "Let my tongue cleave to my jaws, if I do not remember Thee." [8]

[8] Ps. 136:5.

CHAPTER 27 ✐

Love of Neighbor

THE importance of the love of neighbor and the frequency with which it is recommended in Scripture can be appreciated only by those who have read the Bible. Read the prophets and evangelists and you will see how frequently we are admonished to love our neighbor. In Isaias, for example, God places great emphasis on charity and justice toward our neighbor. Thus, when the Jews complained, saying: "Why have we fasted, and Thou hast not regarded? Have we humbled our souls, and Thou hast not taken notice?" God answered them: "Behold you fast for debates and strife and strike with the fist wickedly. . . . Is this such a fast as I have chosen, for a man to afflict his soul for a day? . . . Wilt thou call this a fast and a day acceptable to the Lord? Is not this rather the fast that I have chosen? Loose the bands of wickedness, undo the bundles that oppress. Let them that are broken go free, and break asunder every burden. Deal thy bread to the hungry and bring the needy and the harborless into thy house. When thou shalt see one naked, cover him, and despise not thy own flesh. Then shall thy light break forth as the morning, and thy health shall speedily arise, and thy justice shall go before thy face, and the glory of the Lord shall gather thee up." [1]

From this you can see that God Himself considers love of neighbor a part of true justice and He ardently desires that we act in this way toward our neighbors. And what

[1] Isa. 58:3–8.

shall I say of the writings of St. Paul? Is there any epistle in which he does not highly recommend this practice? How great is the praise that he lavishes on the virtue of charity; how minutely he describes all its wonderful qualities. He places it above all other virtues and says that it is the most excellent path for traveling to God. Not content with this, he states in his Epistle to the Colossians that charity is the bond of perfection; in the Epistle to Timothy, that it is the end of all the commandments; and in his Epistle to the Romans, that he who loves his neighbor has fulfilled the law. What greater praise could be given to any virtue? What man, desirous of knowing the best way to please God, will not be enchanted by this virtue and will not determine to regulate all his actions accordingly?

In addition to these testimonies we have the teaching of St. John the Evangelist, the beloved disciple. He repeats nothing more insistently than the doctrine on the virtue of charity. And when he was asked why he constantly repeated his doctrine on charity, he answered that it was because he realized that if this practice of charity were rightly fulfilled, that would suffice for our salvation. Accordingly, he who truly desires to please God should understand that one of the principal means for doing so is to fulfill the commandment of charity, even when his love seems arid and dry, as long as it is accompanied by the effects and works that true love usually produces. Otherwise, it would not deserve the name of love, as St. John himself testified when he said: "He that hath the substance of this world and shall see his brother in need, and shall shut up his bowels from him, how doth the charity of God abide in him? My little children, let us not love in word nor in tongue, but in deed and in truth." [2]

[2] Cf. 3:17–18.

Accordingly, under the name of charity, we find the following works: to love, to give counsel, to help the poor, to suffer, to pardon, and to give good example. These works are all related to charity, so that he who possesses them more perfectly, will have greater charity, and he who possesses them less will have less charity.

Some persons say that they love but they do not pass beyond this love. Others love and also help their neighbor by advice and good counsel, but they will never open their purse to help the poor. Still others love and advise and help the needy according to their capacity but they do not suffer patiently the injuries and weaknesses of others. Consequently, they do not fulfill the counsel of St. Paul: "Bear ye one another's burdens, and so you shall fulfill the law of Christ." [3] Yet others, although they suffer injuries with patience, do not pardon those injuries, and although they may have no hatred in their hearts, they do not put on a pleasant face. Although they strive in many ways to do well in all things, they fail to manifest a pleasant face to their enemies. And there are others who do all these things but do not edify their neighbor by work and deed, which is one of the loftiest duties of charity.

Each Christian can examine his conscience according to the things we have enumerated, in order to discover how much charity he has or what is lacking in the perfection of this virtue. He who loves is in the first degree of charity; he who loves and also gives counsel is in the second degree; he who helps his neighbor, in the third degree; he who suffers, in the fourth degree; he who pardons and suffers, in the fifth degree; and he who edifies others by his words and his holy life, which is the function of perfect and apostolic men, has reached the height of charity. Such are

[3] Gal 6:2.

the positive aspects of charity regarding our duties to our neighbor.

There are also negative aspects of the love of neighbor, that is, the things we ought not do. For example, we should not judge other people, speak evilly of others, damage their possessions, honor, or wife, scandalize them with our speech, be discourteous, or give them bad example or bad advice. He who observes these things will fulfill perfectly all that is commanded in the precept of charity.

If you wish to keep these things in mind, strive to cultivate the heart of a mother toward your neighbor. In this way you will surely observe the commandment of charity. Observe how the good mother loves her child, how she counsels him in his dangers, hastens to help him in his needs, bears all his faults with great patience or punishes them with justice, because all these virtues are at the service of charity, which is the queen of all the virtues. See how the mother rejoices at the good of her child, is saddened by his evil deeds, and experiences his sufferings as if they were her own. See what great zeal she has for the well-being of her child, how devoutly she prays to God for him, and how watchful she is of him, even more than of herself. She is severe with herself so that she may be tender and kind toward her child.

If you are able to cultivate this kind of attitude toward your neighbor, you shall have reached the perfection of charity. And if at the present you cannot do these perfect works, then at least desire to reach this perfection and let your whole life be directed toward this goal.

If you ask me how it is possible for anyone to have this attitude of charity toward someone who is a complete stranger, I answer that you should not look upon your neighbor as a stranger, but as the image of God. Like yourself, your neighbor is the work of God's hand. How often St. Paul says that we are all members of Christ and that one who sins against his neighbor likewise sins against Christ, and that he who does good to his neighbor, does good to Christ. Consequently, one should not look at his neighbor merely as such and such a person, but as a member of the mystical body and a child of God.

Consider also all the recommendations and praises that we have already mentioned concerning the excellency of the virtue of charity and the insistence with which Christ has urged the practice of this virtue. If you have an ardent desire of pleasing God, you will not fail to strive diligently to do what pleases Him. Consider the love that unites those who are related by flesh and blood, and then be ashamed that grace does not mean more to you than human nature or that a spiritual union is not as important to you as a union based on blood. Consider how noble and excellent is the union described by St. Paul when he says that all Christians have one father, one mother, one Lord, one baptism, one faith, one hope, and one Spirit that gives them life.[4] In other words, all Christians have God as their Father, the Church as their mother, Christ as their Lord, one faith as a supernatural light shared by all, one hope which is one and the same pledge of glory, one baptism in which we are all adopted as children of the same Father, one nourishment which is the Holy Eucharist, wherein we are made one with Christ. In addition to all this, we all share in the same Spirit, which is the Holy Ghost, who dwells in the souls of the faithful to vivify and sustain them.

If the members of one body, although they have different functions and are differently constructed, love one another

[4] Eph. 4:4–6.

because they are all vivified by the same rational soul, with what greater reason should the faithful love each other, for they are animated by the divine Spirit, who is much more noble and much more effective in causing unity and harmony among those in whom He dwells? And if a mere bond of flesh and blood is sufficient to cause such intense love among members of the same family, how much greater should be the love among those who are united by a higher bond? In addition to all this, cast your eyes on that singular example of love which is found in Christ. He loved us so ardently, so tenderly, so steadfastly, and so unselfishly, that, inspired by His example, we may dispose ourselves to love our neighbor in a similar manner. This is the commandment that Christ gave us when He was leaving this earth: "This is My commandment, that you love one another, as I have loved you." [5]

CHAPTER 28 ✍

The Qualities of Mercy

THE virtue of mercy is so beautiful and so highly esteemed by men that scarcely any other virtue is more highly praised. Even those who have little consideration for God have practiced the works of mercy as a means of winning praise and fame among men. As a result, the only obstacle to the practice of this virtue is the love of one's possessions or the fact that men have families of their own to take care of and therefore do not readily part with the things they

[5] John 15:12.

have accumulated at such great effort, only to give them to strangers. So we read in Scripture that Nabal refused to give bread and water and meat to the servants of David because they were strangers.[1]

But the authority of God should suffice to impel Christians to overcome all difficulties and perform the acts of mercy that God asks of us. Moreover, the excellence of the virtue of mercy should suffice to overcome our repugnance to its practice, for it is one of the virtues most pleasing to God and most highly recommended in Scripture. Although the virtue of charity is truly the most noble and most excellent of all the virtues, it is not in any way lessened by the practice of the virtue of mercy. Rather, charity is increased, for mercy is not a departure from charity, but it is joined to it as the stream is joined to the spring in which it has its source. As one theologian has described it, charity is a river that flows between two banks and never deviates from its course, but mercy is the overflow from that river, which irrigates all the surrounding area.

This consideration should help us overcome any unwillingness we may have to practice the virtue of mercy, for if the pagans practiced virtue solely for the sake of virtue, that is, without seeking any reward other than the satisfaction of doing a good deed, how much more should this be true of the Christian? But rather than insist on this argument, I wish to consider the advantages of almsgiving and the other works of mercy. In the first place, let us weigh the temporal loss that results from works of mercy against the temporal and spiritual benefits that accrue from this practice. I am sure that once this has been done, you will not only decide in favor of the works of mercy, but you will

[1] Cf. I Kings 25:10.

be surprised that all men who understand these things do not exert every effort to be as merciful as the saints.

In the first place, the works of mercy make men like unto God in regard to one of His most wonderful attributes, that of mercy.[2] Now, the greatest excellence a creature can have is to resemble its Creator, and the greater the resemblance, the more perfect the creature. Moreover, one of the qualities most proper to God is that of mercy, as the Church signifies when it prays: "O Lord God, to whom it is proper to be merciful and to pardon." It is proper to a creature as such to receive rather than to give, but it is proper to the infinitely rich and powerful God to give and not to receive, which is to have mercy and grant pardon. Not only is mercy proper to God but, as St. Thomas teaches,[3] it is one of His most glorious attributes and for which He is most highly praised and adored. Thus Moses saw the glory of God and saw so many of God's perfections that he felt that he had seen the very essence of God and exclaimed: "O the Lord, the Lord God, merciful and gracious, patient and of such compassion, and true, who keepest mercy unto thousands; who takest away iniquity and wickedness and sin, and no man of himself is innocent before Thee."[4] But God's mercies are so great that they cannot be described, and for that reason it is said that all the earth is filled with His glory, for it is filled with His mercy, as we read in Ecclesiasticus: "The compassion of man is toward his neighbor, but the mercy of God is upon all flesh."[5]

But if God's mercy is so highly esteemed and if it is such a glorious thing for a man to be like God, how

[2] Cf. Luke 6:36.   [3] Cf. *Summa theol.,* IIa IIae, q. 30.
[4] Exod. 34:6–7.   [5] Ecclus. 18:12.

greatly the Christian should esteem the virtue of mercy. "Be merciful," says Christ, "as your Father also is merciful." [6] St. Gregory comments on this passage: "Thank God that He has not placed you in such a condition that you are dependent on others, but others are dependent on you. Therefore, strive to be rich, not in money alone, but also in mercy; not only in gold, but also in virtue, so that you may surpass others in this virtue as you surpass them in wealth. Strive to be like God to the wretched, imitating God's mercy, for there is nothing more divine in men than to do good for others."

The second excellence of the virtue of mercy is that it makes us friends of God. This follows from the first excellence, for if likeness is the cause of love, and mercy is such a godly virtue, then it follows that the merciful man is very much loved by God. Similarly, Aristotle states in his *Ethics* that the wise man, who is much given to the contemplation of divine things, is much loved by God because through this exercise the life of the wise man is similar to the inner life of God. So also, since God is infinitely merciful, He will love all those who are also merciful and will love them as His very sons. What is more worthy of esteem than this? And if men will do so much to gain the favor of a king or worldly ruler, how much more should they practice this virtue which makes them true friends and sons of God.

Moreover, those who are merciful have a special claim on the mercy of God. Scripture gives testimony of this, especially in the words of Christ: "Blessed are the merciful, for they shall obtain mercy." [7] We also read in Tobias: "Give alms out of thy substance, and turn not away thy face from any poor person, for so it shall pass that the face of the Lord shall not be turned from thee." [8] Again, we

[6] Luke 6:36. [7] Matt. 5:7. [8] Tob. 4:7.

read in Ecclesiasticus: "In judging, be merciful to the fatherless as a father and as a husband to their mother, and thou shalt be as the obedient son of the most High, and He will have mercy on thee more than a mother." [9] These and many other passages in Scripture declare how God shall be merciful to him who is merciful toward his neighbor.

But Scripture goes even further and states that he who is merciful makes God his debtor, so to speak. "He that hath mercy on the poor, lendeth to the Lord, and He will repay him." [10] In other words, if he does these things to Christ's little ones, he does it to Christ. And what could be more wonderful than to have God as our debtor?

In addition to this, we can obtain pardon of our sins through the works of mercy, for Scripture states: "Water quencheth a flaming fire and alms resisteth sins." [11] "A secret present quencheth anger and a gift in the bosom the greatest wrath." [12] "For alms deliver from all sin and from death and will not suffer the soul to go into darkness." [13] "But yet that which remaineth, give alms, and behold, all things are clean unto you." [14] But when mercy is lacking, the Christian is in great danger. As a theologian has said, he extends his hands in vain, asking pardon of his sins from God, if he has not extended his hands to help his neighbor when he was able.

Not only is the virtue of mercy a source of pardon, but it also enriches the Christian with new merits. The reason for this is that the works of mercy, so far as they are difficult or laborious, satisfy for the punishment due to sin, but so far as they are acts of charity, they are meritorious. Thus, by one and the same act of mercy the Christian can pay what he owes for his past sins and increase the grace

[9] Ecclus. 4:10-11.   [10] Prov. 19:17.   [11] Ecclus. 3:33.
[12] Prov. 21:14.   [13] Tob. 4:11.   [14] Luke 11:41.

that he already possesses. For this reason, Solomon advises: "Cast thy bread upon the running waters; for after a long time thou shalt find it again." [15] Nothing seems farther beyond recovery than the alms that we give to the poor, yet at the end of our lives we shall see the fruits of our almsgiving and shall receive the reward for our mercy. Consequently, after recommending the practice of the works of mercy, Isaias says: "Deal thy bread to the hungry and bring the needy and the harborless into thy house. . . . Then shall thy light break forth as the morning, and thy health shall speedily arise, and thy justice shall go before thy face, and the glory of the Lord shall gather thee up." [16] Indeed, one of the best titles for the hope of glory is to possess the merit of the works of mercy, and thus the works of mercy are a storehouse of treasures which we shall be able to take with us into the next life. At this point we are reminded of the famous sentence of St. Ambrose: "Those things cannot be called true goods if a man cannot take them with him and for that reason mercy alone is the companion of the dead."

Immediately after their death, the kings and monarchs of the world will find themselves alone and deprived of all their companions and the magnificent splendor of their royal state. Mercy alone will remain at their side and mercy alone will accompany them to defend them on the day of judgment. St. John Chrysostom says that he who performs a work of mercy does not do good but receives good, and sometimes receives much more than he gives, because he actually gives alms to God and not to man. In conformity with this doctrine, St. Gregory says: "Let us give of our possessions to the poor during this life so that we may be enriched with the goods of the next life."

[15] Eccles. 11:1.   [16] Isa. 58:8.

Christ Himself advises us to do this when He says: "Lay not up to yourselves treasures on earth, where the rust and moth consume and where thieves break through and steal. But lay up to yourselves treasures in heaven," [17] In another place He says: "Sell what you possess and give alms. Make to yourselves bags which grow not old, a treasure in heaven which faileth not." [18] Again, He says: "Make unto you friends of the mammon of iniquity, that when you shall fail, they may receive you into everlasting dwellings." [19]

It should be evident from all that we have said how much more the merciful man receives than he gives. St. Augustine says: "Be mindful, man, not only of that which you give, but also of that which you receive, because there is no doubt that a poor man could say to you: 'That which I give you by receiving is much greater than that which you give me. For if I did not receive the alms from you, you would not be able to trade earth for heaven. Have nothing to do with me if there is nothing that you need to ask of Him who made us, but if you must ask anything of God as a result of helping me, you have already earned the grace of being heard. Therefore, give thanks to God, who caused you to buy something so precious at such a low price. You give away something that fades with time and in return you receive something that will endure forever.' "

What better exchange could we make than this? We give the earth and receive heaven; we give bread to men and we shall receive the bread of angels; we give a glass of water and we receive the fountain of living water; we give that which we cannot take with us and receive something that no one can ever take from us. As St. John Chrysostom says: "What greater folly than to store one's goods in a

[17] Matt. 6:19.   [18] Luke 12:33.   [19] Luke 16:19.

place which he must one day leave and not transfer them to a place where he will live forever?" God has left us a good remedy for this in the poor, who are the bankers of these possessions, the merchants of these goods, and the storehouse of the wealth of God. As a result, we save even as we lose our possessions, but we lose everything if we are too anxious to keep them.

In addition to all these benefits, there are many others of great profit. One of these is the assistance of God in our tribulations, for the Savior says that in the measure that we give to others it shall be given to us.[20] It is only fitting that he who has assisted his neighbor in time of tribulation and has given help as best he could, should receive from God the help that he himself needs in time of tribulation. Christ has said that if we perform works of mercy for our brethren, it is as if we had done them for Him.[21] This is one of the blessings of which David sang in reference to the merciful: "Blessed is he that understandeth concerning the needy and the poor. The Lord will deliver him in the evil day. The Lord preserve him and give him life, and make him blessed upon the earth, and deliver him not up to the will of his enemies. The Lord will help him on his bed of sorrow. Thou hast turned all his couch in his sickness." [22]

David did not ask these blessings without reason, for he knew that God Himself had ordained these rewards: "Brethren are a help in the time of trouble, but mercy shall deliver more than they." [23] In another place, we read that God has His eyes on the man who is merciful and will keep this man in mind forever and in the day of his falling there will not be lacking someone to assist him so that he may arise again.[24] And the Lord says through Isaias: "When

[20] Luke 6:38.
[21] Matt. 25:40.
[22] Ps. 40:1–4.
[23] Ecclus. 40:24.
[24] Ecclus. 3:20.

thou shalt pour out thy soul to the hungry and shalt satisfy the afflicted soul, then shall thy light rise up in darkness and thy darkness shall be as noonday." [25] In other words, when a man has been so afflicted by tribulation that there is not a ray of light or hope anyplace, he will be consoled by God in such a way that the darkness of his sorrow will be changed into a happiness as bright as the noonday sun, as was Tobias, who merited relief from his miseries because he was merciful. He was assisted by God in his affliction because he had so often helped others.[26] Tobias understood that all merciful men can expect God's help, and he told his son that if he would practice the works of mercy, he could also expect God's help in time of need.

Another blessing similar to this is that the merciful man will be heard in his prayers. For that reason, after Isaias advises us to give bread to the hungry and give lodging to the homeless and to clothe the naked, he adds: "Then shalt thou call, and the Lord shall hear; thou shalt cry, and He shall say: 'Here I am.' " [27] In other words, if God is more pleased with mercy and especially loves those who are merciful because they have heard the cries of the needy, He will in turn hear their cries for help. Not only will He hear them when they cry unto Him, but He will come to their assistance even when they are silent, for their very works of mercy will plead for them. "Do good to the just and thou shalt find great recompense, and if not of him, assuredly of the Lord." [28] But he who does not hear the voice of the poor, neither will he be heard by God. "He that stoppeth his ear against the cry of the poor, shall also cry himself and shall not be heard." [29]

In addition to the benefits we have already mentioned,

[25] Isa. 58:10.   [26] Tob., chap. 4.   [27] Isa. 58:9.
[28] Ecclus. 12:2.   [29] Prov. 21:13.

there is yet another which is the greatest of all: the strong defense that the works of mercy will afford on the day of judgment. How secure he shall be who stands before God on that day, clothed with mercy! As the holy Tobias has said: "Alms shall be a great confidence before the most high God, to all them that give it." [30] If the devils rise against such a soul, the virtue of mercy will defend it, as we read in Ecclesiasticus: "Shut up alms in the heart of the poor, and it shall obtain help for thee against all evil. Better than the shield of the mighty and better than the spear, it shall fight for thee against thy enemy." [31] And if God Himself should ask the soul concerning the sins it has committed, the soul will answer: "Lord, in recompense for the sins of my life, I offer the works of mercy that I have always performed for love of Thee. Thou hast said that the merciful shall be blessed because they shall obtain mercy and that with the same measure that they mete out to others, it shall be meted out to them.[32] Thou hast promised that alms will deliver from sin and not suffer the soul to go into darkness.[33] Thou hast said that 'mercy exalteth itself above judgment,' [34] which is to say that Thy mercy will prevail over Thy justice, for Thy mercy absolves him whom Thy justice condemns. Thou hast stated that on the day of judgment Thou shalt separate the sheep from the goats. To the former, Thou shalt say: 'Come, ye blessed of My Father, possess you the kingdom prepared for you from the foundation of the world. For I was hungry, and you gave Me to eat; I was thirsty, and you gave Me to drink; I was a stranger, and you took Me in; naked, and you covered Me; sick, and you visited Me; I was in prison, and you came to Me.' [35] And when they ask Thee when they have

---

[30] Tob. 4:12. [31] Ecclus. 29:15–16. [32] Cf. Matt. 5:7; Luke 6:38.
[33] Tob. 4:11. [34] James 2:13. [35] Matt. 25:34–36.

done all these things for Thee, Thou shalt answer: 'Amen I say to you, as long as you did it to one of these My least brethren, you did it to Me.' " [36] What greater reward can be imagined than this? How happy will they be who hear these words from the lips of the Savior: "Come, blessed of My Father."

But why is it that in mentioning the works that are meritorious of heaven, we speak only of the works of mercy? First, consider the remarkable wisdom of God who, knowing man's tendency to seek all things for himself, proposed so great a reward in order to soften the hardness of men's hearts and incline them to be merciful. Secondly, this gives proof of the infinite liberality of God and His desire for our salvation, for glory is the greatest of all goods and money is the least of all created things, but in return for alms He gives us this greatest good. He gives us for money that which He purchased with His blood. Thirdly, we see here the wonderful goodness of God as well as His charity and providence. He knew that there would be poor in the world and in this He was looking both to their good and to ours, for they could gain much by suffering while we could gain much by being compassionate; they, by patience, and we, by mercy. As a remedy for both He expressed these sweet promises: "As long as you did it to one of these My least brethren, you did it to Me." If a king were to be absent from his kingdom and were to entrust his beloved son to some of the nobility, what more beautiful words could he use than to say: "Whatever you shall do for my son, it is as if you did it to me, and I shall be grateful to you accordingly."

How much more highly could Christ recommend the works of mercy than to put Himself in the place of the poor

[36] *Ibid.*, v. 40.

and needy? O remarkable dignity of the poor of Christ, in whom the person of God is represented! The poor man stretches forth his hand but it is God who receives the alms and repays the almsgiver. What could be a better proof of the mercy and goodness of God?

This, then, is one of the greatest reasons for praising the virtue of mercy; it fortifies the Christian against the day of judgment. For that reason St. Paul says that mercy is profitable to all things and bears the promise of the present life and of the life that is to come.[37] One of the commentators on Scripture says of this passage that if a Christian practices the works of mercy, although he may have other faults, he will be punished for his faults but he will not be condemned. We may not understand by this, of course, that the almsgiver is justified in remaining in his vices, because such an action would call down upon the soul the wrath of God.[38] Hence, St. Gregory says that he who gives his possessions to the poor but does not keep his life free from sin, gives his possessions to God and himself to sin. Therefore, there is no promise of salvation for him who perseveres in vice. St. Jerome says, in an epistle to Nepocianus: "I do not remember ever having read that he would die an evil death who willingly gave himself to the practice of the works of mercy. Such a man has so many who intercede for him that it is not likely that the prayers of so many will go unheard." If the virtue of mercy was powerful enough to bring God down from heaven, it is surely powerful enough to raise a man up to heaven.

Perhaps you will say that all the great blessings mentioned above, however great they may be, may invite us but they do not make it necessary for us to practice mercy, for there are many other ways by which one can reach

[37] Cf. I Tim. 4:8.   [38] Cf. Rom. 2:5.

heaven. But I shall show you that it is necessary to practice this virtue when it is possible to do so. We have ample proof of this in Scripture. Christ has invited the merciful to His Father's kingdom and has rejected the cruel and hard-hearted, saying: "Depart from Me, you cursed, into everlasting fire which was prepared for the devil and his angels. For I was hungry, and you gave Me not to eat; I was thirsty, and you gave Me not to drink; I was a stranger, and you took Me not in; naked, and you covered Me not; sick and in prison, and you did not visit Me." [39]

The virtue of mercy opens the gates of heaven to the merciful, but cruelty and inhumanity close those gates to the evil ones. As St. James says: "Judgment without mercy to him who hath not done mercy." [40] And what would happen to man if he were to be judged without mercy? However praiseworthy a man's life, says St. Augustine, alas for that man if he is to be judged without mercy. Alas also for that man who has never practiced mercy, for he will be judged without mercy. St. Basil says: "If you are not merciful, you shall not obtain mercy. If you do not open your doors to the poor, God will not open heaven to you. If you do not give a piece of bread to him who suffers hunger, you shall not receive eternal life." The same Saint says in another place: "Be certain that the fruit must correspond to the seed. Sow bitterness and you will reap bitterness; sow cruelty and this will be your harvest. Flee mercy and it will likewise flee from you. Abhor the poor and He also will abhor you who became poor out of love of men."

These and like warnings pertain in a special manner to those who have much wealth but let the wretched starve in their poverty. They are symbolized by the wealthy glutton in the gospel who was so inhuman that he would not even

---

[39] Matt. 25:41–43.   [40] James 2:13.

give Lazarus the crumbs that fell from his table. The rich ought to take special notice of this parable and consider, as St. Augustine says, that the rich man was not condemned for having taken the possessions of others, but for not having given out of his own possessions. Later, when he was condemned to hell, he was reduced to such a state that he himself had to beg for such an insignificant thing as a drop of water, while on earth he had refused to give even a crust of bread.

We are again reminded of this teaching in the parable of the rich man who had been blessed with many possessions and rich harvests. He stored away his possessions and then said: "Soul, thou hast much goods laid up for many years. Take thy rest; eat, drink, and make good cheer." [41] Commenting on this parable, St. Basil says: "O foolish words! O strange madness! Tell me, I beg you, what more could you say if you had the soul of a pig? Wretched one, take your riches from the prisons in which you have stored them . . . and lay up for yourself treasures in heaven. What prevents you from doing this? Is not the poor man at your very door? Do you not have the possessions from which you can give alms? Is not the reward already promised? Do you not have an express command to do this? And yet with all this, can you say: 'I do not have it; I shall not give to the poor because I am also poor?' Poor you are, for a certainty; poor in charity, in humanity, in faith, and in hope.

"You ask whom you are harming if you keep what is yours. What do you call yours? Did you bring anything with you into this world? Why are you rich and another man poor? Whatever the reason, your wealth is not a reward for your benignity and almsgiving. . . . See what you do in holding to those things that belong not only to you but

[41] Luke 12:16–21.

also to your neighbor. See the bread that you unjustly keep from the poor, the naked who are deprived of clothing, the number of people who go without shoes, and the poor who lack the money which you keep buried in a vault. Understand that riches may mean the salvation of souls. In preserving riches, you cause souls to be lost, but in losing your riches for the sake of God, you save souls.

"I have seen those who fasted and prayed and wept over their past sins and performed all kinds of virtuous works that did not cost money. But they were unwilling to give a penny for the love of God, although they had more possessions than they needed. What did it profit them to be so solicitous in the practice of the other virtues if at the end they did not reach the kingdom of heaven?"

These words of St. Basil make it clear how necessary it is for those who have many worldly possessions to practice the virtue of mercy. And if the many benefits and rewards of the practice of the virtue do not draw them to it, then at least they should be urged through the necessity that is upon them to do so. And if this is not enough, let them recall the fearful statement of St. John: "He that hath the substance of this world, and shall see his brother in need, and shall shut up his bowels from him, how doth the charity of God abide in him? My little children, let us not love in word, nor in tongue, but in deed and in truth." [42] What could be more terrifying than this statement? If the failure to assist the needy results in the death of charity, what must be the condition of so many of the wealthy who do nothing to assist the needy? What is worse, where there is no charity, there is no grace, and where there is no grace, there can be no glory. Then, what kind of joy and peace can a person enjoy who lives in such a state?

[42] Cf. I John 3:17–18.

But if one were to be so much in love with his own self-interest and so attached to the goods of this world that nothing appeals to him except his own interests, we could offer him some of the very benefits he desires. For the goodness of God is so great that He not only rewards the merciful in the next life, but in this life as well. This may seem strange, but we find proof of it in Scripture. I do not refer only to the famous passage in Deuteronomy,[43] where so many blessings and temporal goods are promised to those who observe the law, but also to the words of Solomon: "Honor the Lord with thy substance, and give Him of the first of all thy fruits, and thy barns shall be filled with abundance and thy presses shall run over with wine." [44] In another place we read: "He that giveth to the poor shall not want; he that despiseth his entreaty shall suffer indigence"; [45] and: "Want is from the Lord in the house of the wicked, but the habitations of the just shall be blessed." [46] St. Paul teaches this doctrine even more explicitly when he writes to Timothy: "Exercise thyself unto godliness, for bodily exercise is profitable to little, but godliness is profitable to all things, having promise of the life that now is and of that which is to come." [47]

Do you see that both the goods of this life and those of the life to come are promised to the merciful? Hence, if your heart is not moved to the practice of this virtue by reason of the promise of spiritual goods, here you have what you desire, namely, temporal goods. Heed the words of the Savior when He says: "Give, and it shall be given to you." [48]

This is shown to us very clearly by God's actions toward the widow who shared her poverty with Elias, which con-

---

[43] Cf. Deut. chap. 28.   [44] Prov. 3:9–10.   [45] Prov. 28:27.
[46] *Ibid.*, 3:33.   [47] Cf. I Tim. 4:7–8.   [48] Luke 6:38.

sisted of a handful of meal and a little oil. Thinking first
of mercy and then of her own need and that of her child,
she gave Elias to eat and then she and her son ate. "And
from that day the pot of meal wasted not and the cruse of
oil was not diminished, according to the word of the Lord
which He spoke in the hand of Elias." [49] Ask yourself
whether you believe these things. If you answer no, then
you lack faith and are not a Christian, because you do not
believe the words of Christ, who said, "Give and it shall be
given to you." But if you answer yes, then you must admit
that in giving alms you do not lose anything but you multi-
ply both your temporal and your spiritual goods. See to it
that you do not look for excuses, for you have no excuse.
If you will receive both temporal and spiritual benefits
from the practice of mercy, you have no excuse for not
practicing this virtue.

Let us now return to the beginning and weigh the loss
of one's possessions as a result of almsgiving against all the
goods and blessings that God has promised for the works
of mercy. First, consider the blessings of mercy. It makes
us like unto God in one of His most glorious attributes,
mercy; it disposes us to be dearly loved by God; it gives us
a claim to the mercy of God, which brings pardon for sin,
increase of merits, treasure for the next life, assistance in
time of tribulation, greater efficacy in prayer, defense on
the day of judgment, and the promise of salvation, not to
mention the temporal goods which God promises to those
who share their possessions with the poor.

After placing all these blessings on one side of the scale,
let us place on the other the loss of one's possessions
through works of mercy, and we shall see whether a prudent man would deprive himself of such blessings on ac-

[49] Cf. III Kings 17:9–16.

count of some temporal loss. I think that anyone who considers this matter will be ashamed of himself if at any time he has been stingy with God. For that reason I said at the outset that the lack of understanding is the principal cause of our negligence in this matter. Indeed, who will not consider it a great gain to lose all that he possesses in this world in order to gain such great benefits? What loss could be so great that it would not be amply repaid by these spiritual blessings? And since this is so, it is amazing to see such avarice among Christians. How cold their love has grown!

But if anyone is so blind and obstinate that he still offers excuses for not giving alms, let him listen to the words of St. Cyprian: "You are afraid, wretched one, that you will lose all your possessions if you are generous, but you do not seem to realize that even as you strive to save your possessions, you are losing your life, and while you take care that your possessions do not diminish, you yourself are decreasing. You love money more than yourself and in fearing to lose your possessions, you lose yourself in order to save your wealth. You are afraid that you shall not have enough to eat if you are liberal with the poor. But when was food ever wanting to the just man? Is it not written that the Lord will not afflict the soul of the just with famine? [50] Ravens brought food to Elias in the desert and an angel of the Lord carried Habacuc with food for Daniel in the lion's den. Do you fear that he who works for God and serves God will be wanting in food? Consider, says the Lord, the birds of the air, for they neither sow nor do they reap, and your heavenly Father feeds them.[51] Are not you of much more value than they? If He does not

[50] Prov. 10:3.   [51] Matt. 6:26.

neglect those creatures which lack understanding, how can you think that He will neglect the Christian, the servant of God? Do you think that Christ will not provide for you, when He offers His own flesh and blood as food? Whence comes this lack of confidence? What is a faithless heart doing in the house of faith? How can one bear the name of Christian and have no trust in Christ? Why do you seek to excuse yourself with these vain shadows?

"Admit the true cause of your hardness of heart. The darkness of sterility has invaded your soul. The light of truth has fled and you have become blinded with avarice. You are a slave of your own money; you are bound by the chains of covetousness. You protect your money, which cannot protect you; you increase your possessions, and they crush you with their weight. Fix your eyes on that widow of the gospel, who offered her two mites although she was oppressed with poverty. Be ashamed that widows and the poor surpass you in performing works of mercy."

St. Augustine also addresses those who neglect to give alms or practice the works of mercy: "Christ begs of you in the person of the poor and you give Him nothing, saying that you must save it for your own children. In the poor you are confronted with Christ; will you place your children before Him? What a great injustice to let your God go hungry, for He has said that if you do it to any of these least of His little ones, you have done it to Him."

In addition to all that has been said, there is yet another consideration that should move us to mercy. Even if this virtue were in no way necessary for salvation or did not confer any spiritual and temporal blessings, the debt we owe to God for His great mercies should make us lovers of mercy. St. Paul uses this argument when writing to the

Corinthians: "You know the grace of our Lord, Jesus Christ, that being rich, He became poor for your sakes, that through His poverty you might be rich." [52]

But if God became poor for love of men why should men not do the same for love of God? If Christ let Himself be sold for love of men, should not men sell a bit of their possessions for the love of God? Who will not give part of his possessions in the name of Him who has given His blood? St. Bernard says that if a man were to sacrifice himself a thousand times for the Lord he could not repay the benefits he has received, for what comparison is there between the life of man and the life of God? Then how can you be so parsimonious when you are so much indebted?

"Let us imagine," says St. Cyprian, "that the devil steps forth with all his servants of perdition in order to shame and confound all Christians in the presence of God. 'Look, Christ,' he says, 'at all those who are with me. I did not endure buffeting; I did not endure the scourge; I did not suffer on the cross or shed my blood for them. Neither did I promise them the kingdom of heaven or the glory of paradise. Yet see what great gifts they offer me and how generously they spend in my service the goods that they have gained over a long period of time and with much effort and labor. Now show me, Christ, the creatures that serve Thee and spend all their possessions for Thee. Do the rich and those who have many possessions do the same thing for Thee? Do they sell their possessions for Thee, in order to change them into heavenly treasures and transform them into better goods? In the works of mercy done by Thy servants, Thou art clothed and fed in the person of the poor and Thou hast promised eternal life to all who would do

[52] Cf. II Cor. 8:9.

these things. In spite of all that has been promised, the number of Thy servants can scarcely equal mine, who will suffer great torments.' "

What answer can we give to this? What excuse can we offer when we see that we have not even tried to repay the price of the blood of Christ with a crust of bread for the poor? The best that we can do is point to the saints and holy Christians who have endeavored to repay God's love by works of mercy. St. Elizabeth of Hungary spent her wealth on hospitals and the poor and eventually became so poor herself that she had to support herself with the work of her own hands. St. Paula, when advised by St. Jerome not to be excessive in her almsgiving, answered that she desired nothing more than to go from door to door, begging in the name of God, and to end her life in such poverty that she would not even have a shroud in which to be buried. St. Exuperius, Bishop of Toulouse, gave his own food to the poor and sold the cathedral treasures to raise funds for the poor. After selling all his books for the sake of the poor, St. Dominic offered himself as ransom for the son of a poor widow when he had nothing else to give.

Although it is not possible for all Christians to perform such heroic acts of mercy, many of us are able to do more than we do. And in order that our works of mercy may be truly Christian, let us consider the proper manner of practicing this virtue. The first thing required is that we should be generous and liberal in doing good and not be like those who give to the poor to rid themselves of the annoyance of their begging rather than to help them in their need. "He who gives alms in order to rid himself of the importunity of the beggar rather than to help him in his need," says St. Augustine, "loses that which he gives and also the merit of a good work." St. Paul says: "He who soweth sparingly, shall also reap sparingly, and he who soweth in blessings, shall also reap blessings." [53]

However, the degree of blessings and merit for works of mercy should be judged more from the desire of the heart than the good deed itself. St. Ambrose says that the affection of him who gives makes the giver rich or poor and gives true value to the work done. St. Gregory says that in the eyes of God the hand is not empty of gifts when the treasury of the heart is filled with good desires. St. Jerome points out that no one was poorer than the apostles, but no one has given up more for Christ than they did, because of the great love with which they abandoned all things. Likewise, St. Leo says that the measure of piety is not to be estimated according to the quantity of the gift but by the intention of the giver. The gifts of the rich are great and those of the moderately wealthy are less, but the fruit of each is the same if the desires and intentions are equally good. Although the ability to give may not be equal, their mercy is equal because generosity is not measured by the value of the gift but by the degree of benevolence.

The second requisite for the performance of the works of mercy is that we must observe discretion and moderation, lest our liberality become prodigality, as happens when one gives to whom he ought not or more than is proper. St. Jerome says that this would be to lose liberality because of liberality. St. Paul says that we should not give to such an extent that others are well cared for and we ourselves become needy, but a certain equality should be observed so that he who receives is eased of his condition and he who gives is not reduced to poverty.[54] If a man is too liberal, he may become impoverished, and in this way

53 Cf. II Cor. 9:6.   54 Cf. II Cor. 8:13.

prodigality easily leads to avarice. So it is said that a man seldom is prodigal without eventually becoming a thief.

The third requisite is to give cheerfully and promptly. St. Paul says that we should give, "not with sadness or of necessity, for God loveth a cheerful giver," [55] and St. Peter urges us to practice "hospitality one toward another without murmuring." [56] Hence, a work of mercy is the more valuable as it is done with greater promptness and cheerfulness.

The fourth requisite is to give with compassion of heart. This quality was especially exemplified in our Savior in all the works of mercy that He performed, for it is generally written of Him that He was moved to compassion when He did these things, and He said of Himself: "I have compassion on the multitude." [57]

The fifth requisite is that almsgiving should be done in secret, and this is to be understood in two ways. First, one should not perform the works of charity for worldly motives but for God. Secondly, secrecy should especially be observed in the case of the poor who are ashamed of their condition and for the sake of avoiding vainglory in the giver, although sometimes it is well to give alms openly so that the world may see how a good Christian should act. Christ tells us in this regard that when we give alms we should not let the left hand know what the right hand is doing, so that our alms may be given in secret and the heavenly Father, who sees in secret, may reward us. But those who do otherwise have already received their reward in this world.[58] The Savior has His hand on the pulse of our hearts and He knows how prone we are to vainglory. He also knows that the guile of this vice is so great that

---

[55] Cf. II Cor. 9:7.   [56] Cf. I Pet. 4:9.   [57] Mark 8:2.
[58] Matt. 6:5.

sometimes, without our fully realizing it, it takes possession of our hearts and does great harm. Persons who by reason of their office practice the works of mercy can and should give alms publicly, but they should also take every precaution to avoid scandal and should strive always to have a pure intention.

The sixth requisite is that we should give alms without too much delay, for a gift is doubly helpful if it is given quickly. Hence, the proverb has it that he gives twice who gives promptly. Therefore, "say not to thy friend: 'Go, and come again, and tomorrow I will give to thee,' when thou canst give at present." [59] He who delays in giving, gives unwillingly. Abraham was so prompt to obey that he arose in the night to fulfill God's command to sacrifice Isaac. He was just as prompt in performing the works of mercy, as when he ran after the three young men and brought them to his house to prepare food for them. But if this is so necessary a requisite for mercy, how shall we look upon those persons who let almsgiving go until after their death? St. Lucy admonished her mother in these words: "It is not much to give to God that which you cannot take with you; therefore, while you yet live, share what you have with Christ." St. Basil says of such persons: "You tell me that you wish to enjoy your possessions during your lifetime and that after your death you will leave something to the poor. O wretched man! Do you wish to be liberal and kind to men when you have become a lump of earth?"

The seventh requisite for mercy is that while one should take care to examine the persons to whom he gives alms so that he will not deprive the poor of help while giving to deceivers, he should nevertheless not be like those who hide their avarice and parsimony under the guise of in-

[59] Prov. 3:28.

vestigation. St. Gregory warns: "Do not examine with excessive scrupulosity who is worthy or unworthy of the alms that you give, for it is better to give to those who are unworthy than to place yourself in danger of defrauding the worthy." "Mercy does not judge merits," says St. Ambrose, "but alleviates needs; it does not examine justice, but eases poverty. Where God is, there is His voice, and if you take care to look only to God in everything that He asks of you, you will find Him."

The eighth requisite is that alms should not be given out of the possessions of another, as is frequently done. This is not almsgiving, but sacrilege. God is an enemy of this kind of almsgiving, for we read in Scripture: "I am God, who loves justice and abhors theft, even if it be to sacrifice to Me."

The ninth requisite is that almsgiving must be done with circumspection, which means that we should consider who begs, what he asks, and why he begs. He who begs is not the poor man, but God in the person of the poor, as St. Jerome says: "Whenever you extend your hand to the poor, think that you are extending it to Christ." That which is asked is not your possessions but His, for if Christ is the Lord and Master of all things, His also are your possessions, your life, and your very person. If you consider the reason for the begging, I tell you that the poor beg more for your sake than for their own, because while they ask for themselves some portion of this world's goods, they give you in return the goods of heaven, as Christ said: "If thou wilt be perfect, go sell what thou hast and give to the poor and thou shalt have treasure in heaven." [60]

[60] Matt. 19:21.

CHAPTER 29 🖑

Scandal

IT sometimes happens that the sins of others become ours and that we share in their fault and guilt. St. Paul says of sins of this type: "Neither be partakers of other men's sins." [1] He also writes to the Ephesians: "Have no fellowship with the unfruitful works of darkness, but rather reprove them." [2] Communication in the sins of others may take place in nine ways: by counsel, command, consent, provocation, flattery, silence, negligence, participation, or defense.

One shares in the sin of another through counsel when one advises another to commit some evil, as Caiphas did when he counseled the Jews to kill Christ. Command occurs when one person orders another to do some evil, as David did when he sent letters commanding that Urias be slain. One sins through consent when he approves that others should do evil and as a result of his consent the evil is actually done, as when St. Paul, before his conversion, consented to the death of St. Stephen. [3] Thus, St. Paul writes: "Who, having known the justice of God, did not understand that they who do such things are worthy of death, and not only they that do them, but also consent to them that do them." [4]

One shares in another's sin through provocation when he incites another to wrath, blasphemy, desire for vengeance, or similar vices, as when Job's wife urged him to blaspheme God. [5] Flattery occurs when one praises a person

[1] Cf. I Tim. 5:22. [2] Eph. 5:11. [3] Acts 7:59.
[4] Rom. 1:32. [5] Job 2:9.

210

for his sin, thereby encouraging him to continue in evil. Such was the sin of the preachers to whom Isaias referred: "O my people, they that call thee blessed, the same deceive thee and destroy the way of thy steps." [6] One shares in the sin of another through silence if he does not admonish his neighbor when it is his duty to do so. God calls such persons "dumb dogs not able to bark," [7] and speaking through Ezechiel, He says: "If when I say to the wicked: Thou shalt surely die, thou declare it not to him, nor speak to him, that he may be converted from his wicked way and live, the same wicked man shall die in his iniquity, but I will require his blood at thy hand." [8]

Negligence occurs when we do not punish the wicked when it is our duty to do so. Thus, judges are guilty of sin if they tolerate evils in the state and do not use the power that God has given them for the punishment of evil. Parents and teachers also sin in this way when through too much indulgence they overlook the vices and sins of their children or students, like the priest Heli, who knew that his sons did evil but did not chastise them.[9] Participation occurs when a man joins thieves and other evil-doers and shares their crimes and their booty. This was condemned in Scripture in the following words "If thou didst see a thief, thou didst run with him; and with adulterers thou hast been a partaker." [10] To share in another's sin by defense is to defend, conceal, or protect criminals.

Such are the ways in which one man may sin without being the actual executor of the evil deed. He becomes an accomplice or cooperator in evil and shares in the guilt. It is to be noted that if a person cooperates in any of these ways in sins of injustice, he is bound to his share in making resti-

---

[6] Isa. 3:12.   [7] Isa. 56:10.   [8] Ezech. 3:18.
[9] Cf. I Kings 3:23.   [10] Ps. 49:18.

tution. The principal aggressor or agent is first obliged to restitution, but so also are the others, according as they share in the evil.

Another way in which we may be involved in the sin of another is through scandal. Note well that I do not mean by scandal the astonishment and shock caused by sin, but I use the word in a strictly theological sense to signify any word or deed by which we may offer our neighbor an occasion or motive for sinning. Our Savior referred to the gravity of this sin when He said: "He that shall scandalize one of these little ones that believe in Me, it were better for him that a millstone should be hanged about his neck and that he should be drowned in the depth of the sea. Woe to the world because of scandals. For it must needs be that scandals come, but nevertheless woe to that man by whom the scandal cometh." [11]

When David took to himself the wife of another and killed the husband, God pointed out the scandal of this sin when He said through Nathan: "Thou hast given occasion to the enemies of the Lord to blaspheme." [12] He then declared that the child born of David and Bethsabee would surely die, as it did. In spite of David's fasts and acts of penance and pleas for the life of the child, God would not hear him. Seeing the terrible punishment inflicted by God for this sin, who will not tremble at the thought of giving scandal? It is a particularly detestable sin, for although other sins are also serious, they usually harm only him who commits them. But the sin of scandal harms both him who causes scandal and those who are led into sin. Hence, if such men are lost, they shall be punished not only for their own sins but also for the sins of those whom they have perverted. Now the Christian can begin to understand the

[11] Matt. 18:6–7.   [12] Cf. II Kings 12:14.

significance of Christ's lament when He said: "Woe to the world because of scandals!"

Apart from the sin of direct scandal, there are some Christians who have such an abhorrence and distaste for the exercises of devotion and the persons who practice them that they call such persons effeminate or apply to them some other term of derision. And if one of these devout persons happens to fall, these people are glad and confirmed in their opinion. We can apply to such people the words of condemnation which God spoke through Solomon: "He that rejoiceth at another man's ruin shall not be unpunished." [13]

There are even some preachers who have a dislike for devout persons and it is so evident that they reveal in the pulpit what little devotion they have in their own hearts. Such preachers are like dogs that ought to guard the flock but are actually wolves that devour the flock, for while it is the duty of preachers to encourage the weak and silence the tongues of detractors, they aid the latter by the deprecating remarks they make in their sermons, with the result that they discourage and scandalize the little ones. Let preachers realize that their duty is to encourage the weak and not to discourage them by taking the side of those who, because of their own distaste for devotion, condemn the devotion of others.

These are the people who say that it is sufficient to say an Our Father and to receive Communion once a year and that one should not pay any attention to devotions and pious practices. What shall such persons say to St. Paul, who tells us to pray in every place [14] and to pray without ceasing? [15] And if the words of St. Paul are not sufficient, consider the words of Christ Himself, who states that we ought

[13] Prov. 17:5.   [14] Cf. I Tim. 2:8.   [15] Cf. I Thess. 5:17.

always to pray,[16] "praying at all times, that you may be accounted worthy to escape all these things that are to come, and to stand before the Son of man." [17] Compare these words of Christ with the opinion of those who say that an Our Father suffices. Christ says that we should pray always. Therefore, either Christ is in error or those persons are mistaken. But Christ cannot deceive or be deceived. Moreover, when times are more dangerous, there is greater need of the spiritual weapon of prayer, as Christ demonstrated when on the eve of His death He told His apostles to watch and pray that they fall not into temptation. Indeed, it would be the height of folly to lay down one's arms at the time of battle, for that is precisely when they should be taken up.

Let us now consider those weak Christians who are discouraged and scandalized at seeing good people fall into sin or who abandon prayer and the practice of good works for fear of what the world will think. Christians who feel and act this way seem to live more for the world than for Christ, because they leave Christ on account of the world. They ought to remember that St. Paul teaches that the world is one of the three enemies of the soul and is no less pernicious than the other two. It is to worldly respect that Christ attributed the blindness of the leaders of the Jews, who knew that He was the true Messias but did not dare to confess it openly. "How can you believe," He asks, "who receive glory from one another, and the glory which is from God alone, you do not seek?" [18] What is become of the honor of Christ among Christians when religion makes a man ignoble?

It was this same human respect that caused St. Peter to deny Christ, and yet we can understand how he was

[16] Luke 18:1.   [17] *Ibid.*, 21:36.   [18] John 5:44.

ashamed to be counted as a disciple of Him who was considered a liar and a deceiver. But if you deny Christ, it is much worse, because you are ashamed to be considered a disciple of Him who now reigns gloriously in heaven and is seated at the right hand of the Father. Rightly should we fear that on the day of judgment God will take the hand of St. Lawrence or some other martyr and, showing us the wounds inflicted on His faithful servant, will say to us: "This saint did not hesitate to confess publicly that he was My disciple, although he knew full well how many wounds and how much suffering it would cost him. But you, for foolish reasons or because of a vain fear of the world's opinion, have neglected to show by your works that you are My disciple."

So it is, Lord, that we pay honor to the world and in so doing we desert Thee. If the world had approved of our service to Thee, we would have served Thee, but since the world disdains and condemns this service, we have not given it to Thee.

How is it that we do not see how great is this rudeness to our Lord? He Himself tells us: "He that shall deny Me before men, shall be denied before the angels of God." [19] David says of such persons: "The arrows of children are their wounds," [20] signifying that because they fear the toy arrows of children, they desist from good works and depart from God. For what are the criticisms of the world and the ignominious names heaped on us but the toy arrows of a child? People who are influenced by such things are like timid animals that are frightened and flee at the mere shadow of a danger that does not even exist. Whatever the world may say or do against virtue is so much air and smoke.

But perhaps one of these weak and timid Christians will

[19] Luke 12:9.   [20] Ps. 63:8.

say: "I have seen a person who was very concerned about holiness of life and who actually practiced many virtues, performed good works, and frequented the sacraments. Nevertheless, he fell into a serious public sin. I am afraid that the same thing will happen to me and that is why I am discouraged and dismayed."

But to this I would answer: Think of the countless people in the Church who occupy themselves in pious practices and good works without any pretense and deceit and who persevere until the end of their lives. What foolishness, then, to look upon the one who has fallen and ignore the many virtuous Christians who have persevered. Why should you be more readily moved to discouragement by the weakness of one than to greater efforts by the constancy of the many? The Holy Ghost has never deserted and never will desert the Church. Consequently, there will always be souls who are His living temples and in whom He dwells. They will despise the world with its foolish judgments and be governed by the spirit and doctrine of the Church.

Let me show you how unreasonable you are. Some women die during childbirth, but will you say that this is sufficient reason for parents to refuse to let their daughters marry? Certainly not; for it would be very foolish indeed to forbid women to marry simply because a few die in childbirth. But if this is a prudent manner of judging, why do you not act the same way in regard to your salvation?

Do you wish me to tell you the source of your mistaken judgment? It springs from your inordinate love of the world and temporal things and your small regard for God and spiritual things. Snares and dangers of all kinds do not deter you from seeking temporal goods, but the slightest obstacle makes you lose heart and weakens your love for spiritual goods. How different were the souls of the primitive Christians. They saw the prisons filled with Christians and the streets reddened with the blood of martyrs. They saw Christians strangled, hanged, dismembered, burned at the stake, or thrown into boiling oil, but none of these things deterred them from the love and service of Christ. How far you are from repeating the words of St. Paul: "Who, then, shall separate us from the love of Christ? Shall tribulation, or distress, or famine, or nakedness, or danger, or persecution, or the sword? . . . I am sure that neither death, nor life, nor angels, nor principalities, nor powers, nor things present, nor things to come, nor might, nor height, nor depth, nor any other creature shall be able to separate us from the love of God." [21] It seems that your virtues are stuck to you with pins, if you lose them so easily.

Perhaps you will ask: "Why does our Lord permit scandals at all?" God allows you to be tempted in order to test whether you love Him with all your heart, for it is in temptations that you show whether you truly love God, whether you are loyal and faithful or disloyal and faithless. And one of the greatest fruits you can gain from your temptations is a true knowledge of yourself, which is the basis of humility, the foundation of the whole spiritual life. In times of temptation, says Solomon, "a holy man continueth in wisdom as the sun, but a fool is changed as the moon." [22] And Christ has said: "Everyone, therefore, that heareth these My words and doth them, shall be likened to a wise man that built his house upon a rock, and it fell not, for it was founded on a rock. And everyone that heareth these My words and doth them not, shall be like a foolish man that built his house upon the sand, and the rains fell and the floods came and the winds blew, and they beat upon that house, and it fell, and great was the fall thereof." [23] Again,

[21] Rom. 8:35–39.   [22] Ecclus. 27:12.   [23] Matt. 7:24–27.

we read in Ecclesiasticus: "The furnace trieth the potter's vessels, and the trial of affliction just men," [24] meaning that the well-made clay vessel becomes stronger when placed in an oven, but that which is defective cracks and crumbles in the heat. The same thing happens to evil men when they are tried by afflictions and temptations.

From these comparisons you can understand that the weak Christians who desist from their good works because of the sins of those reputed to be holy are straws carried away by the slightest breeze, defective vessels that crumble in the heat of the oven, and fools who have built their houses upon sand. And if it is important that the weak Christians be tested so that they will be humbled, it is also important that the good Christians be revealed so that great fruits may result. Therefore St. Paul says: "For there must also be heresies, that they also, who are approved, may be made manifest among you." [25] Thus the faithful are purified like gold in the furnace, as the Psalmist says: "Thou hast tried me by fire, and iniquity hath not been found in me." [26]

In conclusion, the Lord permits scandals in the Church so that the perfect and imperfect, the strong and the weak, may be known and recognized. He who is found to be strong should give thanks to God; he who is found to be weak and timid should humble himself and say: "Unless the Lord had been my helper, my soul had almost dwelt in hell." [27]

[24] Ecclus. 27:6.   [25] Cf. I Cor. 11:19.   [26] Ps. 16:3.
[27] Ps. 93:18.

CHAPTER 30 ✍

Envy

ENVY is sadness at the good of another and sorrow at his happiness. The envious man looks upon his superiors as persons he can never equal, his inferiors as those who can never come up to his standards, and his equals as those who compete with him. Thus, the Pharisees were envious of Christ and for that reason they sought His death. Envy is such a vicious beast that it never forgives those who surpass us. In itself, it is a mortal sin because it directly militates against charity, as does hatred, although it frequently happens that the sin is not mortal because the envy is not complete. So also, there is a hatred that is not yet perfectly formed and developed, although it may be well on the way to becoming true hatred.

The daughters that proceed from envy are: hatred, ridicule, detraction, happiness at another's misfortunes, and sadness at another's prosperity. Envy is one of the worst sins and it is especially evident in high places, universities, professional circles, and even in religious orders. Envy caused Cain to kill Abel and was the reason why Joseph was sold into slavery by his own brothers. Truly, it is a sin that holds sway over the world and causes immeasurable harm. Its immediate effect is the persecution of the good, for it is against the virtuous that its arrows are first directed. For that reason Solomon says that all the works and labors of men are exposed to the envy of their neighbors.[1]

Therefore you should arm yourself against this enemy

[1] Eccles. 4:4.

with all care and diligence, asking God's help and avoiding every occasion of envy. And if this vice perseveres in fighting for control of your heart, persevere also in your resistance against it, for as long as your will does not give consent, it makes little difference that you experience the sting of this temptation. If you see that one of your neighbors is more prosperous or more blessed than you, give thanks to God and realize that either you do not deserve as much or it is not fitting for you to have as much. In any case, you do not alleviate your own poverty by being envious of others.

If you wish to know the type of weapons with which you can best combat this vice, I offer you the following considerations. First of all, understand that envious people are like the demons, who are saddened by the good works we perform and the eternal blessings we receive. The demons could never possess such blessings even if men were to lose them, but they are envious that men should possess something that they themselves have lost. For that reason St. Augustine says: "May God take this vice not only from the hearts of all Christians, but from all men, for it is a vice proper to demons and from which they will always suffer. The devils have fallen, but they are envious of man who still stands upright. So also, some men are envious of others, not because they wish to have the prosperity that they see in others, but because they would wish that everyone be as wretched as themselves."

Even if your neighbor did not possess the goods of which you are envious, you would not possess them either, and since your neighbor possesses such things without any damage to you, there is no reason why you should be sad. If you are envious of another's virtue, understand that you are harming yourself, because if you are in the state of grace, you share in the good works of your neighbor. Therefore, you are envious without reason and you should rather rejoice with him for your own good and for his. Realize also what a great misfortune it is that your neighbor should improve while you grow worse. If you truly loved your neighbor, you would rejoice in his virtues as in your own.

Consider also how envy inflames the heart, wearies the intellect, destroys peace of conscience, makes one's life sad, and drives contentment and peace from the soul. Envy is like a worm that consumes the heart and after the heart is corrupted, the bitterness of one's countenance clearly manifests one's internal state. The envious man is his own worst enemy because envy constantly torments its possessor. For that reason theologians have called it a "just" vice, not because it is truly just, but because it justly afflicts the one who possesses it and thus sees that justice is meted out.

Consider how contrary it is to charity and the common good to envy the goods of others and abhor those whom God has created and redeemed. And if you seek a remedy against the poison of envy, love humility and hate pride. Pride cannot endure anything superior or equal to itself and for that reason it easily gives rise to envy, for the proud man feels that he is placed in an inferior position when he sees that others surpass him. St. Paul understood this very well when he wrote: "Let us not be made desirous of vainglory, provoking one another, envying one another." [2]

Rid your heart of all inordinate love for the goods of this world and love only spiritual goods, for they are in no way lessened if possessed by many, but are more increased as more souls possess them. But temporal goods are more diminished as they are divided among many, and that is why envy torments the soul of him who desires earthly goods, for if another acquires that which he desires, he is either de-

[2] Gal. 5:26.

prived of it entirely or his share is lessened. It is only with great effort that we can overcome sorrow when another person has that which we desire.

But it is not enough to avoid being saddened at the goods possessed by another. You should earnestly endeavor to do good to your neighbor and ask God to do for him what you cannot do. Do not hate any man, but love your friends in God and love your enemies for God. Were you not at the beginning of your life an enemy of God? And did He not love you so much that He gave His life in order to rescue you from your enemies? Even if your neighbor be evil, you must not on that account hate him. Be like the doctor, who hates sickness and loves the patient. In other words, love whatever God has made and hate the evil that man has done.

Never say in your heart: "What have I to do with this person or why should I be under any obligation to him? I do not know him and he has never done anything for me." Remember the great mercy that God has shown to you, without any merit on your part. In repayment for this He asks you to be liberal, not to Him, for He has no need of your gifts, but toward your neighbor whom He has commanded you to love. Realize that we are are all brothers. We have a common natural father in Adam and a common spiritual Father in heaven. We have also a common mother, the Church, and Christ is our brother. We have all been called to the same heritage in the heavenly kingdom of our Father, where we shall live in unity and shall rejoice in our common blessings. For charity makes all things the common possession of all. But if we are brothers in Christ and co-heirs with Christ; if we are members of the same body, redeemed by the same blood, and called to the same grace and glory, then there is much reason for one brother to wish well to another, to desire good things for him, to do all the good he can for him, and to rejoice in another's good. But how contrary to reason it is to rejoice at another's adversity and be saddened at his prosperity, for this is proper to the vice of envy.

BOOK FIVE

The Moral Virtues

❧

CHAPTER 31 ✑

Prudence

PRUDENCE is to the spiritual life what the eyes are to the body, the pilot is to a ship, the king is to his kingdom, and the driver is to a cart, for it guides the Christian on his way to perfection and salvation. Without this virtue the Christian would be blind and filled with confusion. Whence the holy Anthony places the virtue of prudence in the highest place, as the guide and master of all the other virtues. Therefore, all true lovers of virtue ought to keep this virtue before their eyes and strive to advance in it as much as possible.

Prudence does not have only one duty in our spiritual life; its functions are many and diverse. It is a general or cardinal virtue which comes into play in the acts of all the other virtues. In the first place, presupposing faith and charity, prudence directs all our acts to God as our ultimate end, examining carefully the intentions for which we perform our actions, to see whether we are doing them for the love of God or for ourselves.

Prudence also directs our actions toward our neighbors so that we shall help them and not scandalize them. It helps us endure the imperfections of others and even to make allowance for the weakness of others, realizing that one cannot avoid all the defects and imperfections that mar human life, especially when we consider the effects of original sin. Aristotle has said that the wise man does not ask for equal certitude and proof in all things, because some things can be clearly demonstrated, but others not. Likewise, the prudent man does not demand that in human affairs everything should be so perfect that there is nothing left to be desired, because some may be so and others not. And he who would demand the contrary would perhaps cause more harm than good, even if he ultimately attains what he seeks.

It also belongs to prudence to enable a man to know himself so thoroughly that he recognizes his own vicious habits, his evil inclinations, and the weakness of his knowledge and virtue. Knowing these things, he will not presume too much and will better understand the enemy against whom he must wage constant war and will appreciate the great need for caution and vigilance. Prudence tells the Christian when to draw back from dangers, how to smell the smoke of battle from afar, and how to fortify himself with prayer so that he may emerge victorious. Such is the advice given in Ecclesiasticus: "Before sickness, take medicine, and before judgment, examine thyself." [1]

Prudence warns the Christian to control his tongue in conformity with the laws and circumstances we have already described, to understand when to speak and when to observe silence, for Solomon says that there is "a time to keep silence, and a time to speak." [2] Prudence teaches us not to trust everyone nor to reveal our souls through excessive speech nor to say all that we think about a certain thing. "A fool uttereth all his mind; a wise man deferreth and keepeth it till afterward." [3] He who trusts in those in whom he ought not to trust will always live in danger and will be the slave of him in whom he has confided.

Prudence enables us to approach our occupations with a moderate spirit so that we shall not be smothered by too much work, for St. Francis says in his rule that all things should serve for our spiritual improvement. It prevents us

[1] Ecclus. 18:20.   [2] Eccles. 3:7.   [3] Prov. 29:11.

from giving ourselves so completely to external works that we lose our peace of soul and neglect the interior acts of virtue. Thus, in our works of love for our neighbor, we should take care not to neglect the exercises of the love of God. The apostles had the talent and ability to perform all types of labor, but they delegated to others certain lesser works so that they could apply themselves to more important affairs.[4] No one should so presume on his abilities and talents as to think that he alone can do everything, for as a rule he accomplishes little who attempts too much.

Prudence gives the Christian a knowledge of the craftiness and deceits of the enemy, and prevents him from believing every spirit or every appearance of virtue, for Satan can transform himself into an angel of light in order to deceive us with the disguise of virtue. Therefore, we should be especially wary of anything that wears the mask of virtue. The devil frequently resorts to this stratagem when dealing with souls who are most determined to advance in holiness.

Prudence also teaches us when to fear and when to attack, when it is to our gain to lose and when it is to our loss to win. It warns us to ignore the judgments and opinions of the world and the talk of worldly persons, which is nothing more than the yapping of dogs that never stop barking and yet have no reason to bark at all. St. Paul says: "If I yet pleased men, I should not be the servant of Christ."[5] Surely, there is no greater folly than to be ruled by a beast of so many heads as is the opinion of the crowd, which manifests no prudence or consideration. It is well not to scandalize anyone and to fear when there is reason to fear, but it is a weakness to be swayed by every wind that blows.

Prudence is also necessary for success in one's affairs and the prevention of mistakes that must be corrected later with

---

[4] Acts 6:1–4.　　　　　　　　[5] Gal. 1:10.

great difficulty and inconvenience, with the result that one loses his peace of mind and the tranquillity of his life. In order to avoid these things, we should bear in mind the following suggestions. We read in Scripture: "Let thy eyes look straight on, and let thy eyelids go before thy steps." [6] This means that we should not rush headlong to the task we are to perform, but should first give the matter serious deliberation and, when necessary, take counsel. In the first place, we should commend our task to the Lord. Secondly, we should give much thought to the matter at hand, considering not only the work itself, but also the circumstances, for the lack of consideration on one point may ruin everything. Thirdly, we should, when necessary, take counsel with others, but these persons should be few and well selected, for although it is well to listen to the advice of many persons so that the matter may be thoroughly discussed, the final judgment should be based on the advice of a few, lest we fall into error. Fourthly, it is important to allow sufficient time for deliberation, even to let the matter settle for a few days. Just as we know persons better when we are with them for some time, so we better understand advice and counsel if we dwell on it for a few days. Moreover, it frequently happens that those who give advice may offer one opinion at the beginning and then a few days later change their mind when they have considered the matter more carefully. Fifthly, one should be on his guard against four principal impediments to prudence: rashness, passion, obstinacy in one's own opinion, and vanity. Rashness does not deliberate; passion blinds the reason; obstinacy closes one's mind to good advice; and vanity stains everything that it touches.

It also belongs to the virtue of prudence to avoid all

[6] Prov. 4:25.

extremes or excesses and hold to the middle course or medium, for virtue observes the golden mean. Therefore, the prudent man does not condemn everything nor does he justify everything; he neither denies nor concedes everything; he does not condemn all for the faults of a few nor does he approve everyone because of the holiness of a few. In all things he follows the rule of reason and never lets himself be carried away by the force of passion.

Prudence does not consider the antiquity or newness of things in order to approve or condemn them, because many old things are bad and many new things are good. On the other hand, the mere fact that a thing is ancient does not on that account make it evil nor does novelty alone make a thing good. Prudence looks first and always at the merits of things in themselves and not at their age, for vice gains nothing by being old except that it becomes more incurable and virtue loses nothing by being new except that it is not yet clearly manifested. Nor is prudence deceived by the appearance of things so that it judges on externals alone. All is not gold that glitters and everything is not good that appears virtuous. Many times thorns are hidden beneath the flowers. And Aristotle says that sometimes a lie has more the appearance of truth than truth itself. So evil may sometimes have more the appearance of good than goodness itself.

Above all, the prudent man will remember that just as gravity and deliberation are the companions of true prudence, so excessive compliance and levity are the marks of indiscretion. Therefore, he will be careful not to be too quick to believe, to concede, to promise, to judge, to converse lightly with other people, or to give vent to anger. In these actions there is a special danger for the compliant and imprudent person. He who believes too readily shows levity of spirit; he who promises too quickly loses his freedom; he who makes concessions too lightly will have much to repent; he who makes quick judgments is often in danger of error; he who is too fond of idle conversations easily falls into detraction and calumny, and he who is quickly aroused to anger shows every indication of being a fool. "He that is patient is governed with much wisdom; but he that is impatient exalteth his folly." [7]

Let us now consider the ways in which the virtue of prudence can be acquired and strengthened. One of the best methods for acquiring prudence is to learn from the experience of one's past failures and successes and those of others. For that reason it is said that the memory of the past is a good teacher of prudence and that today is a student of our yesterdays. As Solomon says: "What is it that hath been? The same things that shall be. What is it that hath been done? The same that shall be done." [8] So we are often able to judge the present by the past and the past by the present.

The acquisition of prudence is also fostered by true humility, but is most impeded by the vice of pride, for it is written that where there is humility, there is also wisdom.[9] Scripture tells us that God instructs the humble and is the teacher of the little ones, to whom He imparts His secrets.[10] But humility need not be so extreme that a person concedes to every opinion or lets himself be influenced by every wind, for this would not be true humility but instability and fickleness of heart. So we are advised in Ecclesiasticus: "Be not lowly in this wisdom, lest being humbled thou be deceived into folly." [11] In other words, in regard to those truths of which a man is certain, he must be constant and

[7] Prov. 14:29.   [8] Eccles. 1:9.   [9] Prov. 11:2.
[10] Matt. 11:25.   [11] Ecclus. 13:11.

not easily influenced as are the weak and timid. Lastly, devout prayer is a great help for acquiring prudence, for one of the principal functions of the Holy Ghost is to enlighten our intellects with the gifts of understanding, wisdom, science, and counsel, and when a man has greater devotion and humility, he presents himself to God as a child to be instructed in these divine lights and filled with heavenly gifts.

CHAPTER 32

Justice

DAVID rightly divided the material of justice into two parts: do good and avoid evil. Under the first part of this precept we are commanded to practice the virtues; under the second part we are commanded to avoid sins of all kinds. The practice of virtue implies the obligation to render that which is his due to God, to neighbor, and to self. The fulfillment of this part of the precept requires that a man be properly observant of the right measure in his relations with these three classes of persons, and in so doing, he merits the title of a just man. The just Christian will be as a child toward God, a mother toward his neighbor, and a judge toward himself. This is what the Lord requires of us. He desires that we manifest sound judgment, that we love mercy, and that we walk circumspectly before Him. In other words, man must show a sound judgment in regard to himself, mercy toward his neighbor, and solicitude in the service of God.

The importance of a Christian's duties toward his neighbor can be appreciated by anyone who reads the Bible, where the practice of justice toward our neighbor is recommended and commanded. In Isaias, for example, God places the perfection of justice in charity toward our neighbor. When the Jews asked God why they had fasted and He had not regarded their fasting or why had they afflicted their hearts when He took no account of it, God replied: "Is this such a fast as I have chosen, for a man to afflict his soul for a day? . . . Wilt thou call this a fast and a day acceptable to the Lord? Is not this rather the fast that I have chosen? Loose the bands of wickedness, undo the bundles that oppress, let them that are broken go free, and break asunder every burden. Deal thy bread to the hungry, and bring the needy and the harborless into thy house. When thou shalt see one naked, cover him, and despise not thy own flesh. Then shalt thy light break forth as the morning, and thy health shall speedily arise, and thy justice shall go before thy face, and the glory of the Lord shall gather thee up." [1]

You will find the same teaching in the writings of Zacharias. When the Jews asked concerning the laws of fasting, the Lord answered through the prophet: "Judge ye true judgment and show ye mercy and compassion every man to his brother. And oppress not the widow and the fatherless and the stranger and the poor. And let not a man devise evil in his heart against his brother." [2]

But perhaps nowhere in the Old Testament do we find stronger testimony of the importance of our obligations to our neighbor than in the words in which God lists the sins of Sodom: "Behold, this was the iniquity of Sodom, thy sister: pride, fullness of bread, and abundance, and the idle-

[1] Isa. 58:5–7. [2] Zach. 7:9–10.

ness of her and of her daughters, and they did not put forth their hand to the needy and to the poor, and they were lifted up and committed abominations before Me." [3] God Himself mentions injustice to one's neighbor as one of the rungs on the ladder of sin by which the people of Sodom descended to the very depths of evil.

In addition to the testimonies from the Old Testament, we can also find ample proof of the importance of this virtue in the teachings contained in the New Testament, which is a doctrine of love. Christ makes fraternal justice and charity the basis of the final judgment, for He shall judge us according as we have practiced the works of mercy. What more could be added to the words in which He states that if we do any of these works to the least of His brethren, we have done it to Him and that the love of God and neighbor is the sum of the whole law and the prophets? In His sermon at the Last Supper, what did Christ recommend more highly than love of neighbor and works of charity toward them? This, He told us, is His commandment—that we love one another as He has loved us. Then, after telling His disciples that the mark of His followers is their mutual love for each other, He prayed to His eternal Father: "Holy Father, keep them in Thy name whom Thou hast given Me, that they may be one as We also are." [4] In other words, the love among Christians must be so supernatural and so far beyond what could be expected of flesh and blood, that it would lead others to believe that Christians are celestial for one another. St. John, the great lover of Christ and beings rather than men, seeing the great charity they have dearly beloved disciple, repeats nothing more frequently than this beautiful doctrine of love. When asked why he repeated this theme so often, he replied that this teaching

[3] Ezech. 16:49–50. [4] John 17:11.

alone, if properly carried into practice, would suffice for
our salvation.

CHAPTER 33 🖋

Avarice

AVARICE may be defined briefly as an inordinate desire
for worldly possessions. A man is avaricious not only if he
steals, but also if he covets the possessions of another or is
inordinately attached to his own. The daughters of avarice
are betrayal, deceit, falsehood, vexation, perjury, violence,
insensitivity, cruelty, and hardness of heart. St. Paul condemns this vice when he says: "They that will become rich,
fall into temptation and into the snare of the devil and into
many unprofitable and harmful desires which drown men
into destruction and perdition. For the desire of money is
the root of all evils." [1]

When you are tempted to this sin, you can defend yourself against it in the following ways. First, consider that
your Lord and your God, when He descended from heaven
to earth, did not desire to possess the riches that you covet.
Rather, He so loved poverty that He chose to assume flesh
from a poor and humble Virgin rather than from a wealthy
and powerful queen. And when He was born, He did not
select a great palace and a soft and beautiful crib, but the
straw of a lowly manger in a cave. All during His life on
earth He disdained wealth and chose poverty. And when
He selected His disciples, He did not call them from among

[1] Cf. I Tim. 6:9–10.

the wealthy and the nobility, but He chose poor fishermen. What a contradiction, then, that a lowly worm should covet wealth when the Lord of heaven and earth was so poor.

Consider also the baseness of your heart if you who are created in the image of God and redeemed by His precious blood, in comparison with which all the wealth and splendor of the world are nothing, would be willing to lose your soul for something that is actually of no value. God would not give His life for the whole universe, but He did give it for your soul. Therefore, your soul is incomparably more valuable than the entire world. The true riches are not gold and silver and precious stones, but the virtues that accompany a good conscience. Put aside the false judgments of men and you will realize that gold and silver and jewels are nothing but clay, which the deceit of men makes precious. That which all the philosophers of the world have disdained, will you, disciple of Christ, consider of such worth that you will become its slave? St. Jerome tells us that he who stores up riches becomes their servant, but he who shakes off this yoke disposes of them as their master.

Understand also that the Lord has warned us that no man can serve two masters. Therefore, no man can serve God and mammon. A man cannot contemplate God if he runs after the goods of this world. Spiritual delights and consolations flee from the heart that is occupied with mundane things, because one cannot mix true values with vanities, the base with the lofty, the eternal with the temporal, or spiritual with carnal things.

Realize that the more you prosper in worldly things, the more you expose yourself to misery, because you run the risk of trusting too much in the false security that such things offer. If you but realized the unhappiness that often accompanies worldly prosperity! The inordinate love of wealth torments a man more with its desire than the actual use of wealth gives pleasure, because it engenders all kinds of temptation. It ensnares him in a net of many cares, it allures him with false delights, it provokes him to sin, and it destroys his peace and tranquillity. Moreover, riches are never acquired without effort, retained without anxiety, or lost without sorrow. What is worst of all, they are seldom attained without offenses against God, as the proverb states: The rich man is either evil or the inheritor of evil.

Consider what madness it is to desire those things which, even if you possessed all the wealth of the world, could never satisfy your desires. Rather, each addition to your wealth increases the desire for wealth, just as each drink of water taken by a person with dropsy increases his thirst. However much you possess, you will always desire what you do not have. Consequently, as the anxious and restless heart acquires the wealth and goods of the world, it wearies but never rests, it drinks but never quenches its thirst, because it pays little attention to what it possesses and concentrates on that which it does not yet have. Its longing for what it does not yet possess is greater than its contentment with what it already has. Rightly did St. Augustine ask: "Why this insatiable desire when even the brutes have a limit to their appetites? Animals hunt when they are hungry and when they have been satiated they cease the pursuit. But the avarice of the wealthy knows no bounds or limits; it is always grasping and never satisfied."

Life is short and death hastens toward us. What do you need for such a brief journey? Why do you want so much wealth and so many possessions when you can travel through life much more easily if you are less encumbered with possessions? And when you reach the end of life's journey, it will not be any the worse for you if you arrive a poor man than if you arrive heavily laden with this world's goods. In fact, if you are poor, you will have less reason to regret the things that must be left behind and less of an accounting to give to God. But the rich will have much sorrow at what they must leave behind and they will render an account to almighty God with fear and trembling.

Think, avaricious man, for whom you accumulate mountains of money and worldly goods, for it is certain that you will leave this world as naked as you entered it. You were born poor and you will die poor. This should be a frequent subject of meditation, for St. Jerome tells us that it is much easier to disdain the things of this world if we frequently recall that one day we shall die.

At the moment of death you will abandon all your worldly possessions and will take with you only the good or evil works you have performed during your lifetime. And if during your life you have considered heavenly things of little worth and have spent all your time and energy on worldly things, you shall lose both at the end. At your death your body will be given over to the worms, your temporal possessions will be given to your heirs, and your soul will be given to the devil. How much better to follow the advice of the Savior and distribute your excess goods among the poor. Consider the goods that God has given you and realize that they were meant to be remedies for human needs and not instruments of an evil life. If things have gone well with you, do not forget Him who has given them to you and do not make the remedies of another's poverty a source of vainglory to yourself.

My brother, do not love the desert more than your fatherland! Do not become so attached to the baggage and equipment of your journey that they become impediments along the way! Do not love so much the light of the moon that you ignore the brilliance of the noonday sun! Do not convert the aids of the present life into the material of eternal death! Be content with your lot and remember the words of St. Paul: "But having food and wherewith to be covered, we are content." [2]

Seek first the kingdom of God and His justice, and all these things will be added unto you,[3] for the God who wishes to give you great things will not deny you the little things. Remember also that poverty is not a virtue, but the love of poverty. They who are voluntarily poor are like Christ Himself who, being rich, became poor for our sake. They who live in poverty by necessity of circumstance, but endure it with patience and do not covet the riches they do not have, make a virtue of their poverty. They who are rich can also be like Christ if they practice almsgiving, for it was not only the poor shepherds who found Christ, but the three kings who brought Him their precious gifts and treasures.

CHAPTER 34 🖋

Theft and Restitution

THE seventh Commandment states: Thou shalt not steal. It forbids us to take the goods that belong to another and it outlaws the vices from which theft springs, such as avarice, covetousness, and envy. In a positive sense, it commands us to have the proper dispositions of heart, to rejoice in the goods of our neighbor, to be liberal; and rather than being

---

[2] I Tim. 6:8.   [3] Cf. Matt. 6:33.

saddened at the possessions enjoyed by another, to be disposed to give of our own should the need arise. He who has these dispositions of heart is well prepared to practice the works that pertain to the seventh Commandment.

They sin against the seventh Commandment who make unjust demands on others, who do not contribute to the Church, who do not pay their employees or who delay payment without reason, so that the employees suffer harm, who do not pay their just debts, who deprive others of that which is rightly owing to them, who falsify or conceal the defects in things that they sell, who draw up unjust contracts, who admit unworthy persons to certain offices and positions, or who are themselves incompetent and yet remain in office. They also sin against this Commandment who do not aid their neighbor in time of need, for in cases of grave necessity the neighbor has a claim on the goods of those who are able to assist him. Thus, the rich man is considered a thief if he deliberately refuses to help those in need. Lastly, they sin against this Commandment and against justice who lose trust in the goodness and providence of God and resort to evil means in order to supply for their needs.

An excessive regard for worldly honor or an inordinate concern for one's own needs is frequently the source of covetousness and many other grave evils. On the other hand, if a man trusts in God's promises and in His providence and mercy, he will understand that God will succor him in his needs by means that are lawful and good. But since sinners and worldly people rely more on their own judgments than on those of God, they are influenced more by what they desire than by trust in God's providence. They fear that God will desert them at the crucial moment and that they will be abandoned to misery and need. They lay their own plans and by their astuteness they seek to carry them through, thinking that they can better provide for their needs through theft and other acts of injustice than by awaiting the liberality of God's providence. It is because of this inordinate self-reliance that loyalty and mutual trust are weakened, superiors exceed the limits of authority, subjects refuse to obey, and all respect for truth and justice is gradually diminished. Nothing is safe from the covetousness of men. Neither duty nor friendship suffice to restrain the works of injustice and even religion is sometimes powerless to prevent such evil.

From what has been said, it is easy to see the various ways in which the seventh Commandment is transgressed. The scope of this work does not permit us to treat in detail of all the sins against justice and the seventh Commandment, but we shall refer to those matters in which men most frequently transgress.

Our first consideration is of those who buy and sell unjustly. Merchants who deceive their buyers are thieves, and no just man will have any part of such dishonest transactions. Scripture warns: "Thou shalt not have divers weights in thy bag, a greater and a less. Neither shall there be in thy house a greater bushel and a less. Thou shalt have a just and true weight, and thy bushel shall be equal and true." [1] "Hear this, you that crush the poor and make the needy of the land to fail, saying, 'When will the month be over, and we shall sell our wares; and the sabbath, and we shall open the corn, that we may lessen the measure and increase the sicle and may convey in deceitful balances; that we may sell the refuse of the corn?' The Lord hath sworn against the pride of Jacob: 'Surely I will never forget all their works. Shall not the land tremble for this and

[1] Deut. 25:13–15.

everyone mourn that dwelleth therein, and rise up all together as a river, and be cast out and run down as the river
of Egypt?' And it shall come to pass in that day, saith the
Lord God, that the sun shall go down at midday and I will
make the earth dark in the day of light. And I will turn
your feasts into mourning and all your songs into lamenta-
tions. And I will bring up sackcloth upon every back of
yours and baldness upon every head. And I will make it
as the mourning of an only son and the latter end therof
as a bitter day." [2]

What greater and more terrifying threats could be given
against this vice? Micheas says: "Hear, O ye tribes, and who
shall approve it? As yet there is a fire in the house of the
wicked, the treasures of iniquity, and a scant measure full
of wrath. Shall I justify wicked balances, and the deceitful
weights in the bag, by which her rich men were filled with
iniquity, and the inhabitants thereof have spoken lies, and
their tongue was deceitful in their mouth? And I therefore
began to strike thee with desolation for thy sins. Thou
shalt eat, but shalt not be filled, and thy humiliation shall
be in the midst of thee. And thou shalt take hold, but shalt
not save. And those whom thou shalt save, I will give up
to the sword. Thou shalt sow, but shalt not reap; thou
shalt tread the olives, but shalt not be anointed with the
oil; and the new wine, but shalt not drink the wine." [3] And
St. Paul says: "This is the will of God, . . . that no man
overreach nor circumvent his brother in business, because
the Lord is the avenger of all these things." [4]

Treating of the holding back of a man's wages, St. James
says: "Behold the hire of the laborers, who have reaped
down your fields, which by fraud has been kept back by
you, crieth; and the cry of them hath entered into the ears

[2] Amos 8:4–10.   [3] Mich. 6:9–15.   [4] Cf. II Thess. 4:6.

of the Lord of Sabaoth." [5] For that reason, God has commanded: "Thou shalt not refuse the hire of the needy and the poor, whether he be thy brother or a stranger that dwelleth with thee in the land and is within thy gates. But thou shalt pay him the price of his labor the same day, before the going down of the sun, because he is poor, and with it maintaineth his life, lest he cry against thee to the Lord and it be reputed to thee for a sin." [6] This is also what Tobias taught his son: "If any man hath done any work for thee, immediately pay him his hire, and let not the wages of thy hired servant stay with thee at all." [7]

On the other hand, laborers should honestly perform the work for which they expect payment. If they do less than that for which they are hired or if they do their work slovenly or carelessly, they are as guilty as if they had stolen their wages.

As to the miserly, the prodigal, and those who beg for alms without truly being in need, no proof is needed to demonstrate that they are all thieves in their own way. Miserly men who spend all their time and effort in storing up wealth and thereby deprive both themselves and their dependents even of the necessities of life, also deprive the poor and needy of the assistance and help they could and should give them. In so doing, they forget that God has made them the dispensers of His goods. Prodigal men, on the other hand, quickly spend their riches and are soon reduced to poverty because of their extravagance and waste. Ultimately they deprive both themselves and the poor of the very needs of life.

In all the various kinds of theft it is important to remember that it is a sin to retain things that belong to another. In other words, it is not only a sin to steal, but it is also

[5] Jas. 5:4.   [6] Deut. 24:14–15.   [7] Tob. 4:15.

a sin to hold the possessions of another against the owner's will. Therefore, it does not suffice to have the intention of making restitution at some future date if one is able to do so at once, for the obligation to restore the goods of another obliges from the moment that those goods are unlawfully possessed and the actual restitution must be made as soon as possible. However, if one cannot make restitution at once or if he is totally unable to do so because he has fallen into poverty, the obligation does not bind, for God does not command the impossible.

St. Gregory says: "Remember that riches that are unjustly possessed must remain behind, but the sin committed in stealing those riches will go with you beyond the grave. Therefore, what greater foolishness than to leave behind you the benefit of your theft and to take with you the harm it has caused; to leave behind the satisfaction and to take with you the torment? You oblige yourself to suffer in the next life for that which others will enjoy after you have gone."

What is more foolish than to have a greater appreciation for your possessions than for yourself and to suffer injury to your soul rather than diminish your worldly goods? How much this action resembles that of Judas, who for a few pieces of silver sold justice, grace, and his own soul! And if you are obliged to make restitution if you wish to be saved because you have the means to pay what you owe, what greater folly than to choose to live in sin and to run the risk of losing everything after death? A man who acts in this way seems not to be a man at all.

Strive, then, to pay what you owe and not to do injury to any man. Do not make your employee come repeatedly to beg for his wages, so that it is harder work for him to get his pay than to earn it. If you are the executor of a will, do not defraud the souls of the dead; if you have servants, be open and honest in your dealings with them. Take care to owe nothing to any man and you shall have peaceful sleep, a tranquil conscience, a happy life, and a fearless death. Restrain your desires and do not strive to acquire all that you would like to have or spend more than you can afford. If you measure your wants by your capabilities and not by your desires, you will never have reason to be indebted to anyone. Keep in mind the admonition of St. Paul: "Let every man abide in the same calling in which he was called." [8] Do not try to be more than what God has wished you to be, and you will live in peace. It is when you try to go beyond the station in which God has placed you that you lose your peace of soul, because no man can have good fortune if he goes against the will of God.

CHAPTER 35 🖋

Sins of the Tongue

THE eighth Commandment states: Thou shalt not bear false witness against thy neighbor. This precept forbids the various acts of injustice that are committed through speech; for example, false testimony, deception by those in high positions, and injury to the reputation of others through malicious speech. A false witness is one who in any way conceals or distorts the truth. Whether he himself speaks or whether he persuades another to do so, he sins against this Commandment. Moreover, a judge who twists the law,

[8] Cf. I Cor. 7:20.

misinterprets the testimony of another, or does not exert himself sufficiently to discover the whole truth is likewise guilty of sin against the eighth Commandment. If men but realized the gravity of sins of speech, they would not commit them so readily. To bear false witness under oath is equivalent to calling God a liar, because God is called as a witness to the truth of one's statements.

God knows all things; He knows who speaks the truth and who does not. And since He is the source of all truth, we must have special reverence for His veracity. But God desires that we also give credence to men, especially if they represent Him or have positions of special authority. But if those persons who take the place of God by reason of their office tell us lies instead of the truth, is this not equivalent to making God a liar? Speaking in the name of God, Moses emphasized the obligation of speaking the truth at all times: "Hear them and judge that which is just, whether he be one of your country or a stranger. There shall be no difference of persons; you shall hear the little as well as the great; neither shall you respect any man's person, because it is the judgment of God." [1] In other words, a man is obliged to be truthful as God Himself is truthful, and particularly when he testifies under oath. Not to be so would be an injustice to God and an intolerable blasphemy.

Although the eighth Commandment is a negative precept, it also implies positive obligations. Thus, it obliges us to cultivate simplicity of heart and a mind free of all malice and human respect, because if these things are preserved, there will be little danger of false testimony. Simplicity of heart will prevent us from judging hastily or always interpreting things in their worst light. We must

[1] Deut. 1:16–17.

have the prudence of serpents in avoiding occasions of sin and keeping watch over ourselves, but the simplicity of doves in dealing with our neighbors, striving to appreciate their labors and to be so favorably inclined to them that we always speak well of them and overlook their faults whenever it is possible.

As a negative precept, the eighth Commandment prohibits every word by which one's neighbor may be injured. It is, therefore, a brake applied to the tongue, and rightly so, for men are most quick to use the tongue and frequently it is used thoughtlessly and to the detriment of one's neighbor. It is an instrument of anger, pride, flattery, lying, murmuring, and vainglory. It is the weapon with which we most readily seek revenge, and while its effects are most harmful, few persons realize the injustice or attempt to make amends. This is why God has given us this precept for the restraint of the tongue.

Not only they sin against this precept who tell lies in giving testimony as witnesses, but they also who reveal the faults of their neighbors to others who were ignorant of them. Even if the accusations are true, this action is against the law which states that we should not do to others that which we would not wish them to do unto us. It is likewise against the natural law which permits us to preserve silence concerning those secret faults which may prove prejudicial to others, unless there would be greater good in revealing them than in keeping silent about them. Consequently, they frequently sin against the eighth Commandment who hold themselves up as censors of evil and great enemies of vice, because in practice they do nothing but spread evil reports about those in high places. It is the function of superiors to administer corrections and punishments, and of preachers to condemn evil and point out the way to virtue. And even these should not be rash and imprudent, but should use their authority temperately and discreetly.

Moreover, they sin against this Commandment who murmur and complain, who have a loose and false tongue, or who are hypocrites, pretending one thing and doing another. Likewise the flatterers and vainglorious sin against the eighth Commandment, because these things are closely related to lying.

One sin that needs to be especially avoided is that of murmuring or destructive criticism. It is so prevalent in the world today that no home, no religious congregation, or no group of persons is exempt from it. Although this vice is practiced by all sorts of persons, since the world itself offers many occasions for the good to lament and the indifferent to complain, there are some people who seem to have a greater natural inclination to it than others. For just as some persons have no taste for sweet things, but prefer bitter or spicy things, so some persons are so melancholy and dyspeptic that they find no delight in praising others, but do nothing but ridicule, criticize, detract, or treat others with disdain. On all other subjects of conversation they are silent, but when this chord is struck, they seem to come to life and to revive their spirits in order to contribute their share to the criticism of others.

If you want to cultivate a hatred for this horrible vice, consider the three evils that result from it. First of all, criticism is very close to being a mortal sin, because it is only a short step from criticism to detraction and it is easy to pass from one to the other. Thus, it frequently happens that when a man begins to complain or criticize, he easily passes from a discussion of his neighbor's common faults to particular faults, from public sins to secret sins, and from small faults to serious sins, with the result that the other person's reputation is stained and blackened.

Once the tongue begins to wag, it is as difficult to restrain it as it is to quench flames that are fanned by the wind or to check a runaway horse. The backbiter does not conceal anything from anybody and he does not stop until he has penetrated the most secret depths of another's character. We read in Ecclesiasticus: "Who will set a guard before my mouth and a sure seal upon my lips, that I fall not by them and that my tongue destroy me not?" [2] He who wrote these words understood very well how difficult it is to protect oneself from this vice and he trusted in God alone, who is the true physician for curing this evil, as Solomon testifies: "It is the part of man to prepare the soul and of the Lord to govern the tongue." [3]

Consider the life and character of your neighbor as a forbidden tree which you must not touch. Moreover, be as careful not to say anything good of yourself as not to say anything evil of another, because the first is vanity and the second is detraction. Let everything that comes from your lips be virtuous and honorable and never let it be said that people think evilly of another person because of what you have said. In this way you will avoid a multitude of sins and much remorse of conscience and you will be more loved by God and men. As you honor others, so shall you be honored. Keep a constant watch on your tongue and always be ready to swallow any critical or injurious words that come to your lips. This is one of the best forms of prudence and discretion and one of the most salutary precepts you can impose upon yourself.

And do not think that you can excuse yourself from this vice by first praising him whom you intend to criticize or

[2] Ecclus. 22:33.   [3] Prov. 16:1.

condemn. People who do this are like the surgeon, who first deadens the nerves and then makes the incision with his knife. The Psalmist says of such persons that their "words are smoother than oil, and the same are darts." [4] And if it is a great virtue to refrain from all types of backbiting and criticism, it is especially virtuous to observe this restraint in regard to those who have offended us, because in such cases the desire to speak evilly of others is much stronger. For that reason we should exercise the greatest vigilance when speaking of those who have offended us, lest we yield to the inclination to retaliate by speaking evilly of them.

Not only is it wrong to criticize others but it is also wrong to listen to such speech from others. In this regard we should strive to follow the advice given in Ecclesiasticus: "Hedge in thy ears with thorns, hear not a wicked tongue, and make doors and bars to thy mouth." [5] In other words, it is not enough to close our ears, but we should try to stop the words of the backbiter by showing our displeasure at his speech, as Solomon signifies when he says: "The north wind driveth away rain, as doth a sad countenance a backbiting tongue." [6] St. Jerome says that the arrow shot forth from the bow will not penetrate hard rock but will rebound and wound the one who shot it. Consequently, if the backbiter is a subject of yours or a person whom you can silence without giving scandal, you ought to do so. If this is not possible, you should discreetly introduce a new topic of conversation or show by your countenance that this talk is displeasing to you, so that the backbiter will realize that he is doing wrong and will desist from his speech. But if you manifest an eager and happy countenance, you are encouraging him to proceed with his evil

---

[4] Ps. 54:20. [5] Eccles. 28:28. [6] Prov. 25:23.

talk and therefore you are no less guilty of sin than he is. It is a serious sin to fan the flames started by another when you should strive to extinguish the fire.

But of all kinds of backbiting and criticism the most grievous is that which is levelled against those who are good and virtuous, because this results in the intimidation of those who are already weak in the life of virtue and closes the door to those who are scrupulous and fearful. And although this type of backbiting is not usually a scandal to those who are strong in the spiritual life, it cannot be doubted that criticism of holy persons is a scandal to the little ones. And lest you think this is a small thing, recall the words of Christ: "He that shall scandalize one of these little ones that believe in Me, it were better for him that a millstone should be hanged about his neck, and that he should be drowned in the depth of the sea."[7] Therefore, consider it a kind of sacrilege to speak against the servants of God, because even if they were what evil persons say they are, at least by reason of their title they deserve honor and respect. Remember what God said of those who serve Him: "He that toucheth you, toucheth the apple of My eye."[8]

All that has been said of backbiters applies equally as well to those who are guilty of reviling, tale-bearing, derision, and similar vices. These latter vices have all the evil of the former and sometimes add to it the sins of pride, presumption, and contempt for others. But the evil of these vices is so evident to all that we shall not discuss them in detail. Let us, rather, proceed to discuss the sin of lying.

Theologians generally distinguish three types of lies. The first is the lie that results in harm to one's neighbor or is told with the intention of injuring another. This type

[7] Matt. 18:6.　　　　　[8] Zach. 2:8.

of lie is a mortal sin, unless there is lack of due deliberation or it concerns some small matter. The second type of
lie does not cause any harm nor was there any intention of
doing so, but is told for one's own advantage or profit.
This type of lie is generally a venial sin. The third type
of lie is that which is told in a joking manner, as a pastime
or recreation, without harm or profit to anyone. Nevertheless, if it is a true lie, that is, an abuse of speech, then it is
a venial sin.

The Christian should especially avoid any lie that is
harmful and the more so if it is detrimental to another's
reputation or honor. Indeed, a person can harm another
just as seriously by sins of the tongue as if he had committed
homicide, adultery, or theft. For he who destroys his neighbor by lying is a murderer, an adulterer, and a thief; a
murderer, because he has mortally wounded his neighbor
by the arrow of his poisonous tongue; an adulterer, because
by his shameful lie he has perverted and corrupted the
beauty of truth; a thief, because by his lies he has robbed
his neighbor of his good name or may be the cause of the
neighbor's losing his home and family.

In addition to the sins already mentioned, we must speak
of another that is closely connected with them: rash judgment. It frequently happens that backbiters and critics
speak not only of things that are actually evil, but also of
things that they merely suspect or judge to be so. If there
is nothing for them to criticize, they will make something by their rash judgments and suspicions or by giving
an evil interpretation to things that could just as readily be
interpreted well. Our Savior has commanded us to refrain
from rash judgment in the following words: "Judge not,
that you may not be judged." [9] This sin may very easily

[9] Matt. 7:1.

become mortal if that which is rashly judged is a serious matter and the judgment itself is without sufficient foundation. However, if it is a question of false suspicion and not an actual judgment, the sin is usually venial.

Such are the sins of the tongue that men most frequently commit against their neighbor and which we should seek to avoid with all diligence. Only by so doing can we preserve the divine grace which gives us light and strength for all things and instructs us in regard to all goods.

CHAPTER 36

The Virtue of Religion

OUR obligation to worship God rests on the countless blessings He has bestowed on us and the infinite perfection and excellence that are His as the Creator. Even the tongues of angels could not fittingly describe the greatness of our obligation to worship God, for the obligation is as great as is the God to whom worship is due, and since He is infinite, so also are the love and honor and reverence that we owe Him. Moreover, all the reverence and love we owe to other creatures have their foundation and terminus in God. Hence, the obedience we owe to those who govern us, the reverence due to our parents, the respect we give to men of eminent holiness and virtue, and the gratitude we show to benefactors—all are in some way rooted in God. Therefore, whatever reverence and respect we owe to eminent persons, we owe also to God. This obligation is the most holy, the most just, the most beautiful, and the most serious that can be imagined. There is no nation so barbarous that it does not acknowledge the existence of God and does not worship Him in some fashion, although there may be many errors in its religion. So great is the love and service we owe to God that if the love and reverence of all the blessed in heaven, of all the cherubim and seraphim, and that of the Blessed Mother were added together, they would still fall short of the love that is due to God. For all these loves, however perfect, are still finite, while He to whom the love is due is infinite. Therefore, only God can love Himself as He deserves to be loved, and only in God is the law of charity perfectly fulfilled in an absolute sense.

According to this excellence of love that is proper to God alone, theologians measure the baseness of any offense against the sovereign Majesty. And since sin is an offense against the infinite God, it has an infinite gravity. Therefore, in justice, it merits an infinite punishment, which is the deprivation of the infinite good, although even this punishment does not perfectly satisfy for the offense.

Once we understand the gravity of an offense against God, we should also understand how necessary is the practice of religion. According to the rules of philosophy, as a thing is more evil, it is more opposed to that which is good. Therefore, if we realize how evil it is to commit any offense against God, we realize what a great good it is to honor and serve Him, and this is the proper function of the virtue of religion. Indeed, all the divine laws and even nature itself impel us to the practice of religion. It follows from this that there must be some true religion by which God can be fittingly worshipped and venerated, otherwise this natural inclination to worship God would be vain and useless.

The virtue of religion, as distinct from an organized religious sect, a body of doctrine, or liturgical ceremonies, has as its object the proper worship of God and as such it is a virtue that perfects the individual. By reason of its object it is the most excellent of all the moral virtues and it imperates many particular acts. For lack of space we shall not treat of all the acts of religion, but shall speak only of those which are of special importance to the generality of Christians. First we shall speak of that internal act of religion which is called devotion.

Devotion is something quite distinct from that which many people understand by the word. Many persons think of it as a certain tenderness which is sometimes experienced while they pray or as a sensible delight in spiritual things. Neither of these things is devotion. As a matter of fact, men who are absolutely sensual or even in the state of mortal sin may sometimes experience this tenderness and sensible delight. On the other hand, it has often happened that great saints and other holy souls have experienced nothing but aridity and loneliness, and yet they possessed true devotion. Consequently, devotion is not tenderness of heart nor spiritual consolation, but a promptness of will in fulfilling the commandments and precepts of God and performing those acts that pertain to His worship and service. Considering the significance of the word itself, the devout man is one who is dedicated and prompt in the service of God.

In addition to this, we call devotion that which accompanies good and holy prayer or the promptness in the performance of good works, although in either case tenderness of heart or spiritual consolations may be lacking. After having taken refreshment, the traveler is invigorated and strengthened for continuing his journey, although he may not have taken any pleasure in the taste of the food he has eaten. So also prayer, which is a spiritual food of the soul, causes a promptness and animation for traveling along the road to God, although many times the traveler experiences no delight or consolation in his prayer. This is manifested in the prayer of Christ in the Garden of Olives, from which He rose to meet His enemies, who were cast to the ground at the first word He uttered to them. And yet we know that Christ's prayer in the Garden was not accompanied by consolations and delight, but that it was a prayer of such agony that it caused Him to sweat blood. He wished it to be so, not because His grace increased or decreased with prayer, for He was full of grace at all times, but to give us an example in His own person of the efficacy and power of prayer. He wished to teach us that even when prayer does not bring delight and consolation, it can always bring us a promptness and courage for the yoke or burden that God deigns to give us, and the strength to carry it.

However, we should observe that very frequently there is born of devotion a spiritual consolation, which uninformed persons call devotion simply and which serves to increase true devotion. Thus, spiritual consolation serves devotion as a good daughter serves her mother, so that the Christian is the more prompt for the service of God as he is more joyful internally. In like manner, the love of God arouses hatred of sin, while hatred of sin serves as an excellent disposition for the greater love of God. In a sense, devotion is a kind of general virtue which affects all the other virtues, so that all seem to be part of the same pattern: devotion, prayer, contemplation, the practice of the love of God, spiritual consolations, and the loving knowledge of God. All these virtues are seen as distinct and separate in textbooks and in the classroom but in practice they are all joined together in a remarkable manner. Wherever there is perfect prayer, there is perfect devotion, spiritual consolation, recollection, and the actual love of God. They are so intimately connected that there is an easy transit from one to the other.

To treat of the various steps to perfect devotion is equivalent to treating of the various steps to perfect prayer and contemplation or to the perfect love of God and that most blessed union with God in this life which is the goal of our spiritual life. This is the most lofty theology and most excellent doctrine that one could study, for here he is shown the ladder by which to ascend in order to pluck the fruit of perfect happiness so far as it is possible in this life.

Since perfect devotion is so excellent and so great a good, it is not surprising that it should be difficult to attain, for those things that are more noble and more excellent usually present greater difficulties. It is not an easy task to restrain and control our restless and fickle imagination; in fact, it cannot be done without perfect prayer and perfect devotion. For that reason, it has been said that there is no more important work in the spiritual life than the practice of prayer. Many persons practice and persevere in such things as fasting, almsgiving, vigils, and other good works, but are unable to persevere in the practice of prayer. It is strange that this should be so when we consider that in the practice of prayer we have the Holy Ghost as our consoler, the angels as our ministers, the saints as our companions, and the sacraments and Scripture as stimulators and sources of inspiration and grace.

Difficulty in prayer and devotion springs from three sources. First, the human nature has been so weakened by the effects of original sin that man does not have complete control over his lower powers as he had in the state of innocence. As a result, the imagination is like an unruly child that will not obey our wishes. Secondly, some persons have the bad habit of giving complete freedom to their imagination so that it is only with great difficulty that they can fix their mind on one thing. They may desire to meditate devoutly on the passion of Christ but as soon as they begin their meditation, their mind scatters in a thousand directions, so that they cannot even keep their attention on the crucifix that is before them. They cannot control their imagination because they have become accustomed to let it run wild. The third reason for difficulty in the practice of prayer is the malice of the devils, who are so envious that they especially torment those who practice prayer and try to deprive them of any fruit from this holy exercise.

Against these difficulties we have the help of grace, which is the most powerful of all weapons. In order to make the best use of grace in our combat, we shall point out certain means by which, with the help of God, that which is difficult will become easy. But because the practice of true prayer and devotion is the work of grace and the Holy Ghost, we do not intend to make any general rule nor to restrict the soul so that it cannot select some other way to reach God. Neither do we presume to understand all that is required for perfect prayer, but we are merely offering certain counsels so that the soul may put them into practice and start out on the right road. Once the soul has made a good beginning, its own experience and the help of the Holy Ghost will be better guides than our teaching.

The first thing required for the attainment of true devotion is the sincere and efficacious desire to attain it. The reason why this is so important is that the desire for an end or goal is that which moves all things to operation. Moreover, the greater the desire for the end, the greater the care and diligence with which one seeks to attain it. Why did Alexander the Great undertake such labors and struggles and wage incessant war unless it was his intense desire to make the world his empire? Why did Jacob endure seven years of servitude but for his love for Rachel? But if the love of created things exerts such a powerful influence on men, what will the love of God do to the lives of men?

Considerations of this type should arouse in your heart a strong desire and spiritual avarice for heavenly things. See how they conduct themselves who are avaricious, lovers of honor, or infatuated with the beauty of some creature. They can think of nothing else by day or by night except how to achieve that which they desire. In like manner you should strive to possess God. See how carefully the captains of war plan their battles. Do likewise in your struggle to win heaven, for it is written that the kingdom of God suffers violence and the violent bear it away.[1]

He who seeks God in this way already possesses Him in part and has the assurance of possessing Him entirely in the end. The prelude to finding God is to seek Him, and He already has the pledge of the Holy Ghost who seeks God with holy and ardent desire. When the hunter sees that his dog is running faster than usual and is pursuing a straight course, he knows that the dog has the scent of the hunt and rejoices in the hope of capturing the quarry. So also when you see these things in your spiritual life, you can be more secure in the hope that you are on the right path and that if you persevere in your straight course, you will reach Him whom you seek.

Desire must also be accompanied by great diligence and fortitude so that we can overcome the difficulties that threaten the success of our pursuit. Nature has provided animals with two types of passion: the concupiscible, by

[1] Matt. 11:12.

which the animal desires those things that pertain to the preservation of the individual and the species, and the irascible, which inclines the animal to attack dangers or overcome obstacles that threaten the attainment of its desires. These same two types of appetite are necessary for the preservation and protection of one's spiritual life and the attainment of the good that is sought. Therefore, one must have that intense desire of which we have spoken, and also the courage to attack and overcome the obstacles that impede the attainment of the goal.

The foregoing doctrine points out the imperfection of those who have good desires but lack the courage to put them into effect. They who lack courage cannot preserve their spiritual life. Frequently they are lazy and slothful, the wishful thinkers of whom we read in Scripture: "The sluggard willeth and willeth not; but the soul of them that work shall be made fat." [2] When they consider the beauty of virtue, they desire it; but when they realize the difficulties and labors connected with the attainment of virtue, they do not desire it.

But it should also be noted that while our desires must be accompanied by fortitude, lest they be inefficacious, our fortitude must be accompanied by humility, lest we become proud and self-sufficient. We should work as best we can and put forth all our efforts, but we must do so with the realization that it is not so much our personal efforts but the aid of divine grace and God's mercy that enable us to attain our goal. So we read in Ecclesiastes: "The race is not to the swift, nor the battle to the strong, nor bread to the wise, nor riches to the learned, nor favor to the skillful." [3] Grace is given to the humble, and in this respect, humility is more important than courage for attaining our goal.

[2] Prov. 13:4.   [3] Eccles. 9:11.

The next important aid to perfect prayer and true devotion is custody of one's heart. A guitar must be well tuned if the musician is to play it well. In like manner, the heart must be in tune and well moderated before the Holy Ghost can produce in it the strains of heavenly music.

Another forceful reason for maintaining custody of the heart is to be found in the incredible fickleness of the human heart. One of the great miseries of man is the extreme difficulty he encounters in being recollected. The heart is so easily distracted that a man must exert great effort to acquire any degree of devotion, and it is easily lost after it is acquired. Vision is impaired by the slightest speck of dust in the eye and a little steam suffices to blur a mirror; so also, the slightest things can sometimes cloud the soul, obscure its vision, and despoil it of its holy affections and devotion. It requires great diligence to protect so precious and so fragile a treasure.

In order to maintain custody of the heart, great care should be exercised to avoid vain thoughts and inordinate passions. As painters are accustomed to clean and prepare the surface on which they are to work, so the table of our heart must be scraped clean before the image of God can be painted thereon. Therefore, let the servant of God look to himself in this respect, for this is one of the principal differences between the good and the bad Christian. The heart of the evil man is like a public square or busy street which is never closed by day or by night, but the heart of the good Christian is an enclosed garden.

In addition to freedom from vain thoughts, it is also imperative to keep the passions and affections under control, for there is nothing so disturbing to the heart as the passions. They are like heavy winds that stir up the sea, clouds that obscure the light of the heavens, or weights that drag the spirit earthward. They weary the heart with anxieties, exhaust it with affections, enslave it with earthly attachments, and confuse it by their inordinate inclinations. The soul cannot contemplate the eternal light if it is clouded by rebellious passions.

Those who live under the sway of their passions are as fickle and changeable as the moon; they are like a weathervane, turned by the slightest breeze. Such persons will never possess a balanced and stable character. Now they are happy, now they are sad; now peaceful, now disturbed; now serious, now giddy; now devout, now dissolute. They are like the chameleon, which changes its color to suit its environment, and nothing of any consequence can be expected of them. Indeed, they are unworthy to be called men because they have an effeminate and weak spirit; they deserve the description given in Ecclesiasticus: "A holy man continueth in wisdom as the sun, but a fool is changed as the moon." [4]

The Christian who guards against useless thoughts and inordinate passions will acquire the peace of soul that the philosophers identify as the principal means for attaining true wisdom and which the saints describe as the goal of the spiritual life. It is the last disposition required for the contemplation of divine things, as Christ has told us: "Blessed are the clean of heart, for they shall see God." [5]

The surest guaranty of maintaining custody of the heart is to walk always in the presence of God, not only during prayer, but in every time and place. Some Christians are like students, who are attentive and well-behaved as long as they are in the classroom, but as soon as the class is ended, they scatter in whatever direction their whims or fancies lead them. The true servant of God will not act in

[4] Ecclus. 27:12.　　　　[5] Matt. 5:8.

this way, but will strive to preserve the warmth of prayer and maintain a holy recollection. Otherwise, their whole life may be spent in weaving and unweaving, without ever reaching a definite goal.

It will be a great help to recollection if you recall that God is present in every place, not only by His power and presence, but also by His essence. The king is throughout his kingdom by his power and in his castle by his presence, but it is only in his own body that he is present by his essence. But God is in all places in these three ways, as can be demonstrated in the following argument. God gives being and life to all things, for He is the cause of all things. And since the cause must necessarily have some contact with its effect it follows that if God is the cause of all things, He must in some way be joined to them. But in God there is no distinction of parts; whatever is in God is God. Hence, wherever there is anything of God, there God is also. But the being of a thing is that which is most intimate; therefore, God is more intimately related to things than they are to themselves. Is it, then, so difficult to keep before your eyes Him who carries you in His arms, sustains and guides you by His providence, and in whom you live and move and have your very being? [6]

God is a witness to your entire life and the constant companion of your journey. He should have a share in all your interests; to Him you should recommend yourself in all your difficulties and dangers. Consider God Incarnate under various aspects: now as beatifying the angels in heaven; now as conversing with men on earth; now as abiding in the bosom of the Father; now as resting sweetly in the arms of His Blessed Mother; now in the flight to Egypt; now in prayer in the Garden of Olives; now as carrying His

[6] Cf. Rom. 11:38.

cross to Calvary; and always as dying on the cross for you. When you are at table, let the salt of your food be a symbol of the vinegar and gall that was given Him on the cross; when you lay yourself down to rest, see your bed as the wood of His cross and the pillow as the crown of thorns; when you dress or undress, think of how He was ignominiously stripped of His garments during His passion. This is one of the ways of following the Lamb with those sacred virgins who follow Him wherever He goes.[7] This is the way to be His true disciple and to walk always in His footsteps; and on every step of the way, speak to Him in words tender and humble, for this is the way He wishes to be addressed.

Speak to Him not only when you are engaged with the work of your hands, but even when conversing with others, reading, or attending to your other duties, for you can frequently withdraw your mind from what you are actually doing and enter into the temple of your heart to adore God. Once you have acquired this habit of recollection, you will be able to attend to external affairs and yet very easily withdraw into your heart for a moment with God. Be solicitous in this matter of preserving custody of the heart and of being recollected in God and you will walk with greater circumspection and be careful not to commit any act that would be offensive to God.

He who cannot fulfill the counsels given above, will find it most profitable to use those short prayers or invocations which were used by the hermits of the desert in the midst of their manual labors so that the warmth of their devotion would not grow cold. People who live in cold regions try to remain as close as possible to their stoves or fireplaces in order to keep warm, and those who are not able

[7] Cf. Apoc. 14:4.

to do so, will often approach the fire to warm themselves and then return to their tasks. The Christian should do the same, for he lives in a world in which charity has grown cold and malice has been inflamed. Therefore, these short prayers or ejaculations are most profitable, for they are like so many arrows that sweetly pierce the heart of God and awaken the soul to the love of God. The verses of the Psalms are especially useful for this type of prayer and therefore the Christian should be familiar with this part of Scripture. But it is not so beneficial constantly to repeat the same verses or phrases, for the soul may weary of the same words and its needs will vary from time to time. But there are words in Scripture suitable for every need and every taste. Moreover, the times and places and the various affairs which occupy us will frequently offer us the occasion or inspiration to raise our hearts and minds to God, for he who truly loves God, sees God in all things and all things arouse his love of God.

Spiritual reading is another great help for cultivating custody of the heart and the spirit of recollection. St. Bernard says that the mind is like a mill which always turns out whatever is put into it; if wheat, wheat; if barley, barley. Hence, it is well to accustom oneself to the reading of good books, for when a man wishes to think of something, he will normally turn to those things with which his mind has been most occupied. St. Jerome recommends the reading of Scripture, as we see from the following passage of his letter to Demetria: "One thing I wish to advise you, virgin of Christ, and to repeat again and again, is that you occupy yourself in the love and study of Scripture and not let the good earth of your heart be sown with bad seed." And at the end of the letter he again returns to the same subject, saying: "I wish to join the end of this letter with the beginning, because I shall not be content with having admonished you once. Love Scripture, and wisdom will love you; give yourself to it and it will protect you; embrace it and it will honor you."

Custody of the heart is also maintained to a large degree by custody of the senses, for the senses are the gates through which all things enter and leave the mind, and if the gates are well guarded, all will be safe and secure. Hence, the devout Christian will be deaf, blind, and mute, so that his soul will always be pure and properly disposed for the contemplation of divine things. And since it is sometimes necessary to hear and see many things that could easily cause distraction, one must keep such things at a distance and not let the heart and mind pay too much attention to them. The servant of God should be like a well-calked boat; it glides smoothly through the water and although the waves wash against it, they cannot enter and sink the ship. Those who keep such a watch over their senses will always be recollected and devout, but those who open their doors to every distraction soon become involved in the attractions of the world and bring to their hours of prayer the anxieties and distractions that have beset them in the world. Those who spend their time in the pastimes of worldly men and are always curious about worldly affairs return home with their minds filled with air and empty of devotion. Such people are vagabonds at heart and restless in body and soul. They cannot sit still for a moment or remain in one place, but must be running here and there, from one place to another, and when they have no place in particular to go, they will be carried by the whim of their fancy or curiosity to find some distraction and recreation, because they have lost the ability to find peace and recreation within their own minds and souls. Unfortunately, it often happens that it is the devil who leads them in their comings and goings and as a result they frequently find themselves in an occasion of sin.

Solitude is another great help for acquiring custody of the heart and repression of disorderly passions, for it not only eliminates many sources of distraction and occasions of sin, but it disposes a man to enter into himself and converse with God. St. Bernard says: "You will have solitude if you do not harbor common and vulgar thoughts, if you do not desire present goods, if you disdain the things that the world holds dear. You will be able to reject what the world desires if you keep yourself from contention, if you take no account of temporal losses and gains, and if you do not reckon with injuries. Otherwise, although you may be alone, you will not enjoy true solitude." In other words, it is possible to be alone even in the midst of others, while one may not be alone at all, although he is alone in body. But if you wish to enjoy solitude in the company of others, take care that you are not curious, that you do not inquire into their affairs, and that you do not judge others rashly.

Solitude is not something reserved only for religious, as some persons may think, but it is necessary for all who truly desire to please God and travel along the way to perfection. Therefore, St. Jerome advised a noblewoman: "I wish you to take such care of your household as to give yourself time for prayer and recollection. To this end, it would be well to have a small oratory or some private chamber away from the distraction of the family, which shall be for you a quiet port, removed from the tempests of the cares and anxieties of the world. I would have you use this oratory for nothing but prayer, the reading of the Bible, and devout recollection. I do not advise these things to take you from your family, but that you may here learn how to conduct yourself with your family. And if you were to ask me how many times a day you should recollect yourself in this manner, I would not know how to give you any definite rule, because all persons do not have the same opportunities of time or disposition, but I do think that you can formulate some kind of rule from that which God Himself has given in Leviticus,[8] when He commanded that there should always be fire burning on His altar and that it should be fed twice daily, in the morning and at night."

But these exercises in solitude should not be practiced as a chore or as something that must be done, come what may. They should be practiced in the same spirit that a wounded or sick man approaches the physician so that he may be cured. Those who do not have the disposition or time to practice this exercise twice daily should at least recollect themselves in prayer or pious reading once a day, and if even this is impossible because of occupations and other duties, I can only advise them to make use of those short prayers or ejaculations of which we have spoken, for these prayers can be said in the midst of any occupation. Many Christians have been spiritually sustained by such brief prayers when their duties in life or sickness did not permit them to do more. But we should remember that as a general rule these invocations seldom suffice.

For any practice of prayer, however, perseverance is of paramount importance. Some persons never seem to be able to carry anything through or to persevere in any practice, but are constantly winding and unwinding the thread like Penelope. They will take up some new method for a few days and then will lose interest and become negligent so that when they return to the exercise, they are so cold and disinterested that it is as if they had never started.

[8] Lev., chap. 6.

They make new resolutions and begin again, but when they have gone on for some time, they again become weary or think that they are well enough along, and again abandon the exercise. So they pass their lives building up and tearing down. Half way up the mountain, they turn around and go back to the bottom, to start all over again.

St. Bonaventure says that perseverance in the exercises of prayer and the other exercises of the spiritual life enables one to arrive most quickly at perfection, for however short a distance one may travel each day, if the traveler perseveres in his journey, he will soon arrive at his destination. But if he spends most of his time resting or making fresh starts, he will never reach the end of his journey. Therefore, if it happens that sometimes you must cut the thread of these exercises, because of affairs which cannot be put off, let it be done in such a way that you never lose sight of the road that lies before you, lest you lose the will to continue your journey. And if at any time you should fall or become weak, do not on that account give in to despair or lose heart. If you should fall a thousand times a day, rise up a thousand times and try to mend the thread where it has been broken.

It is important to be constant in the method or manner of performing our spiritual exercises. Some Christians are faithful in the daily practice of their exercises, but each day they find new resolutions and methods, so that today they follow one way and tomorrow, another. They are constantly changing their guides, with the result that they are not steady in anything. Sometimes they begin by a consideration of the Passion; at other times they abandon this to take up other meditations. Sometimes they will ascend to the heavens and try to penetrate divinity itself; then they will leave this to consider their sins, with the result that they never carry anything out to completion and therefore they never arrive anywhere. They resemble the dog of a hunter when it comes upon a group of rabbits. It chases after one and then another and yet another, with the result that it catches none of them.

There are many paths and ways by which a man may travel to perfection and many subjects of meditation and prayer by which he can raise his mind and heart to God. Therefore, each Christian should consider which is most profitable and best suited to him. Once having decided, he should follow that method through to completion, because that is the best method for him, considering his circumstances and dispositions. But he should also be careful not to fall into the common error of those who, because they have found God by traveling along a certain path, think and talk as if there were no other way to God but the one that has succeeded for them. The truth of the matter is that there are as many ways of going to God as there are ways that lead to Him, for the Holy Ghost, who is the guide of the spiritual life, leads each one along his own path.

To conclude our consideration of the aids to true devotion and the practice of prayer, we shall mention briefly such secondary helps as time, place, manner, austerities, and works of charity. According to St. Bernard, "a quiet and peaceful time is best suited for prayer, especially when the sleep of night has silenced all things, because prayer is then more pure and attentive than at other times." We read in Scripture [9] that we ought to rise with the morning sun to bless and adore God. Consequently, morning and night would seem to be most suitable times for prayer. But if by reason of old age or infirmity or one's occupations it

[9] Wisd. 16:28.

is not possible to pray at these times, one should select that time which will be most conducive to prayer. As a rule, if one wishes to make a good prayer in the morning, it will be helpful if he has prayed before retiring the night before. A solitary and quiet place is most convenient for prayer, and for that reason our Lord was accustomed to go off to a deserted place at night when He wished to pray, not because He found it necessary to make use of a particular place, but to give us an example of how we ought to pray. Moreover, the light should be subdued, for we read that St. Anthony of the desert lamented that the brilliance of the rising sun impeded his contemplation of God.

The posture of the body can also be of assistance in our prayer and help to arouse devotion. Whence the Church prescribes certain bodily postures in her rubrics. So also, although it was in no way necessary for Him to do so in order to arouse His devotion, Christ frequently knelt or prostrated as He prayed, in order to teach us what we should do. But we should observe that it is not necessary to remain on one's knees all during prayer or whenever one prays, for the exhaustion or discomfort of the body may cause us to lose devotion. Although it is profitable to suffer some little penance in our prayers in atonement for our sins, this is not the principal purpose of prayer. In comparison with the light that God gives to us in prayer, the penance of the body is a very minor thing. Therefore, the body should be as composed during prayer as health will permit so that the soul will be best disposed to give itself to God, especially if the period of prayer is to last for some time, for few persons can keep the body in an uncomfortable position without being distracted from prayer.

Devotion is aided by the use of corporal austerities, such as a hard bed, fasting, self-denial in legitimate pleasures, and other forms of self-abnegation. Such practices are the initiation to devotion and without them devotion soon dies. It is seldom that people possess true devotion if they do not practice self-denial; and it is seldom that the practice of penitential exercises is not accompanied by devotion. As to the works of mercy, they not only foster true devotion, but they are a source of merit. It would seem that the devout soul would become distracted and lukewarm through such occupations, but the works of mercy generally make devotion even more intense. God is such a rewarder of the merciful that He will protect the portion of His faithful servant who leaves the table to relieve the needs of another.

Having spoken of the helps to devotion, let us say something about the impediments to devotion. The principal impediment is sin, not only mortal sin, which is an obstacle to any good of the soul, but also venial sin, which lessens the ardor of charity. Venial sin does not destroy charity, but deprives it of the wings on which it takes its flight and leaves the soul weak and ineffectual for many good works. Therefore, the devout man must wage constant war against venial sins, for although they may seem small, they cannot be considered insignificant. St. Jerome says that the servant of God should not look at that which is commanded, but at God who commands, and since God is not insignificant, none of His commandments can be considered unimportant, especially when we shall have to render an account on the day of judgment.[10] He who fears God neglects nothing, however small.[11]

Another impediment to devotion is the excessive sorrow which some persons experience over their venial sins. This sometimes causes more damage than the sins themselves, for although remorse of conscience is commendable, some per-

[10] Matt. 12:36. [11] Cf. Eccles. 7:19.

sons become excessively despondent and lose all heart for good works. Sometimes this excessive remorse is the result of pusillanimity; at other times it may be caused by a hidden pride which gives a man the notion that he should no longer have any defects or imperfections. But the truly humble man believes himself capable of any evil and for that reason he is not astonished when he falls. Therefore, let the timid soul strive to realize the value of the merits of Christ so that he will not lose hope in God's mercy, even if he should have the misfortune to fall into grievous sin. St. John says: "My little children, these things I write to you that you may not sin. But if any man sin, we have an advocate with the Father, Jesus Christ the just; and He is the propitiation for our sins, and not for ours only, but also for those of the whole world." [12]

How can you lose confidence under the protecting wings of such a Mediator? What satisfaction could you offer God for your sins that would not be far surpassed by that which was borne on the shoulders of His Son? In comparison with the infinite merits of Christ, all the sins of the world are like straw in a raging fire. Why, then, shall you be despondent, when such merits and satisfaction are available to you through Christ?

Perhaps you will say that you commit sin practically every day, without ever amending your life as you would wish to do. But tell me, if Christ were to suffer anew each day for your sins, would you still give in to despair? Then be certain that His passion and death are of no less help to you, although they occurred many centuries ago, than if He were to endure them today. Does not St. Paul tell us that with the one offering of this High Priest He sanctified us forever?

[12] Cf. I John 2:1-2.

You may say that you still sin every day in spite of all the mercies you have received from God and that you cannot endure such a situation without feeling despair. But I tell you that just as nothing gives greater evidence of a man's evil than the fact that he multiplies his sins amidst so many blessings, so nothing gives greater evidence of God's goodness than that He continues to confer benefits on him who sins. St. Paul tells us that our malice makes God's goodness more manifest because the goodness of God is nowhere more evident than when He forgives sinners. Even if you cannot endure your sins and are weary of the suffering they cause you, God never wearies of pardoning you. Be consoled by the consideration of the divine goodness rather than being despondent over your imperfections.

Scrupulosity is another obstacle to true devotion because of the uneasiness which it causes. Scrupulous persons are forever tormenting themselves and trying to decide whether they consented to evil or not, whether they prayed or not, or whether they made a good confession or not. If, as we read in the Canticle, the bed of the Bridegroom is a bed of flowers, how shall He recline in a heart that is filled with the thorns of scruples and the nettles of anxiety and doubts? But since it is not enough to tell people to rid themselves of scrupulosity without showing them how to do it, we shall discuss the origin of scruples and their cure.

God sometimes permits this affliction, as He permits sickness and trials, as a purgation from sin or a source of greater merit. If this be the origin in a given case, the only consolation and counsel are those which are offered for any other kind of cross or affliction that comes from God.

At other times scrupulosity is the result of a melancholy temperament, which afflicts the imagination and arouses the passions of sorrow or fear, with the result that the person experiences much uneasiness of conscience. When this is the cause of scrupulosity, the soul has greater need of a doctor, says St. Jerome, than of a spiritual director.

Again, scrupulosity is sometimes born of self-love or the inability to distinguish between temptation and consent, with the result that the one is mistaken for the other and the person thinks himself guilty of sin. When a man loves himself inordinately he is unreasonably afraid of danger and this fear, together with the ignorance to which we have referred, causes him to be afraid without cause. Scrupulosity may also be the work of the devil, for if he cannot destroy the soul's fear of God, he will try to pervert this holy fear so that the soul is afraid not only of true dangers, as is reasonable, but of those which are only apparent.

Lastly, scrupulosity may result from the soul's misunderstanding of God's goodness and His great desire for our salvation. Scrupulous persons underestimate the goodness of God. They look upon God as a severe judge, looking for small points in the law so that He can punish the guilty. They do not appreciate how much God desires the salvation of men, nor do they understand that what God asks of us is a resolute heart in the performance of good and the avoidance of evil at any cost. The Christian who is conscious of this and, through the mercy of God, possesses these qualities, will seldom be afflicted with scrupulosity.

What are the remedies for scrupulosity? The first and most important one is humble submission to the direction of another person. Our Lord, who did not fail us in necessary things and has given us a remedy for every evil, has taught us that if we cannot cure ourselves by our own knowledge and prudence, we should be cured by another. The scrupulous person cannot be his own judge, for he is too intimately involved in the affair; he should not try to be his own doctor, because he is the one who is sick. He must be cured by another and obey in all things that pertain to his affliction.

It is also a great help in curing this disease to ignore one's scruples as much as possible and not to follow what they command or suggest. Scruples are such that as soon as we give in to one, we open the door to a thousand others and run the risk of scruples for the rest of our lives.

Since scrupulous persons generally have difficulty with confession, it will be helpful to consider what Cajetan says about this matter. He states that although persons are usually advised to confess doubtful sins, scrupulous persons are not obliged to do so. If I, for example, were to doubt whether I had committed a certain sin or whether I had confessed it, I would be obliged to resolve the doubt one way or the other. But a scrupulous person would not have an obligation to resolve the doubt, for it is presumed that if scrupulosity has frequently caused him to doubt where there is no reason to doubt, perhaps the same thing has happened in this particular instance. Therefore, it is sound advice that once a scrupulous person has confessed his sins, he should never under any circumstance give way to doubts that may arise later concerning that confession. If he has carefully examined his conscience before confession and can reasonably believe that he confessed his other sins, it is most probable that he included the sin about which he now has a doubt. This is the way in which the soul should quiet any scruple about confession, especially if it has a holy desire to do God's will. And even if the scrupulous person had actually forgotten some sin in confession and yet has this preparation to do God's will, what has he to fear? God did not institute the sacrament of penance as a snare for consciences, but as a means of relieving them and giving them peace. But confession would surely be a snare if it were weighted with so many obligations and difficulties as scrupulous persons imagine.

The inability to distinguish between temptation and the actual sin is also a cause of scrupulosity, and it is therefore necessary to discuss this point. As regards evil thoughts, a person may find himself in any one of four situations. If, as soon as the evil thought arises, the person has recourse to the fear of God and recollection of Christ crucified and thus drives the thought from his mind, he has not sinned. If he deliberately retains the thought, the retention is culpable and there is a more or less serious sin, depending on the length of time that attention has been given to the evil thought. However, a penitent need not tell in confession the exact length of time or other minute details; it suffices to say that he harbored some thought of anger, vainglory, pride, or lust and that he did not reject it as soon as he should have done, but retained it for a short time. If the person consents to the evil thought, in the sense that he would actually perform the external deed were he given the opportunity, he is guilty of mortal or venial sin, depending on the gravity of the matter represented by the thought. Anyone should be able to see the difference here between a simple thought and deliberate consent to the thought. The fourth situation is what theologians call morose delectation and it signifies deliberate consent, not to the performance of the deed if it were possible, but to the delight that is caused by thinking about that which is evil. A person deliberately takes pleasure in some evil thought, although he does not desire or intend to perform the actual deed. He is like the man who does not drink in the tavern, but spends much of his time there.

It is especially in regard to morose delectation that scrupulous persons become confused and upset. For their instruction, we must note that for such delectation to be mortally sinful it is required that a person give deliberate consent to the delight of thinking about some matter that is in itself mortally sinful. I say deliberately, because if it happens that a man entertains sinful thoughts without realizing what he is thinking about, and then suddenly realizes what is in his mind and immediately rejects it or refuses to consent to such thoughts, he is not guilty of mortal sin. The same thing is true if, after a man realizes what is in his mind, he tries to reject it but cannot, because the thought is already well fixed in the mind. He is not guilty of mortal sin as long as he can truthfully say that the thought is there against his will. This sometimes occurs as a result of previous passion, and if the passion itself was spontaneous and not voluntary, then neither the passion nor what follows is sinful. There are many delicate points in this matter of evil thoughts, but such sins are usually found only in those who have little fear of God and if they do not perform the external act, it is not out of any respect for their conscience, but for fear of their reputation, the opinion of the world, or lack of the opportunity. Since they cannot commit the external act, they content themselves with sinful thoughts and enjoy mentally what they cannot enjoy physically. Scrupulous persons should apply themselves to one or another of the remedies we have listed and should remember that this affliction is not incurable, especially if they submit humbly to proper direction.

Another obstacle to true devotion is the bitterness of heart that arises from anger, envy, rancor, or similar vices. Sweetness and bitterness are contrary qualities, and the heart cannot contain the bitterness of vice and the sweetness of devotion. Therefore, we should not harbor bitter or envious thoughts, and if any should enter the mind, we should reject them as quickly as possible. It is not necessary to discuss this impediment at length because it is evident from experience that devotion weakens and dies if one's heart is filled with bitterness and his mind is a tangle of uncharitable thoughts.

An outstanding impediment to devotion is the desire for sensible consolations, for it closes the door to a true appreciation of spiritual consolations. Human or sensible consolation is not compatible with spiritual consolation; the one must leave before the other can enter the soul. Some persons are anxious to find delight in their prayers and also wish to have their recreations, social life, and all their other human associations. They want consolations in prayer but they also want to enjoy the things of this world. They do not seem to realize that they cannot take a step toward spiritual consolation as long as they follow the ways of the world. Therefore, St. Augustine advises them: "Leave all, and you will find all, for he finds all things in God who leaves all things for God."

Excessive anxiety is another impediment to devotion and is no less harmful to the soul than sensible delights. St. Bernard says that personal needs and sensual delight are the principal sources of all the evils in the world, for all evils spring either from the needs that afflict us or the pleasures we seek. Anxiety sometimes takes such a hold on the mind that it does not let the individual think of anything else. The remedy against over-anxiety is to work as best you can to rid your heart of attachment to created things and this presupposes the suppression of sensual love. Do not love inordinately and you will not be afflicted. Do not seek your delight in created things and you will not be saddened by created things. Secondly, place all your cares in God's hands and have the faith to believe that He will see them to a happy solution. With this provision alone St. Francis of Assisi sent forth his friars, saying to them: "Cast thy care upon the Lord and He shall sustain thee." [13] But how few Christians are able to do this! "Many men are called merciful but who shall find a faithful man?" [14]

In addition to the cares and anxieties of spirit, excessive labors can also be an impediment to true devotion. They may so distract the soul that it cannot pray, either because there is no time or because there is no inclination to pray. This is particularly true of excessive study, even the study of theology, because no exercise is more contrary to devotion than pure speculation. It consumes the mind's energy and leaves the will so sterile that it neither experiences nor tastes God. Manual labor is not incompatible with devotion, but intellectual labor usually impedes the functioning of the will. However, if rightly used as a help and not a hindrance, the study of sacred truth can serve to increase devotion. But whatever the occupation, it is necessary to observe the proper measure so that Martha will not interfere with Mary, who has chosen the better part.

Prudence and fortitude are especially important in this matter of manual and intellectual labor. Prudence is necessary so that we may know our own strength and the daily demands in time and energy. Once this is recognized, we shall need the constancy and fortitude to refuse other labors that are offered to us apart from this, lest we assume tasks that we know we cannot discharge. Those who let themselves be influenced by pleas and human respect and take too much work upon themselves, will ultimately fall beneath their heavy burden and will not accomplish what they should have done nor what they have voluntarily accepted.

[13] Ps. 54:23.   [14] Prov. 20:6.

When it is too late, they will realize that the harm they have done themselves is the result of their own indiscretion.

Those who live under the vow of obedience have less reason to examine themselves on this point, because obedience excuses them from making their own decisions, which is a great blessing. But they should be careful not to do their own will under the guise of obedience, as sometimes happens when persons are commanded to do something that they already desire to do and like to do. These persons will often excuse themselves from religious exercises by saying that they have been commanded to study, to preach, or to take care of some other matter of the apostolate. Therefore, they say, they have no time to spend in religious exercises or monastic observances. This is a very grave deception. No one in the world has greater obligations and more varied tasks than the Pope. Nevertheless, St. Bernard advised Pope Eugene to take time each day from the cares and government of the Church in order to occupy himself in pious exercises, at the risk of not doing other tasks well.

What I say to religious, I say also to all Christians in regard to avoiding excessive labors and allowing some time for pious exercises, especially prayer, each day. Man's misery is so great, the world is so evil, and dangers are so numerous that if we withdraw from God even a little, we may be lost. Moreover, our heart is so inclined to the things of the flesh that if we take it away from God, who is pure spirit, we may easily become completely carnal.

The vice of curiosity is another great obstacle to devotion, and it takes many forms. First, there is the desire to know all about the lives and affairs of others, so that the mind is filled with useless thoughts and the heart becomes so beset by anxieties that all peace and tranquillity are destroyed. This is the curiosity of slothful and lazy men, who do not mind their own affairs or perform the tasks to which they are obliged, but prefer to interfere in the affairs of others. There is also an intellectual curiosity, which is found in those who are eager to know merely for the sake of knowing. They devour books of history, profane subjects, curiosities, fiction, and useless information. If they read the works of more serious authors, it is not to acquire true wisdom, but for the sake of curiosity. They seek only the artificiality and eloquence of high-sounding words or a familiarity with facts that will amaze others but which serve of little or no profit to themselves. Persons of this type are like a broken vessel that can hold no wisdom.[15] They manifest a certain cleverness and brilliance, perhaps, but St. Augustine warns that we should not be in love with words, but with the truth that is contained in them.

A third kind of curiosity is called sensual curiosity and it proceeds from the intense desire to see one's possessions well made and well preserved. The accumulation of such things merely causes greater anxiety and distraction, and a man becomes so involved with their maintenance that he must neglect other matters that are of much greater importance. This type of curiosity is an impediment because devotion requires freedom from care. For that reason, among many others, evangelical poverty is highly praised, because it deprives us of all such luxuries and provides only the bare necessities, in imitation of the Lord of all creation, who had a manger for His crib and a stable for His birthplace.

A rather common impediment to devotion is to cut short one's pious exercises without sufficient reason. Of all the defects of the human heart, one of the worst is that it is so easily inclined to anything evil but so cold and indifferent to good. It takes but an evil thought, passing swiftly

[15] Cf. Ecclus. 21:17.

through the mind, to inflame our hearts and sometimes our bodies; but to arouse a little devotion, it is sometimes necessary to move heaven and earth and to seek God's help. The student who studies faithfully every day and attends the lectures in the classroom can hope to reach a high degree of perfection in his studies; but if he studies only at intervals and interrupts his hours of study for the slightest reason, he will never achieve anything, and when he does return to his books, he will have forgotten what he had studied and will have to start again from the beginning.

However, if the interruptions to our pious practices are brief and for some necessary reason, it will be possible quickly to recover what has been lost, so that one can return to fervent prayer after his work is finished. Moreover, those who are more perfect run less of a risk because of interruptions than beginners do, because they who are more perfect have a greater reserve from which their devotion can be nourished. The perfect are like trees that grow in sandy ground, and even if it does not rain for many days or weeks, their leaves remain fresh and they can produce fruit; but beginners are like trees that need much irrigation and if water is lacking, they will loose their beauty and their leaves will wither.

Devotion is also impeded by excessive eating and drinking. Hence, fasting and prayer are almost always mentioned together in Scripture and the monks of the desert were noted for their fasting and abstinence. Consequently, fasting and sobriety help the soul rise to God, but excessive food and drink cast it down. On the other hand, St. Bernard points out that excessive fasting, bodily weakness, or any other extreme such as hunger, cold, or heat, can easily lessen or kill devotion. There is such a close relationship between body and soul that when the body is badly disposed, the soul cannot give itself to prayer and the contemplation of divine things, at least not with the desired facility, because in the suffering of any affliction, the mind gives its attention to the pain or discomfort. Therefore, the devout man will moderate his mortifications and will take reasonable care of his health. He will not stupefy himself by excessive food and drink, nor will he exhaust himself by the weight of mortifications and sufferings. If the strings of a guitar are too taut, they will break; if they are too loose, they will not make a musical sound. Likewise, if we wish to draw heavenly music from our soul, we must be neither too lax with ourselves nor too severe, for the one is as much an impediment to devotion as the other.

Be convinced, then, that the ultimate goal of your life is familiar and intimate converse with God. Close your eyes to everything else and employ your efforts in this one activity. This is the purpose for which you were created and it is the most excellent work to which you could dedicate yourself. It is the better part, which Mary chose; it is the work of the contemplative life, which is far more excellent than the active life; it is an exercise in which the heart is actually engaged in the love of God, which is the best of all our good works, for St. Thomas says that the interior act of charity is the greatest and most meritorious of all the acts of all the virtues. If you are desirous of knowing and possessing true wisdom, be assured that in the practice of the love of God He will teach you more in one hour than all the masters of the world can teach you in a lifetime. And the wisdom that He will impart to you will be so lofty that the gold of human wisdom will seem but a grain of sand by comparison. "For if one be perfect among the children of men, yet if Thy wisdom be not with him, he shall be nothing regarded." [16]

[16] Wisd. 9:6.

CHAPTER 37 🖎

Vocal Prayer

PRAYER, as the spiritual writers tell us, is the raising of our hearts to God. Prayer lifts the soul above created things to unite it to God; it is the going forth of the soul to meet God when He approaches with a new grace, to receive Him into the soul as in His temple, there to possess and love Him. Prayer places the soul in the presence of God; it is a spiritual colloquy in which the soul, seated at the feet of God, hears His teaching and receives the influence of His grace, saying with the bride of the Canticle: "My soul melted when He spoke." [1]

St. Bonaventure tells us that during prayer God inflames the soul with His love and anoints it with His grace, so that once it is anointed, it is raised in spirit, and being lifted up, it contemplates Him, contemplating Him, it loves Him, loving Him, it tastes Him, tasting Him, it reposes in Him, and in this sweet repose is to be found the greatest glory that can be attained in this world.

Prayer is a salutary healing of each day's defects, a daily exercise of the virtues, death to the sensual appetites, and the source of all good desires and intentions. It is the milk of the beginners, the food of the proficient, the port of those who are engaged in battle, and the crown of those who triumph. It is medicine for the sick, strength for the weak, a remedy for sinners, a reward for the just, a help to the living, a suffrage for the dead, and a common help for the entire Church.

[1] Cant. 5:6.

He who truly desires to travel along the road to perfection and to root out his vices and cultivate the virtues should practice prayer, and he will find that it opens the door to all things else. One of the greatest blessings of prayer is that it awakens the activity of the other virtues. The soul is cleansed of its imperfections, charity is inflamed, faith is strengthened, hope is fortified, the spirit is gladdened, the heart is pacified, truth is discovered, temptations are conquered, sadness is dispelled, virtue is restored, sloth is banished, the dross of vice is consumed, and the burning flame of divine love enkindles a desire for heaven.

St. Bonaventure writes very beautifully of prayer in these words: "If you wish to bear adversities and the miseries of this life with patience, be a man of prayer. If you wish to acquire virtue and the strength to overcome temptations, be a man of prayer. If you wish to mortify your will in all its inclinations and desires, be a man of prayer. If you wish to know the wiles of Satan and defend yourself against his snares, be a man of prayer. If you wish to live joyfully and travel with ease along the path of penance and labor, be a man of prayer. If you wish to drive from your soul the importunate insects of vain thoughts and anxieties, be a man of prayer. If you wish to be sustained by solid devotion and keep your soul filled with good thoughts and desires, be a man of prayer. If you wish to fortify your heart on the road to God, be a man of prayer. If you wish to rid your soul of all its vices and plant in it the flowers of the virtues, be a man of prayer."

"All you that thirst, come to the waters; and you that have no money, make haste, buy and eat; come ye, buy wine and milk without money and without any price." [2] Come, all of you from every state, to drink of this fountain,

[2] Isa. 55:1.

priests, religious, the married, and those in the world or out of the world. If you live in the world, you will be fortified by the practice of prayer; if you live out of the world, you will be made more perfect. If you are a sinner, you will learn to weep for your sins; if you are just, you will be more justified still. If you are in the midst of battle, you will find your victory; if you are living in peace, your peace will increase like a flowing river. If you are beset with doubts, you will find your solution; if you are blind, your path will be enlightened; if you are sick, you will be cured; if you are lukewarm, you will be inspired; if you are sad and afflicted, you will find rest and consolation. If there is anything you desire, you will attain it through prayer; if there is anything you possess, you will preserve it through prayer.

If you are a religious, it is for the practice of prayer that you have left the world; if you are married there is no greater help to enable you to carry the burdens of your state. Are you a child? Then in prayer you will find milk and be carried in safe and protecting arms. Are you a grown man? In prayer you will find nourishment for even greater strength. Do you wish to be wise? This is the path to true wisdom. Do you wish to be more humble and simple? Here you will learn true simplicity of heart. Are you partial to gifts and consolations? Then there are no greater gifts under heaven than those to be received through prayer. Do you like to work? In prayer you will receive the strength to fulfill your tasks.

For this did the holy men go into deserts; for this have religious left their families and the world; for this was his humble monastic cell more sweet to Pope Gregory than the chair of the pontificate. All good exercises of the spiritual life are in one way or another directed to the practice of prayer: spiritual reading, fasting and abstinence, choral prayer, vigils, and penances of all kinds.

There are two types of prayer: one which is made with the heart and mind, as when we attentively consider the things of God and present our needs to the Lord, to whom the language of the heart is no less intelligible than the language of the tongue; the other, which is the prayer of the lips, called vocal prayer. This second type of prayer is beneficial for all classes of people and especially for beginners, if it is recited with proper attention and devotion. The words of a prayer, says St. Augustine, are like spiritual arrows which sweetly wound the heart. Consequently, those who through lack of knowledge do not have material for meditation or those who through lack of devotion do not have the words with which to speak to God can make use of the words and phrases that will raise their hearts and minds to heavenly things. In so doing, they will be like infants that as yet cannot walk alone and are placed in little walkers or other vehicles so that with the help of the walker they can move around, although they could not have done so on their own power. Similarly, those who know not how to speak with God in words of their own can use the words of others and thereby awaken their devotion. And when the affairs and labors of this life weigh down and oppress our hearts and minds, holy and inspiring words of prayer can again lift them to heaven, because the mere reading of these words will captivate the intellect and not let it be distracted by other external matters.

Vocal prayer is useful not only for beginners, but it also helps the proficient and perfect, especially when the distractions of their duties or exhaustion of the body prevent them from raising their minds and hearts to God as they would wish. In those times they can arouse devotion by reading fervent prayers. Hence, we read of St. Augustine that ten days before he died he ordered that the seven penitential psalms should be written out and hung on the wall near his bed so that he could read them, and as he did so, he shed copious tears. In like manner, the Church has commanded the chanting of the psalms and other prayers in the Divine Office so that those inspired words would arouse the devotion of those who chanted. And not only the significance of the words, but also the sweetness and melody of the chant penetrate the heart and awaken devotion. St. Augustine frequently was moved to tears and experienced a great sweetness of soul when he listened to the hymns and chant of the Church, for music is naturally delightful to the soul and even infants in their cribs are silenced and put to sleep by the lullabies crooned to them by their mothers.

But while the beautiful words of vocal prayer are helpful for awakening devotion, they may impede devotion once it is aroused. Once the soul is moved to the love or fear of God or admiration at His wonderful works, it wishes to remain for a time in that state. When the soul begins to take delight in this blessing which God has given it, the tongue becomes mute and the other powers of the body and soul are incapacitated for any other occupation or interest.

When the soul finds itself in this condition and perceives that the reading or recitation of words would be an impediment to its devotion, it should put aside vocal prayer, as St. Thomas tells us,[3] for it would be unreasonable to let that which has been used as an instrument become an obstacle to the very thing for which it has been utilized. Whence, they do wrong who, when they read pious books or recite inspiring prayers and experience a noticeable devotion and sweetness in them, leave the passage that has awakened de-

[3] Cf. *Summa theol.*, IIa IIae, q.83.

votion and pass on to other material. They are fleeing from the very thing they are seeking, for one of the reasons for prayer is to arouse our devotion, and vocal prayer is of more or less benefit as it serves to accomplish this end. Of course, this must not be applied to public prayers, which are ordained to the edification of the people, nor to those prayers which a person is obliged to recite by reason of his office or state in life, but only to those prayers that are said personally and voluntarily to arouse devotion. And since we are usually lukewarm at the beginning of prayer, it is generally advisable to begin with vocal prayer and to terminate in mental prayer.

It is a principal in philosophy that causes communicate their power according to the disposition of the subject on which they operate. Thus, fire will burn more brightly and more quickly if the wood is dry and the impress made on wax will be more clearly defined if the wax is soft but firm. But God is the first and universal cause of all things and the dispenser of grace. In accordance with the above principle, man will receive more grace from God as he is better disposed, and the better his dispositions, the more grace he will receive. Accordingly, if we consider the nature of prayer, we can see that when rightly used, it is a most useful disposition and preparation for grace.

In addition to this, prayer is a remarkable means for uniting man with God, so that they may become two in one spirit. God is the cause of the perfection of all things and for that reason man will be the more perfect as he is more closely united with God. This union is not attained by steps of the body but of the spirit, by which we share more and more intimately in His life. So St. Augustine states that we approach God, not by walking, but by loving, not with steps of the body, but by movements of the heart.

As the soul more closely approaches God in prayer, it shares more and more in God's light and gradually becomes more perfect. God is infinite goodness and He desires to communicate His goodness and will give Himself to those who first give themselves to Him. "He hath loved the people, all the saints are in His hand, and they that approach to His feet shall receive of His doctrine." [4]

If, in spite of obstacles and impediments, we approach God in prayer, we shall begin to experience an internal warmth and a happiness of soul; but if we depart from Him, we shall increase our coldness and indifference. God is the source of light and heat and just as he who approaches the fire receives warmth from the fire but gets colder and colder as he moves away from the fire, so the soul's warmth or coldness will be determined by its distance from the divine fire.

Aristotle teaches that one of the principal differences between sensible and intellectual things is that sensible things, as they are more intense, corrupt the external senses that receive their impressions, as is evident in the case of a strong light which blinds the eyes or a powerful sound which deafens the ear. But intelligible things, as they are more excellent and lofty, perfect the intellect that receives them. Consequently, as the mind of man becomes base and vile by dwelling on lowly things, it is ennobled and perfected if it meditates on lofty matters, and especially if it thinks of God. For that reason, it is not surprising that prayer should be so effective in perfecting the soul, for its primary function is to fix our minds on Him who is our perfection. If a man gazes on sensible beauty, he is gladdened and fortified. What will it be to gaze upon Him who is beauty itself? And if we gaze on Him, He has promised

[4] Deut. 33:2–3.

that He will in turn look upon us with love: "Turn ye to Me, . . . and I will turn to you." [5]

Another marvelous effect of prayer is that it nourishes and sustains the soul. All living things must have nourishment in order to sustain life. Some creatures live on the fruits and produce of the earth, others, on lower creatures, but men and angels are spiritually nourished by God, through the contemplation of His beauty. Our souls are spiritual substances and they must be sustained by the vision of God so far as it is possible in this life. As the vision of God is, so is the life that results from it; and since the angelic vision is clear and ours on earth is imperfect, the angels enjoy the life of glory while we on earth can at best enjoy the life of grace. But the life of grace is spiritual life, the life of charity. And if the spiritual life consists essentially in charity, what is of greater help to its preservation than the frequent consideration of the divine perfections? As fire is sustained by the wood on which it feeds, so the divine flame of charity is sustained by the fuel of these devout considerations.

If we consider the matter further, we shall discover that prayer is not only the sustenance of the spiritual life, but it is a remedy for our wounds, for there is no other spiritual exercise in which the wounds of the soul are more quickly manifested or more readily cured. As dark colors are more accentuated when set against lighter ones and the crooked is more manifest when compared with the straight, so also when the soul is in the presence of God, who is the light and guide of all things, it can readily perceive its obscurity and deviations and ask a remedy of Him who is the model of all rectitude and beauty.

Nor would he be in error who would say that prayer and

[5] Zach. 1:3.

meditation are the very life and soul of faith and the substance and foundation of all our good. We have already observed that one of the things that predominates in the practice of prayer is the consideration of the mysteries of faith. When this consideration is aided by charity, it animates our faith, enabling us to ponder the divine truths and to appreciate something of their grandeur. Prayer reveals that which is hidden and unfolds that which is contained in the mysteries, and as our intellects are enlightened in regard to the mysteries, our wills acquire greater efficacy and power for good.

Prayer has yet another effect: it enables us to taste and enjoy the divine sweetness of spiritual consolation, which is one of the greatest helps to virtue and one of the principal effects of the fruits of the Holy Ghost. Indeed, the Holy Ghost is called the Paraclete or Consoler because His principal function is to give consolation to the soul and fill it with such wondrous spiritual delights that it will more readily disdain mundane pleasures. But the greatness of these spiritual delights and consolations can be understood only by him who has experienced them and for that reason we shall not attempt to explain or describe them. He who has not yet experienced these spiritual joys is not able to understand them, no matter how much we say about them. Nevertheless, spiritual delights are used by God to raise a soul from earth to heaven and make it reject all the things of the world. The soul will gladly throw away all mundane pleasures when it discovers the delights of the spirit. Thus, divine providence is like the prudent mother who, when she sees the child chewing on something dirty or harmful, takes it away and then, to pacify the child and stop it from crying, gives it something much more tasty. The heavenly Father knows our selfishness; He knows that we do not like to give anything unless we shall receive something in return. So He offers us spiritual delights so that we shall throw away mundane delights and, as St. Bernard says, once the soul has tasted spiritual delights, all other delights become insipid.

We have seen that prayer disposes the soul for grace, leads to greater union with God, and raises the mind to the contemplation of His beauty. It is the nourishment of the virtues, the principal instrument by which faith probes the divine mysteries, and the source of the spiritual delight which accompanies the contemplation and the love of God. If a Christian conscientiously and faithfully practices prayer, his entire life will become integrated and properly ordered, his conscience will be purified, his spirit joyful, his heart strengthened, and his soul will be filled with good intentions and holy resolutions. Gradually he will become more and more aware of the presence of God and the power of grace working within him. It is as if he were being carried on the shoulders of another or on the wings of eagles, for God is now guiding the soul along the path to sanctity. "I will bring them through the torrents of waters in a right way and they shall not stumble in it." [6] But if through his own fault the Christian cuts the thread of this holy practice, little by little his soul will become indifferent, weak, and sterile. Its good intentions and desires will vanish and the passions, which were dormant under the control of reason, are re-awakened and begin to stir. The soul then finds itself filled with vanity and fickleness, a friend of laughter and useless conversation. The passions of vainglory, envy, ambition, and all the others begin to revive, like flames kindled from glowing coals fanned to life by the bellows or a slight breath of air.

[6] Tob. 31:9.

The Christian who is faithful to the practice of prayer is like a traveler walking in a heavy fog, which is so dense that he can scarcely see his hand in front of his face. But when the rays of the sun dissipate the fog, other shapes and objects gradually become visible until the fog is finally lifted and all things are seen clearly. Prayer is like a spiritual fog which surrounds the soul and as long as it lasts the soul cannot see anything but God and is so occupied with this vision that it scarcely thinks of anything else.

It is often remarkable to observe the sudden change that the practice of prayer causes in persons who dedicate themselves to it. A man may be very distraught, vivacious, depressed, or indifferent, but if he takes up the practice of prayer and perseveres in it even for a short time, the change may be so great that he will think he is a different person entirely. A plant that has been without water for days is dried and withered and almost dead; but pour a few glasses of water on it and you will see that almost immediately the leaves regain their shape, and the stem becomes erect again, and it is like a different plant. Prayer is the spiritual rain that irrigates our spiritual life and even if our hearts are like the sterile earth which will never produce any plants no matter how much it is watered, the water of prayer can arouse a desire for the flowers of virtue.

Many religious are more or less enclosed in their monasteries and occupied with the observances and austerities of the religious life. They offer Mass daily, fast for a good part of the year, assist at choral recitation of the Divine Office, and occupy themselves in other religious observances and tasks. They live in the state of perfection, separated from the cares and anxieties of the world. But if these religious lack interior prayer, they will become so dry, so indifferent, and so remiss in their love of God that little by little they will return to the things of the world and become so alien to the exercises of the religious life that for all practical purposes they will be nothing more than laymen wearing a religious garb.

On the other hand, you may find a married woman, burdened with the cares of children and the household and unable to perform many of the pious practices that are observed by religious, because her duties and state of life do not permit it, who manages to be recollected for a certain amount of time each day, who practices prayer, and receives the sacraments regularly. Perhaps she possesses such simplicity of soul, such purity of intention, such chastity, such devotion, so intense a love of God and a true disdain for the things of the world, such mercy and compassion toward her neighbor that she amazes us and makes us ashamed that we ourselves are so far from her degree of holiness. How is it that many religious are dry and indifferent in the midst of their many pious exercises while a woman burdened with many cares has become very holy without utilizing those exercises?

Many reasons could be given, but I think that one of the principal reasons is the inestimable power of the sacraments and the practice of prayer. If prayer is so important a disposition for grace, the more one practices prayer, the more he will grow in grace and, consequently, in all virtue and perfection. Thus, the practice of interior prayer is the breath of the spiritual life, for it gives a man the fervor and strength to grow in devotion; it arouses him to do good and gives him a taste for the good that he does, which will not be so if he lacks devotion and prayer. If one does not believe this, I have no stronger argument whereby to convince him than to ask him to spend a few hours in prayer before the altar, conversing with God and lamenting his sins. Then he will see that all we have said on prayer is very little in view of the praise it actually deserves.

We can see from this the error of those religious superiors whose whole effort and insistence in government is merely on external observances, without taking any account of these interior exercises. Such superiors do not seem to realize that the observances and precepts of the religious life, such as fasting, cloister, silence, and the rest are ordained to this one end: to raise the mind and heart to God and enable the soul to give itself to the contemplation of God. Therefore, what profit is there in expending all one's energy in external observances if one neglects the cultivation and practice of interior prayer? What is more similar to the deceit and error of the Jews, who in their malice embraced the means but rejected the end, that is, they observed the ceremonial law, but rejected Christ; they kept the dead letter and ignored the spirit.

Many religious today are in the same state of error and self-deception. They wear only the habit and external appearance of religious. They keep the observances and ceremonies that are seen by the eyes of men, but they lack the core of true religion which is seen only by the eye of God. One of the worst results of this error is that it makes us pharisaical. We think ourselves to be something by reason of external observances but we disdain anything that pertains to the interior. St. Bernard says of such a religious: "Strangers have devoured his strength and he knew it not. The evil religious, seeing himself in the habit and tonsure of a monk, chanting the Divine Office, and observing the rules of fasting, thinks that he is something on this account, but he does not realize that interiorly he is empty and spiritless and that his heart is far from God." All the beauty of religious life and all the great virtues have their source in interior devotion. Show me a heart that is devout and recollected, and I will show you a disciplined body, fasts, silence, vigils, and moderation in all things. For just as the health of the body is manifested in the complexion and figure of a man, so internal discipline and self-control will foster a moderate and controlled body. But to try to have the second without the first is like the ugly woman who strives, with the use of cosmetics, to make her face beautiful.

If man had remained in that joyous state in which he was created by God, he would have little need of arguments and persuasions to incline his heart to God and raise him to the contemplation of heavenly things. As the eagle naturally soars on high and builds its nest in the loftiest summits, so man, had he remained in the state of innocence, would always have soared to lofty and divine things and would have found his delight in such things. But man, at the instigation of the serpent, has bartered heaven for earth and has become so immersed in the things of earth that he has become little more than a lump of clay. He loves earth, he eats earth, he speaks of the earth, he has placed all his treasure on earth and has so sunken his roots in the earth that he can only with difficulty break the bonds that hold him.

Having spoken of the utility of prayer, we shall speak briefly of its necessity, which is a stronger link than the one preceding, in the hope that we may show that prayer is so necessary that the Lord has made it a special command: "We ought always to pray, and not to faint." [7]

What remedy is there for man in such a miserable state as that of fallen nature? What remedy is there for a man who has no possessions and no way of acquiring them? He has no other recourse but to beg. That is precisely the condi-

[7] Luke 18:1.

tion of man, for original sin has left him so impoverished that he can do nothing but beg at the gates of divine mercy. "But I am a beggar and poor; the Lord is careful for me." [8] The little bird newly hatched has neither the strength to fly nor any way to sustain its life. It can do nothing but fill the air with its chirping so that the parents will provide for its needs. So also man must cry out to God in his helplessness and ask his Father to provide for him. Ezechias says: "I will cry like a young swallow, I will meditate like a dove." [9]

Prayer is one of the surest means of obtaining all that you wish to receive from God. If you seek friendship and grace, pardon of your sins, mortification of your passions, consolation in your afflictions, fortitude in your temptations, spiritual consolation, or help in temporal needs, then pray.

How true it is that prayer is everything since through prayer we can attain everything. Prayer is all the virtues and through prayer we gain all the virtues. He who prays, possesses God, for it is through prayer that we reach God. Therefore, it should not astonish anyone when we say that prayer can accomplish more than all the other virtues. If a castle were surrounded by enemies and on the verge of being surrendered, when a soldier who had escaped to seek help from the king returned with reinforcements, could we not say that this soldier has accomplished more than all the rest, since his intercession availed more than the weapons of the others? But what is prayer but a messenger that we dispatch from earth to heaven in order to seek God's help? How often it has happened that when our virtue failed us and we were on the verge of consenting to sin, prayer brought us new courage and help from heaven by which we successfully defended the castle of our soul against the

[8] Ps. 39:18.   [9] Isa. 38:14.

enemy. How often it has happened that when our heart was troubled and oppressed by affliction and all the virtues of the soul were insufficient to raise it up, we called upon God and began to live again because of the help that came to us through prayer.

What miracle was ever performed except through prayer? What gifts of grace were ever received except through prayer? How did the saints cure the sick, cast out devils, tame wild beasts, quench flames, or subdue the elements of nature, except through prayer? How did Moses, Josue, Gideon, David, Ezechias, Josaphat, the Machabees, and all the friends of God triumph if not through prayer?

All these things demonstrate the necessity of prayer. As Christ has told us, we must always pray and not faint. And since prayer is the gate through which all blessings enter our lives, what is a Christian without prayer but a soldier without arms, a writer without a pen, or a surgeon without instruments? Therefore, he who desires to be a true Christian will arrange his life so there will be time to converse with God in prayer. And not only temporal affairs but spiritual works as well should be undertaken in such moderation as always to leave time for this holy exercise of prayer. For if prayer is one of the primary instruments for the performance of good works, and no man is so strictly bound to restitution that he must sell the tools with which he makes his livelihood in order to repay his debt, so the law of charity or any other office do not oblige to such an extent that we should entirely abandon the life of prayer. Without prayer we cannot rightly discharge our duties nor can we preserve our spiritual life; with prayer we can do both.

Some souls, realizing the difficulty of perseverance in prayer because of their many tasks and duties, say that one can make his external works of the apostolate a continual prayer and that will suffice. The truth of the matter is that he will seldom work well who does not pray well. Therefore, while it is true to say that good work is good prayer, this is not what Christ meant when He told us to pray always, for He explicitly told us to pray; He did not use the word work. If He had meant that good works replace prayer, He would have said that we could let work suffice for prayer, but He said that we should pray.

If at a given time it is impossible to fulfill the command, there is no need to be anxious, for Christ never demands the impossible. Christ wants us to pray as frequently as we can and to put aside those things that interfere with prayer. In other words, He wants us to do all that we can whenever we can. So also, when we are told in the Psalms to meditate on the law day and night, we are not to understand this literally, but morally, as common sense would interpret it, meaning as often as possible.

But continual prayer can be much more frequent than worldly men are inclined to believe. A man is always absorbed in the thing or person he loves, so that this is in his mind constantly, although for short periods he may be distracted from it or may deliberately turn his attention to other duties. Why, then, should not the soul that has been touched by divine love and divine beauty keep its heart and eyes fixed on its treasure?

Some souls measure the time for prayer as if they were measuring out doses of medicine, taking what they think will suffice to cure the wounds or sickness of the soul, and only that amount. Actually, it is not possible to set a definite amount of prayer that would suffice for all. Much depends on the extent to which an individual is under the sway of his passions, the number and severity of the occasions of sin in his life, or the greater or less need he has for this or that virtue. Some souls are of such good disposition or so blessed by divine grace that even with a little prayer they can walk safely and securely; others are so constituted that as soon as they are deprived of prayer they lose all their vigor. Undoubtedly, the latter have a greater need of prayer, just as the more seriously ill have greater need of medicine. The same thing is true of dangers from without, for if one is in the land of the enemy, he must walk with greater caution, or in time of winter he must be better protected against the cold. Likewise, those who live in more danger or occasions of sin need more frequent prayer.

Theologians commonly teach that the value and merit of our good works does not depend so much on the substance of the works themselves as the manner in which they are performed. One theologian has pithily stated that God does not reward verbs, but adverbs, meaning that God looks not so much to what we do as to how we do it; for example, whether we perform our works with charity and devotion. This is especially true of prayer, because if prayer is not practiced properly, it will bear little or no fruit. St. James tells us: "You ask, and receive not, because you ask amiss." [10] Thus, charity is required if prayer is to be meritorious; confidence, if it is to be true petition; attention, if it is to be prayer at all; and actual attention, if it is to give spiritual joy.

Let us now consider the requisites for perfect prayer. The first is that one should pray with attention. Our Lord said that when we pray we should withdraw to an inner chamber and there pray in secret to our Father in heaven. In other words, Christ would have us rid our souls of all worldly cares and thoughts so that we can give our minds

[10] Jas. 4:3.

to God in silence and recollection. For prayer is conversation with God and it requires great attention and reverence. If one observes great reverence and attention when discussing earthly matters with rulers of nations, much more so when one addresses the King of heaven and earth concerning the affairs of eternity.

Attention is required by the very nature of prayer, because prayer which lacks attention should be called distraction rather than prayer. Hence, Cassian says: "He prays little who prays only when on his knees; he prays not at all who, although he is on his knees, is voluntarily distracted." Against such persons St. John Chrysostom says: "You do not hear your own prayer, and do you expect God to hear it? You say that you are in the church on your knees. That may be true, but your mind is distracted. Your body is in a holy place, but your mind wanders all over the world. Your mouth speaks to God, but perhaps you are thinking on evil things."

Prayer that lacks attention is not efficacious for obtaining mercies from God; it may even be a sin. Cajetan says that although it is true that a man is not obliged to pray at every instant, one must pray with reverence and attention when he does pray. And if he deliberately refuses to pray with the proper dispositions, he is not excused from at least venial sin. In accordance with this doctrine, St. Basil says that the divine favor should not be asked in an indifferent manner and with a distracted mind, for he who asks in this way not only does not receive what he seeks, but He angers God.

Consequently, it is of great importance that persons take care how they pray. Some persons recite their Office with so little attention and reverence that they seem to be chanting the verses of Vergil rather than the Divine Office. If such persons would reflect on what they are doing, to whom they are speaking, and the words they are saying, they would pray with much more attention.

However, if distractions are not voluntary or do not arise through the fault of the individual, he should do the best he can in spite of them, for the weakness of human nature is such that it is not completely subject to reason at all times. Indeed, to continue in prayer in spite of distractions may be very fruitful and meritorious. For prayer has three distinct benefits: it is a meritorious work, it is a work of impetration, and it arouses devotion. Of these three benefits, only the third demands actual attention, because devotion proceeds from the consideration of divine things. But for the first two benefits, merit and impetration, good will and the proper intention suffice. Therefore, when a man begins to pray and his mind involuntarily becomes distracted, there is no sin. This is a great consolation to humble and devout souls who become over-anxious when they find themselves distracted in prayer.

The second requisite for perfect prayer is true humility. "The prayer of him that humbleth himself shall pierce the clouds, and till it come nigh, he will not be comforted, and he will not depart till the Most High behold." [11] Humility enables a man to recognize his nakedness and poverty, the abyss of miseries into which he has been cast as a result of original sin, and the malice and ruin he has added to this by his own personal sins. He who is so weakened, should cry out to God with the Psalmist: "Save me, O God, for the waters are come in even unto my soul. I stick fast in the mire of the deep and there is no sure standing." [12] And when he considers the evils that have befallen him because of his own malice, he will cry out again with the Psalmist: "Save me, O Lord, for there is now no saint; truths are decayed

[11] Ecclus. 35:21.   [12] Ps. 68:1.

from among the children of men." [13] And as a man more clearly recognizes his poverty and need, the more frequent is his prayer.

The greatness of God's majesty should also arouse our humility, for if countless angels serve and adore God, how great should be the fear and reverence and humility with which a mere man presents himself before such great majesty. This is the spirit in which the publican prayed, not even daring to raise his eyes to heaven, and for that reason his prayer was heard. Christ Himself prayed in this manner when He lay prostrate in the Garden in an attitude of complete abasement and perfect humility. But if He who is innocence itself and infinite majesty humbled Himself in prayer, how much more he should abase himself who is but the sweepings of this world.

The third requisite for perfect prayer is faith and confidence, for if humility teaches us not to trust in ourselves, faith teaches us to trust in God. St. James refers to this when he says that we should pray with faith and without doubting, otherwise we shall not obtain what we desire. And the Lord Himself has pointed out the importance of this quality by saying: "All things whatsover you shall ask in prayer, believing, you shall receive." [14]

But perhaps you will ask how you can have that kind of faith and confidence when you have done so little for God. The answer is that the principal foundations of faith and confidence are not the services that one has given to God, but the merits of Jesus Christ and the goodness and mercy of God. And if you ask how great are the goodness and mercy of God, they are commensurate with the divine substance, which is infinite. Therefore, God is infinitely merciful, and since He has an infinite treasury of riches to communicate,

[13] Ps. 11:1.   [14] Matt. 21:22.

He is infinitely generous in bestowing them. Therefore, when you approach God to ask pardon and mercy, do not be afraid or timid, thinking that you will vex Him. It is as fitting for God to be merciful as it is for the sun to shine and for fire to burn. Nor does He become angry, as some men do when we ask them for help or favors. Men become upset at being asked for things because they realize that in giving to others, they themselves lose something. But God loses nothing when He bestows favors or answers our requests, but He is glorified in so doing.

Our confidence in prayer rests on the merits of Christ; hence, we have a right to pray with utmost confidence because all that He did and suffered on this earth was done for us. This is His heritage to us. He had no need of any of these things for Himself. He was innocent and had nothing for which to atone. We can obtain all blessings if we seek them in the name of Jesus.

But even faith is not sufficient; it must be accompanied by good works and a good life. Sometimes God in His infinite mercy will hear the prayer of a sinner and grant his petition, but generally the statement of the blind man is true: "Now we know that God doth not hear sinners, but if a man be a server of God and doth His will, him He heareth." [15] All good works are aids to prayer, but fasting and almsgiving are especially so. It is God's law that it shall be meted out to us as we have meted out to others. As we are merciful to others through almsgiving, God will be merciful to us. Fasting, however, aids prayer in another way. It tempers the body by means of moderation in food and disposes it to dwell on heavenly things. It castigates the flesh which rebels against the spirit and when a man purifies himself as best he can, he is disposed for the passive purification

[15] John 9:31.

that comes from God. Moreover, he who chastises his body, proves that he truly seeks God and shall surely find Him.

The fifth requisite for true prayer pertains to the matter of prayer itself, and especially the things for which we may lawfully pray. God desires that we ask great things of Him, that is, spiritual and eternal goods. The goods of this world may also be the object of prayer, so far as they can serve the spiritual life, but we must be careful to leave everything in God's hands, because He knows better what is for our good than we do ourselves. What seems profitable from our point of view may prove dangerous to our salvation and in this case God mercifully refuses to grant us the things for which we plead so earnestly. Therefore, we should ask for temporal goods under this condition and leave all to the providence of God; but we may pray for spiritual goods without any conditions whatever. And of these spiritual goods, let us pray first for pardon of our sins, then for the strength never to commit mortal sin in the future, and finally, for whatever virtues are particularly necessary in our state of life.

The last requisite for true prayer is patience and perseverance, so that we shall not become discouraged and abandon our plea, no matter how long the Lord may delay in answering us. "Although He should kill me, I will trust in Him." [16] Christ recommends this to us when He relates the parable of the man who knocked at the door of his friend in the middle of the night to borrow three loaves of bread. When the friend excused himself by saying that he was already in bed, the importunity of the man at the door finally caused him to rise and grant the request. Jesus concludes by saying that if we persevere in knocking at the door of divine mercy, it will be opened to us.

Perseverance is necessary in prayer because sometimes the

[16] Job 13:15.

Lord delays in order to test our faith, to see whether or not we shall abandon prayer and seek a solution by unlawful means, to let us realize our need, to arouse greater fervor in our prayer by this delay, or for other reasons that He knows best. Some souls are very fervent in prayer for a short period and they place much confidence in prayer, but while they may be patient in other matters, they cannot suffer any delay in getting an answer to their desires. For that reason they become discouraged and abandon their demands.

CHAPTER 38 ✍

Mental Prayer

UP to this point we have been discussing vocal prayer, which is the easiest kind of prayer and that which is most generally practiced by the faithful. Now we shall discuss mental prayer, which is somewhat more difficult and as a rule is habitually practiced by those who are more advanced in the grades of prayer. When a vine is young and fragile, it needs a pole or tree upon which it can lean as it grows, but after it has reached full strength, it no longer needs a support. So it is with beginners in the spiritual life; when they want to converse with God they need the help of vocal prayers so that they can raise their hearts and minds to Him and know how to address Him, but after they are well established in the spiritual life and have acquired a bit of devotion, their love speaks for itself and finds the words with which to express the sentiments of their hearts.

There is no essential difference between vocal and mental prayer, for they are both very lofty and excellent acts of the virtue of religion. However, the one speaks with the heart alone and the other speaks with the heart and tongue. The difference is purely accidental and as our devotion becomes more intense, our prayer becomes more excellent and lofty. Moreover, the best prayer for the individual is that which is accompanied by the greatest devotion and for that reason, if praying with beads or a book arouses greater devotion, then that is a better prayer for the individual.

Mental prayer is any form of meditation or consideration of the things of God, even when we do not actually petition God for anything. Meditation is of inestimable benefit to the soul, for as the study of the human sciences is the principal means of acquiring human wisdom, so the consideration of divine things is a very important means for attaining to divine wisdom, which is the greatest of the gifts of the Holy Ghost. Moreover, meditation is a great help for cultivating true devotion, which makes a man prompt for the performance of virtue.

Another great blessing of this type of prayer is that it gives an awareness of divine things. He who recites the Office or says the Rosary passes quickly and lightly over the prayers, but he who meditates takes no account of when he shall finish or whether he shall cover a certain amount of matter. He will spend his time on a phrase or sentence of Scripture, on a mystery in the life of Christ, or on some divine truth and dwell on it as long as he gains benefit from it. So we read of St. Francis of Assisi that he spent an entire night repeating the one sentence: "Lord, that I may know Thee and that I may know myself." It is much more profitable to the soul to consider a mystery or truth in this way than to pass over many truths superficially.

This same practice should be followed by those who meditate with the help of a book, reading until they come to an inspiring passage and then pausing for as long as is profitable or as long as the Holy Ghost gives them an interior awareness of that which they read. So it happens that some persons can spend a long time in the recitation of the Our Father or the Creed, meditating on the various mysteries or truths represented. Not only is this type of meditation very profitable, but it is relatively easy.

Since mental prayer deals with the truths or mysteries of God, it will be helpful to enumerate some of the particular points that are suitable for meditation. Any subject is suitable for meditation if it serves to arouse in us a love or fear of God, hatred of sin, disdain for the things of the world, and such sentiments. Therefore, Scripture, the lives of the saints, or a consideration of the structure of the created universe are all excellent subjects for meditation. But St. Thomas Aquinas mentions two subjects that are especially suitable to arouse devotion: the perfections of God and our own defects and sins.[1] The first disposes us to grow in the love of God and the second arouses true humility, both of which are necessary for progress in the spiritual life. The following observations are those of Cajetan in his commentary on the *Summa theologica:*

"To the first (meditation on the divine perfections) pertains the consideration of the goodness, mercy, justice, charity, and beauty of God or His other attributes and perfections, especially His love for men and for each human being in particular; or the consideration of the divine benefits, such as creation, redemption, baptism, the Eucharist, divine inspirations, . . . the fact that He has waited so

---

[1] Cf. *Summa theol.,* IIa IIae, q. 82, a. 5.

long for you to do penance, that He has mercifully preserved you from many dangers of body and soul, that He has deputed His angels to take charge over you, and many other benefits.

"To the second part (meditation on our own defects) pertains the consideration of one's defects and miseries, his present and past sins, his inclinations to sin, the misuse of the abilities and natural talents that God has given him, the perversity of his sensitive appetite, his poverty of virtues, the spiritual wounds in his soul, such as blindness, malice, concupiscence, and sloth, his carnal impediments to the performance of good works, the fact that he lives in darkness and does not even seem to be aware of it, that he does not hear the voice of the Good Shepherd who calls him interiorly, and above all, that he has so frequently put enmity between himself and God by committing mortal sins and has thus done Him such a great injury that it would seem that he no longer wanted Him for his God but had made gods of his stomach, money, honor, delights, and other such things.

"Such meditations, which should be the daily practice of religious and of all spiritual persons, can engender true devotion and all the other virtues if one puts aside the vocal prayers which are not of obligation. They do not deserve the name of religious or holy persons who do not occupy themselves in this kind of prayer at least once a day. An effect cannot be produced without a cause nor can the end be attained without using the means to that end. Neither can a man cultivate the virtue of religion if he does not perform the acts of religion and use the means by which it is attained."

When Cajetan says that one should abandon vocal prayer to practice meditation, he does not mean to condemn the use of vocal prayer. For if it is a holy thing to call upon God with all one's heart, how could it not be holy to add one's tongue to the words of the heart? Cajetan is not condemning the use but the abuse of vocal prayer, as when a person prays so rapidly and with so little attention that he reaps little or no benefit from his prayer. And would to God that so many Christians were not guilty of this fault. Anyone who observes the way in which some priests recite the Divine Office—in public or in private—will see clearly with what good reason Cajetan has reprehended the abuse of vocal prayer. Moreover, Cajetan means to say that one should not use purely vocal prayer when he is able to practice mental prayer. Strive, therefore, to observe what Cajetan teaches by putting aside a certain period each day in which you can consider your sins and the divine benefits or the life of Christ.

St. Bonaventure, who was an outstanding doctor of theology and renowned for his devotion, religious observance, and prudence in governing, arranged a series of meditations on the life of Christ, and he did this because he appreciated the benefits of meditation. They who meditate at regular intervals will make greater progress in the service of God and along the path of virtue and will be more prompt in performing the works of mercy and the austerities of penance and mortification. They will be more solicitous to keep themselves as far as possible from the occasions of sin.

To summarize, there are three general subjects especially suitable for meditation. The first is the divine perfections, such as God's goodness, charity, beauty, justice, mercy, providence, and the others. The second comprises the divine benefits, especially that of redemption, which embraces all the phases and mysteries of the life of Christ. The third is the knowledge of oneself, that is, of one's defects and wretchedness, from which one acquires contempt for self and true humility which is the foundation of all the other virtues.

Some persons, however, are so busy that they cannot meditate more than once a day. They will do well to meditate on some event or mystery in the life of Christ or one of the divine perfections or attributes and to do this daily until they have gone over the entire life of Christ or all the attributes of God. They may even begin again once they have completed the cycle. But those who have more leisure, as religious and clerics or professional people, may find the time to meditate two or three times a day and should arrange their periods of meditation by assigning certain subjects for each meditation period. We mention these things so that a person will not meditate on the same subject each day, for this could become tedious and monotonous even to the perfect. Moreover, a change in the subject of meditation is a great help for arousing devotion, as St. Thomas points out in one of his minor works. This is the reason why beginners often have greater fervor and sensible consolation than those who are more advanced, because the novelty of things experienced for the first time arouses greater admiration and feeling.

We should also observe that two things may precede meditation and two things may follow it, with the result that there are five elements in this practice of prayer: preparation, spiritual reading, meditation, thanskgiving, and petition.

It is as necessary to prepare ourselves for that holy exercise as it is to tune the guitar before playing it. "Before prayer prepare thy soul, and be not as a man that tempteth God." [2] To tempt God is to expect Him to work in an

[2] Ecclus. 18:23.

extraordinary manner when something can be accomplished by other means. And since the preparation of the heart is so essential for attaining devotion, he who would expect to attain it without this means would for all practical purposes be tempting God.

The first step in preparing for meditation is to select the time and place convenient to one's condition or state of life. In general, the best time is in the morning or late at night and the best place is one that is solitary and obscure so that as many distractions will be avoided as possible. Once arrived at the place selected and having blessed ourselves, we should consider these three points: what we seek, what we are about to do, and to whom we are about to speak. As to the first, we should realize that we are about to seek grace and glory and whatever will help in the acquisition of these two things. We shall recall the importance of the requisites for prayer that have already been enumerated, particularly attention and humility, because without these two qualities prayer is fruitless.

Secondly, we shall understand that we are about to consider the things of God and that proper attention is of great importance, for although virtual attention suffices for petition, it does not suffice for arousing devotion.

Thirdly, we shall realize that we are about to converse with God, and this requires the humility and reverence due to His infinite majesty. Once we have made our reverence to God, we should accuse ourselves of our sins and humbly ask pardon for them. In doing this, it would be well to recite either the Act of Contrition or some psalm such as the *Miserere* or the *De profundis*. But one should not delay too long at this point, as some do, for although it is always necessary for beginners, it should not infringe on the time necessary for other things. Therefore, this is not

the time for a detailed consideration of one's sins, especially if the recollection may prove a source of temptation
or distraction.

Once the preparation has been made, beginners at least
should read the passage which is to be the material for their
meditation. After a time they will find that a book is no
longer necessary, for they can proceed immediately to
meditation, but at the start they will not know how to meditate without the aid of a book.

The reading, should not be done hurriedly, but more
slowly and with great attention, applying the mind to that
which is read and striving to arouse the will to react to it.
When they come upon some inspiring passage, they should
pause for a while and meditate on what has been read.
So St. Bernard advises: "Sometimes it is necessary to take
something of spirit and devotion from that which one is
reading and to interrupt the reading by a short prayer by
which the heart and mind are raised to God, according to
one's sentiments and the material that is read."

The reading should not be so lengthy that it occupies
the greater part of the time and thus prevents other more
important acts. St. Augustine says that it is good to pray
and to read if we can do both at the same time, but if we
cannot do so, prayer is better than reading. But since prayer
involves effort and reading is more easy and enjoyable,
we often refuse the effort and choose that which is more
pleasant.

If a man does not have white bread, he will eat any kind
that he can obtain, rather than go without food; so also, if
the soul is so distracted that it cannot pray, one may spend
more time in spiritual reading or combine meditation with
reading. In this way the mind which is attentive to that

which is read will not so easily be distracted by useless thoughts or imaginations, as would be the case if it were left to itself. It would be better, of course, to spend the whole time wrestling with God, as Jacob did, and at the end to receive His blessing.

After the reading, comes the meditation proper. We should note here that sometimes the material of the meditation can be represented by the imagination, as happens in meditations on the life of Christ. At other times the material is intellectual, as when we meditate on the attributes of God. Either the intellectual or the imaginative meditation can be used to great advantage, depending on the material at hand. And when we are meditating on some phase of the life of Christ or on anything else that can be pictured in the imagination, such as the last judgment, paradise, hell, we should represent these things as present to us here and now, so that the meditation will be more vivid. But we should beware lest we use our imagination too extensively, for this will not only weary us, but we may deceive ourselves to the extent of believing that we really see something when it is only our vivid imagination that is at work.

Once the meditation is completed, we should give thanks for the benefits we have received. Indeed, this spirit of thanksgiving should accompany all our prayers, as St. Paul advises: "Be instant in prayer; watching in it with thanksgiving." [3] As St. Augustine remarks: "What greater thing could we think in the mind, speak with the mouth, or write with the pen, than 'Thanks be to God'? Nothing is more quickly said, more sweet to the ear, more joyfully understood, or more fruitfully done." In order not to make too abrupt a change, if we are meditating on some mystery of

[3] Col. 4:2.

the life of Christ, we can address our thanks to Christ rather than attempt to turn our minds away from Him in order to give thanks to God as pure spirit.

The last step, that of petition, should contain two elements. The first is connected with our thanksgiving, wherein we not only thank God for benefits received, but express the desire that all creatures should serve and glorify Him. We should then petition for the needs of the whole world, that all nations may know and serve Him, and for the needs of the Church so that all the faithful will walk in the service and knowledge of God. We should pray for the various classes of members of the Church: the just, that God may conserve them; sinners, that God will pardon them; the deceased, that they may be taken to eternal glory. Moreover, we should pray for all our debtors, friends, benefactors, and all who suffer tribulation. We should ask for our own needs as well, for some persons never ask God for anything in particular, but only that His will be done. But we know from the lives of the saints that they frequently prayed for particular things, such as growth in virtue, remedies against vice, control of their passions, and similar needs.

It is truly lamentable to hear some persons say that they do not know what to ask of God. Wretched indeed is the man who does not know how to ask for a remedy for his wretchedness. What animal is so insensible that it cannot in some way signify its needs? What person is so sick that he cannot tell where he is suffering pain? Look at yourself. Look at the passions which most frequently afflict you; whether it is a question of avarice, anger, vainglory, hardness of heart, stubbornness of will, looseness of tongue, lust, love of honor and fame, inconstancy in good resolutions, self-love, or some other pestilence of soul. Expose these wounds to the heavenly Physician so that He may cure them with the ointment of His grace. Above all, once you have petitioned a remedy for your vices, ask also for the virtues necessary for your salvation.

We shall now give some suggestions for the actual practice of meditation and first of all concerning the subject matter. Although it is good to assign in advance a topic for meditation for the day or week, if some other subject presents itself as more profitable, one should not ignore it in order to comply with some schedule. It is most unreasonable to reject the light that the Holy Ghost offers in order to occupy ourselves with something else that may not be as beneficial. Moreover, since the end of meditation is to arouse devotion and an awareness of divine things, it would be folly to seek this devotion and awareness by some other way when we have the means at hand for finding it. However, neither should we be so fickle and inconstant that we too readily take up the consideration of whatever presents itself to our minds. Let us be always guided by the profit to be gained from one or the other and choose that which promises to be of more spiritual help to us.

Secondly, we must at all costs avoid too much speculation in our meditation. We should strive rather to arouse affections and sentiments of the will than demonstrations and proofs. It is true that the intellect helps the operations of the will, but it may also be an impediment to our love and the awareness of divine things. The intellect should guide the will, giving it a knowledge of the things to be loved, but if there is too much speculation, this operation of the will is impeded or prevented entirely. The reason for this is that the human soul is finite and the more its power is applied to one thing, the less remains for application to other things. If the intellect absorbs all the power of the soul, little remains for the other faculties. Hence, if a man gives much or most of his time to speculation, he will be weak in affection.

It is evident from the foregoing that they are not on the right path who meditate on the divine truths as if they were studying theology or preparing a sermon. The end of their meditation period will find them dry and without any savor of devotion and they will be no better spiritually then they were before. They have not prayed at all, but have studied or prepared a sermon, which is something quite distinct from praying. Such persons should remember that when we meditate we come to listen rather than to talk. "I will hear what the Lord God will speak in me." [4]

Consequently, we should not try to stimulate equally both the intellect and the will in our prayer and meditation nor try to make the one faculty keep pace with the other. Particular dexterity is required to arouse the will and silence the intellect so that it will not impede the activity of love. The intellect must consider the truths but it should then offer these truths to the will so that they can be tasted and can arouse the soul to devotion and holy desires. This being so, devout but uneducated persons sometimes gain much more profit from their mental prayer because they do not spend their time in speculation, but exercise their will in love. If you wish to learn how to do this, whenever some holy thought or ardent affection arises during prayer, immediately go with it to God, like a child who runs to his mother with everything he finds.

However, we should not let the will become too active or too ardent. The devotion we seek is not obtained by force, as they seem to think who work themselves to a state of tenderness and tears when they meditate on the passion

[4] Ps. 84:9.

of Christ. Such antics do nothing but dry up the soul and make it less disposed for the visitation of God. They may even harm their health and leave the soul so terrified at the unpleasantness it has experienced that it hesitates to return to an exercise that has been so painful. If the Lord grants the gift of tears or similar things in prayer, they should be accepted with all humility, but it is not prudent to try to seize them by force. Let the Christian be content with doing his part, which is to meditate on what Christ has suffered, but let him not try to force anything that the Lord has not given him.

He who experiences great fatigue in this exercise should not try to proceed further, but should humble himself before God with all tranquillity, asking the grace to proceed along the path of prayer without so much effort. If the Lord should grant this peace of mind, the soul will experience greater devotion than it would have experienced by its own efforts. It will also find that it is able to pass long periods of meditation and prayer without feeling any exhaustion or tedium. Hence, it is well to avoid vehement movements of sensible feeling, and if they should arise, one should not give in to them, but should moderate and control them, restraining the thoughts that gave rise to them. In this way devotion will last for a longer time and its consolation will be more profound. But external manifestations such as sighs and groans usually do nothing but dim the interior light and serve as obstacles to that which should transpire in the soul. Beginners are less able to control these sensible feelings, for the novelty of mental prayer causes them to react with admiration and astonishment. But after they are more accustomed to this exercise, the heart should become more calm, and while their love is then more intense, it is not accompanied by much sensible fervor.

In spite of the importance of proper attention during mental prayer, it also must be moderated lest it do harm to the health or impede devotion. Some persons exhaust themselves by the effort they exert to be attentive during meditation, while others are so lax and slothful and indifferent that they are distracted by the slightest thing. To avoid these two extremes we should take care that our attention is not so forced that we weary our heads nor so careless that we let our thoughts wander where they will. Some persons have practiced meditation for years with little profit because of the coldness with which they pray, while others have lost their health and their minds because they exerted too much force in this exercise. It is especially important that beginners do not weary themselves because they may then lose the spirit to continue.

But of all the counsels, perhaps the principal one is that he who prays should not lose heart nor abandon his exercise when he does not feel the devotion he desires. The human heart is like muddied water, which cannot be cleared up suddenly, no matter how much one tries. Time must be given for the sediment to settle before the water will become clear again. So also, our hearts become muddied by the affairs of daily life and it cannot become settled and tranquil unless we give it time to do so. For that reason, the end of prayer is better than the beginning.

We must faithfully wait for as long as God desires and in the meantime be consoled by the counsel given in Scripture: "If it make any delay, wait for it, for it shall surely come and it shall not be slack." [5] This is a stage in which devout souls are tested and if they succeed in this, they will prosper in all that follows. And if it seems that the time spent in prayer is lost, they should take up some devout book

[5] Hab. 2:3.

and exchange prayer for spiritual reading, often interrupting the reading in order to pray. This is a very profitable practice and is easy for beginners.

But we should not be content with any little fervor that is experienced during prayer and think that we have completed our prayer when we have shed tears or experienced some tenderness of heart. This is not enough, any more than a summer shower suffices to irrigate the arid soil. All it does is settle the dust and wet the surface of the earth. The soul may appear devout, but its devotion is only superficial.

Hence, it is rightly advised that we should allow as much time as possible for meditation and mental prayer, and it is better to have one long period than two short ones, for if only a brief time is allotted, most of the period is spent in quieting the heart and repressing the imagination, and by the time we are finally settled down to meditate or pray, it is time to rise and go. It seems to me that an hour or even two hours is not too long a time to be spent in prayer, for it sometimes takes a half hour to quiet the imagination and the heart. But if meditation is held after some other pious exercise, such as the chanting of the Office, Mass, spiritual reading, or vocal prayer, the heart and mind are or should be already disposed for prayer and therefore the period of prayer may be shortened. Or when the period of prayer is held early in the morning it can also be shorter because one is usually better disposed for prayer in the morning. But he who is pressed for time because of his many occupations should not neglect to give what time he can to mental prayer, and as long as he does not neglect prayer through his own fault, God will provide for his needs.

If the Lord should visit the soul either in or outside of prayer, the soul should not render that visitation futile, because with help given directly by God the soul can make more progress in an hour than in many days. Remember how the apostles had fished all the night and had caught nothing, but when they let down their nets at the word of Christ, they were scarcely able to draw the net back into the boat, for the large number of fish that were in it.[6] The same thing may happen to us spiritually if we know how to make the most of the divine visitations. Much can be accomplished if we are alert to opportunities, but in the practice of prayer more than in any other. And they who do not profit from God's visitations will be punished by not finding Him when they seek Him, since when He sought them He did not find them ready.

Let us now consider some of the temptations encountered in the practice of prayer and point out some of the remedies. The principal temptations are: lack of spiritual consolations, distractions, blasphemous thoughts, temptations against faith and hope, and presumption.

The Christian must never abandon the practice of prayer because of the lack of consolations. No matter how dry and seemingly fruitless the prayer, let the soul place itself in the presence of God and examine its conscience to see whether this is due to its own culpable negligence. Then let it ask God's pardon and beg Him to manifest His patience and mercy by pardoning one who knows how to do nothing but sin. In this way the soul will draw benefit even from its aridity. Even if it finds no consolation in prayer, it should remember that those things that are profitable need not necessarily be pleasant. If a man perseveres in prayer, doing the best he can, he can be consoled by the thought that at least he has done his part so far as he was able. There is nothing remarkable in remaining faithful to prayer when one receives great consolation from it, but it is something to do so when there is little or no consolation or delight in

[6] Cf. John 21:6.

it. In times of dryness it is also necessary to walk with greater care and vigilance, for when spiritual consolation is lacking, it is necessary to supply for this lack with greater circumspection.

As for distractions in prayer, one must wage a battle against them with perseverance and courage. Yet this should not be done to such an extent that one becomes exhausted, for prayer is not so much a battle of violence as one of grace and humility. Therefore, when a man finds himself beset by distracting thoughts, he should remember that as long as such thoughts are involuntary, they are not sinful. Let him, therefore, turn to God with all humility and realize that little else can be expected in the garden of his soul but thorns and thistles. And if the distracting thoughts remain in spite of his efforts to reject them, let him realize that he gains much more ground by this resistance than by enjoying the delights of prayer.

If blasphemous thoughts come to mind, it is consoling to know that few temptations are so distressing as this and few are less dangerous. The best remedy is to pay no attention to such thoughts, because sin is not in the awareness of temptation but in consent to temptation. As a rule there is no delight in such temptations, for they are more of a pain than a fault. Consequently, it is best to disdain such temptations rather than to fear them, for if they are feared too much, the fear itself may cause them to rise again.

When tempted against faith, the Christian should think of the insignificance of man and the greatness of divine mercy. Let him think more of what God commands than scrutinize closely the works of God, which exceed our power of comprehension. He who wishes to enter the inner sanctum of the mysteries of God must do so with great humility and reverence and be as simple as the dove and not as wise as the serpent. Let the Christian be like a child, for to such does God reveal His secrets. Close the eye of reason and see only with the eye of faith, for this is the way one must consider the works and mysteries of God. But since this temptation is generally distressing and distasteful to the man of prayer, let him use the same remedy here as against blasphemous thoughts and pay no heed to it. For there can be no sin where there has been no consent.

Temptations to despair are best overcome by the realization that it is not our powers and forces alone that bring success in prayer, but divine grace, and that grace is more speedily obtained as one relies less and less on his own powers and depends more on the goodness of God in whom all things are possible. The remedy against presumption is to realize that there is no greater proof that a man is far from holiness and perfection than for him to presume that he is very close to it. Let the Christian look into the lives of the saints as into a mirror and he will discover that by comparison with them, he is a dwarf in the presence of a giant. This will warn him not to be presumptuous.

CHAPTER 39

The Path to Perfection

SINCE the end is the first and principal circumstance in moral actions and the foundation of all things else, if a man makes an error concerning the end, he will err in everything else. For that reason it is important to note that the end or goal of the Christian life is the fulfillment of the law of God by obedience to His commandments and most perfect conformity to His will. St. Paul states that the end of the law is charity, but this is not contrary to our statement, because these two virtues are so closely connected that we seldom find charity without obedience nor obedience without charity, as is evident from the words of Christ: "If you love Me, keep My commandments." [1] Whence, perfect obedience and perfect charity amount to the same thing, because he who truly loves cannot help but obey what the beloved commands and he will not obey unless he loves.

This type of obedience demands mortification and denial of our own will, because we cannot give the divine will first place in our hearts unless we deny our own will, and this is accomplished by mortification and the practice of the moral virtues. Indeed, most of the moral virtues have as their function the modification of the passions. Hence, the end of all our Christian practices is obedience, love, and mortification of our evil inclinations. That is why prayer is highly praised; not because of what it is in itself, though it is an act of the virtue of religion, which is the most excellent of all the moral virtues, but because of the help which it gives us in reaching our goal. In a word, prayer is not an end in itself but a means to an end, as medicine is a means for regaining health. Hence, if one is much given to prayer but in spite of this is no more virtuous or mortified, he is like a sick man who is always using medicine but never gets better.

Another important counsel is that we must not seek delights and consolations in prayer, because this is a source of many deceptions. Some persons find sweetness in prayer and difficulty in mortification and therefore they leave the bitter for the sweet and the laborious for the delightful, with the result that they spend all their time in prayer and little time in mortification. The human heart is so partial to

[1] John 14:15.

pleasure that it frequently becomes the source of much evil, since many persons neglect their duties or choose evil in search of delight.

The inclination for pleasure is so strong in man that when one pleasure is denied, the heart will seek an outlet in another. Human nature is crafty and subtle and often seeks itself even in the most noble practices. This is the root of many errors in the path of prayer. One's very intention for good is sometimes corrupted by a desire for delight, when our only goal should be God. This is what most frequently perverts our good deeds and prevents us from acting entirely for God. Many persons who pride themselves on the good deeds they have performed for the love of God will discover, if they examine them closely, that they are not pure gold but are covered with the dross of self-love.

Thus, some persons, in the practice of prayer and spiritual reading, seek nothing but consolation and delight, thinking that as long as prayer gives delight there can be no danger in it. They do not consider that self-love may play a very prominent role and that spiritual gluttony, spiritual avarice, and other appetites enter in all the more as the delights are greater and more desirable. It may happen, of course, that there is more culpability when the pleasure sought is more carnal, but there is greater deception in regard to spiritual consolations that are sought for their own sake.

You may say that you do not believe that many souls are deceived in this manner because few people are so blind as to seek only delight in prayer and pious practices. But I believe that many are thus deceived because, while many persons are constant in these practices, if there is an opportunity for a work of mercy or obedience or some other virtue, they will turn their back on it or defer to someone else. This is a manifest sign that they do not seek the will of God, for when He offers them the opportunity to perform a great work, they spurn this in order to turn to that which gives them greater satisfaction.

Another grave deception is to spend a great deal of time in prayer and little or no time in the practice of mortification. Since there is delight in the one and difficulty in the other, the human heart embraces that which gives pleasure and rejects that which is painful. Hence, many persons are eager to attend many Masses and sermons, recite prayers, confess and receive Communion frequently, or spend long hours talking about spiritual subjects. But in spite of all these pious practices, they are still very eager to follow their own will and to defend their every right. They will not yield an inch and will not humble themselves for anyone. They like to eat and drink and dress well, and with all this they think they are pleasing God. But if at any time they should cease to find sweetness and delight in their prayer and pious practices, they would immediately become disinterested, lose patience, and shed tears, not of devotion, but of impatience and disgust. Well may they weep at finding themselves still filled with anger, pride, impatience, avarice, and empty of humility and charity and the other virtues which are more necessary than all the tears of devotion.

It sometimes happens that those who make so much of their devotion do not fulfill many of the duties to which they are obliged in justice. If they have not heard daily Mass or have not carried out all the practices of piety on their schedule, they feel they cannot eat or sleep, but they have no difficulty in sleeping when their closets are filled with costly garments and their coffers are crammed with idle money while so many poor go in want. They can sleep with a conscience that is filled with debts and frauds. They can sleep without having fulfilled their duties of state or their obligations to home and family. And if they have the opportunity of performing a good work, especially if there is labor connected with it, they refuse on the pretext that their hearts and minds will be too distracted and confused by such activities and that as a result they will not be recollected in their prayers. They do not realize that they are cutting off their head to save their foot when they prefer recollection of heart, which disposes for prayer, to obedience to the law of God, for which prayer itself is a disposition. Apparently, persons such as these have never heard or read the words of Christ: "Not every one that saith to Me, Lord, Lord, shall enter into the kingdom of heaven, but he that doth the will of My Father, who is in heaven, he shall enter into the kingdom of heaven." [2]

Devotion without the foundation of justice is one of the greatest deceptions in the life of prayer and is also one of the most common. It destroys the entire order of the spiritual life. The end of the spiritual life is perfect fulfillment of the law of God and prayer is one of the means of attaining this end, but if the end becomes a means and the means become an end, the whole order is reversed. Although it is found more in some than in others, few souls are completely free of it.

Another subtle deceit is to measure one's spiritual progress by the sentiments and feelings that he has for God rather than by the virtues he has acquired. Many people, when they shed a few tears or experience spiritual consolations, judge themselves to be better and more spiritual than others and sometimes even look down on others as carnal men who do not know how to taste and experience God. Such persons ought to consider that these consolations and

[2] Matt. 7:21.

feelings for God are not virtue itself but merely dispositions to virtue. They are like spurs to the rider, arms to the soldier, and books to the student. But of what value are spurs if the rider is slothful? What value are arms to a coward? What good are books to a student who never opens them?

Spiritual consolations may result from any one of three sources. They may come from the Holy Ghost, who uses them to wean us away from the things of the world and urge us to take up the life of virtue. Secondly, they may be the effect of the subject matter of one's meditation, as when certain philosophers are delighted by the contemplation of the beauty and construction of created things and through them rise to a consideration of God or when Christians contemplate the works of God in the order of grace or of nature and experience a great sweetness and consolation; or they may result from a tender disposition. In this second instance, persons should not deceive themselves into thinking that the measure of their charity is proportionate to the sweetness and consolation they experience, for a person has as much charity as he is willing to deny himself for God, and no more. As St. Gregory says, the love of God is never idle, but it works great things. If it ceases to work, it is not love. Thirdly, consolation may proceed from the evil spirit, who seeks to deceive the soul and make it think that it is better than it is, or to aggravate its errors, as sometimes happens with heretics who experience a great sweetness in reading the Bible and even possess a great knowledge of Scripture. Consolations of this sort make the soul more proud, less submissive to the advice of others, and sometimes incorrigible.

Whatever the source of spiritual consolations, a man has no reason to consider himself anything solely on that account. If they come from the Holy Ghost, he should fear the accounting that he will one day have to give of them. If they are the natural result of the subject matter of mental prayer, one should not exaggerate their value, for they are purely natural effects. If they proceed from the devil, a man has even more to fear, like the animal that approaches the trap of the hunter because it sees the bait but does not suspect a snare.

If we should not desire spiritual consolations for our own selfish delight, much less should we desire visions, raptures, revelations, and such things, for these are most frequent sources of deception on the part of the devil. Let no Christian feel that he is being disobedient to the Lord in this matter if he closes the door to such things, because when God wishes to reveal anything, He will find a way to do it that will leave no room for doubt as to its origin. Thus, God called Samuel three distinct times and then revealed what He desired of the boy.

It is also advisable to be silent about the gifts and favors that God imparts to the soul during prayer. St. Bernard insisted on this so strongly that he said the devout man should have written on the wall of his room: "My secret for me; my secret for me." St. Francis of Assisi was so reticent in these matters that not only did he not reveal to others the gifts that God had bestowed upon him, but he tried to dissimulate by words and actions so that no one could guess what had transpired during his periods of prayer.

Contrary to this, there are some who cannot contain themselves but emit the bubbles of devotion from their mouth. They make a great show of their piety by groans and sighs. They are like little children who, when they have received new clothes or a new pair of shoes, have to run immediately to show them to all their playmates. The more outward show, the more emptiness within. Others, under the guise of charity, immediately tell everything they have experienced of God, when they should be silent about their gifts lest they become vainglorious. They should be even more anxious to hide these things than they are to hide their faults. Therefore, we should be silent about all things that could serve as an occasion to vainglory. The Lord commanded this when He told His apostles to be silent about His transfiguration and other miracles.

The Christian should also be advised to address God in prayer with the utmost humility and reverence. "Serve ye the Lord with fear and rejoice unto Him with trembling." [3] This is indeed a strange thing that is asked of us: to mix joy with trembling and fear, yet both are necessary when we converse with a God of such goodness and majesty. And the more pure the soul is, the more agreeable will humility be to it. Nor should one fear that the fire of his love will be extinguished by fear, for when he considers the immensity of God's greatness and the abyss of his own vileness, he will marvel at the incomprehensible goodness that moves God to find delight in such a wretched creature. And as admiration increases at the divine goodness, love and joy and gratitude for such great benefits likewise increase, together with all the other fruits and inspirations of the Holy Ghost who dwells in such souls, as He signifies in Isaias: "To whom shall I have respect, but to him that is poor and little, and of a contrite spirit, and that trembleth at My words?" [4]

We have said that the pious Christian should always strive to have a set time for prayer each day. Now we say that in addition to the daily practice of prayer, a man should retire from time to time from his regular affairs of the world, even of holy tasks, in order to give himself entirely to prayer and meditation and give his soul the opportunity to be

[3] Ps. 2:11.   [4] Isa. 66:2.

spiritually nourished and to regain what has been lost through the defects of daily life. People of the world, in addition to the periods of respite at the end of each day's work, have their holidays and vacations when they take extended periods of rest and recreation. So the good Christian, in addition to his daily prayer, should set aside spiritual holidays and retreats when his soul will not feed on the customary spiritual fare, but will taste the sweetness of God and be rejoiced at the abundance of His Father's house. This is especially necessary in times of tribulation, after long journeys, or affairs of great anxiety and importance. It may happen that souls gain greater graces and gifts during such times than by the labor of many days.

But some people manifest so little discretion in their spiritual exercises that when all goes well between them and God their very prosperity becomes an occasion of danger. There are many who seem to think that God gives graces to those who already have their hands filled with gifts and they find conversation with God so sweet and agreeable and they spend such long hours in prayer and vigils that they fall through exhaustion. As a result, they become incapacitated, not only for manual labor, but even for the practice of prayer itself. Therefore, one must exercise great discretion and caution in these things, especially at the beginning of the spiritual life, when fervors and consolations are greater and prudence is weaker.

St. Bonaventure raises a question concerning those who are favored by God but find themselves failing in health and unable to persevere in these holy exercises. It would seem that they ought not close the door to God's grace and gifts nor resist His calls, but they must also consider their natural needs and the weakness of the body. St. Bonaventure answers that it is better to love and enjoy God for a longer period, although perhaps with less vehemence, than to enjoy a sudden deluge of His gifts and run the risk of growing cold and losing everything. After persons have lost their health, they frequently pity themselves excessively and begin to live delicately and even dissolutely. To avoid this and to continue one's progress to perfection, it is better to go from a little to the fullness of perfection than to start with the fullness and then decrease gradually to the point of nothingness.

The other extreme is found in those who are highly gifted by God and, under the guise of prudence, are always driving the body to work. This is dangerous for most people, but especially for beginners. It is not easy to determine which of the two extremes is worse, but Gerson says that indiscretion is more incurable, because if the body is strong there is still room for hope, but if the body is already exhausted by indiscretion, it will be difficult to find a cure.

Another danger in this matter, and perhaps greater than the preceding, is that many persons, after having experienced the inestimable power of prayer and having seen by experience how the whole spiritual life is dependent on it, conclude that prayer alone is everything and that prayer alone suffices. As a result, they gradually neglect the other virtues and become remiss in the other activities of the spiritual life. The more time and attention they give to prayer, the more they neglect everything else, and having too great a vigilance over their life of prayer, they leave everything else exposed to the enemy.

But since all the other virtues in one way or another aid the life of prayer, if the foundation is lacking, so also is the superstructure. The result is that although the soul spends much time in the practice of prayer, it actually attains very little through these practices, for it is certain that as the life of prayer disposes for mortification, so mortification and the other virtues likewise dispose for prayer, so that the one is never found without the other. Therefore, what kind of prayer can he have who does not observe custody of the heart, the tongue, the eyes, and the other senses, both interior and exterior? What manner of prayer will be found in him whose body is stuffed with food and whose mind is filled with the interests and cares of the world? Hence, he works in vain who strives to cultivate one virtue without the others, for they are so intimately connected that one cannot be had perfectly without the others, nor the others without the one.

If a man is careless in preserving custody of the heart in the beginning of the day and begins to think of some evil or useless matter, he cannot give himself to prayer as long as such thoughts reside in his mind. And since morning prayer sets the pattern for the entire day, if it has been omitted, the whole day may be upset and many faults may occur during it. Moreover, morning prayer disposes for evening prayer, and evening prayer for that of the following morning. But the greatest danger is that if a new tempest or distraction arises, the soul is not prepared for it. The origin of all this may have been the moment of carelessness when some evil or useless thought was admitted.

It is also fitting to remark here that what we have said concerning the helps to devotion and prayer should be understood as preparations by which man disposes himself for divine grace, putting all his confidence in God and not in self. I say this because there are some who consider these rules as mechanical devices, thinking that he who observes the rules of prayer will by that very fact attain what he desires. Such an attitude makes sanctifying grace purely mechanistic and artificial and attributes to human rules and regulations that which is a gift of the mercy of God. This error has been fostered to a great extent by certain spiritual books which are so insistent on rules and methods as to infer that by the rules alone, and not by grace, one can attain the life of perfect prayer. The writers of these books tell the Christian to follow a particular method and he will reach the perfect love of God. This is a bad method of instruction and far removed from that used by spiritual writers and the saints. It is likewise prejudicial to divine grace, because the art of prayer is a gift of God and therefore should not be treated simply as an art but as a grace. If prayer is understood as a gift of God, the Christian will realize that one of the principal means to attain true and perfect prayer is to dispose himself by profound humility and a knowledge of his own misery, trusting with great confidence in the divine mercy. If a man enters by the gate of humility, he will attain what he desires through humility and will not rely on himself alone nor on any method as such.

However, one should not neglect the counsels and directions concerning the practice of prayer, for although they who plant and water are not the ones who make the plant grow, God desires that men do their part so that He may give the increase. Therefore, while it is not proper to teach prayer as an art, it is necessary to give sufficient instruction so that the soul will not fall into error. Some persons make little progress in prayer even after many years; others spend a good part of the day reciting an endless series of prayers but they never stop for a moment to think of God or of the meaning of the words they recite. In both instances it is necessary to provide instruction so that their prayers will be more fruitful.

Moreover, while it is very helpful for beginners to follow a definite series of meditations, they should not confine themselves to any set method after they are proficient in prayer. Rather, they should let the Holy Ghost lead them where He will. Thus, some souls pass from meditation on the life of Christ to meditation on the divine perfections. Others find sufficient material for meditation in their own lives or in the lives of others. For if a man considers himself from the day of his birth until the present hour, he will find many things on which to meditate. Other souls are so advanced that God closes the channel of speculation and opens that of the affections so that the intellect remains at rest and the will delights in God and spends all it's love on Him. This is the lofty state of contemplation for which we should all yearn. There the soul is no longer on the road to perfect prayer but it has reached the end of the journey. No longer does it seek incentives to love through meditation, but it delights in the love that has been found, saying with the spouse in the Canticle: "I found Him whom my soul loveth. I held Him and I will not let Him go." [5]

Although it is profitable for beginners to follow some sequence of meditation, we should mention that a plan or schedule of meditations is not always possible nor is it suitable for all classes of people. Those who are ill, especially if they have some sickness that affects the nervous system or brain, cannot give themselves to meditation without injury to their health. Those who are already advanced in the practice of prayer will find less difficulty or harm in continuing this practice even should they fall ill. Others are so occupied with obligations and duties which cannot be neglected under pain of sin that they cannot spend much time or a regular period at meditation. Still others are so restless in mind, so lacking in devotion, or so arid of spirit that no matter how hard they try, they seem to gain nothing

[5] Cant. 3:4.

from meditation. These people should not immediately give up the struggle but should keep knocking at the door of Him who never fails to answer those who persevere with humility. And even if the door remains closed, let them not become discouraged, but realize that mental prayer is a gift of the Holy Ghost and if He does not give it to them, they should content themselves with prayers such as the Rosary or the Stations of the Cross and little by little they can introduce short meditations on the life of Christ. It will also be helpful for them to read pious books, if they read them slowly and with great attention and pause from time to time to raise their hearts and minds to God. This is one of the best remedies for persons who find themselves lacking in devotion and it is the way in which the Lord frequently opens the door to true mental prayer.

Some persons spend most of their time thinking of their sins, not daring to dwell on the life of Christ or any other truth that would give them joy and strength. To them we say that there is no reason for the Christian to be so sad and discouraged. There are others who forget their past sins entirely and want to ascend immediately to the most lofty thoughts. They are certain to fall, like a building without foundations. Later, if they wish to think of more humble things, they cannot, because they are already satiated with more tasty meditations. Therefore, it is better at the beginning to occupy oneself with thoughts of one's sins and then gradually ascend to loftier thoughts. But if some souls find no devotion in any of the things we have mentioned and feel that they would gain more by meditating on something else, let them enter into prayer by the door that they find opened to them, because that is the way God wishes them to enter.

CHAPTER 40 ✍

The External Acts of Religion

IN accordance with the command of God, which stated that they were not to make any images of sacred things, the Jews never permitted images or idols in their homes or temples. The Christians, however, have always made use of images of various kinds, although they were frequently accused of idolatry for this practice. The truth of the matter is that Christianity is far from such a sin. Think of the countless martyrs who gave their lives rather than worship idols or even touch food that had been sacrificed to idols. We use images in order to arouse devotion through the memory of the saints and the representation of the sacred mysteries. Who does not experience devotion when he looks at pictures of the birth of Christ, His glorious resurrection, His agony in the Garden, His scourging and crowning with thorns, the carrying of the cross, or His crucifixion?

Moreover, reverence is not directed to the image as such, but it passes beyond the image to the person or mystery that is represented. The same is true of the courtesy and respect shown to the representatives of kings and rulers; it is not directed to the individual as such but to him whom the ambassador represents. So also, we adore the Cross as the symbol of our redemption and our adoration is directed to the Lord who used it as an instrument of our redemption. Even in human affairs it is customary to attribute to an instrument the effect of the principal cause, as when we say: "This is the sword that conquered Seville."

If God forbade the Jews to have any images, it is because

the world at the time was infected with the adoration of demons through statues and other images. Moreover, the Jews were especially inclined to idolatry and God, as a most wise Legislator, tried to rid them of this occasion of sin. But now that we are so far removed from those times, what dangers is there in images?

From what we have said, it is evident that it is merely a question of defaming our holy religion when persons accuse us of idolatry because we make use of images. We would rather die a thousand times than commit such a sin. Therefore, those who desire to know the truth of the matter, should not believe these false accusations but should ask the teachers and masters of our religion for an explanation.

Another point that deserves consideration under the external acts of religion is that of taking the name of God in vain. This may be done in various ways or for various reasons, such as to use it in a loose fashion, to use it to testify to a lie, or to use it irreverently and in matters of no importance. God is supreme truth, and from Him come all our blessings. And since there is nothing in the universe in which we can have such hope and confidence, the name of God should not be used by men except to give thanks to Him, to make petitions to Him, to lead men to a knowledge of Him, to give testimony to others that we are speaking the truth, or to show by our words the esteem we have for God in our hearts.

One of the gravest sins regarding the use of God's name is to use it in swearing to a lie, for this is directly against God. In itself, it is much more grave than any sin we could commit against our neighbor. This is true not only when we take an oath in God's name, but also if we swear by the Cross, on the Bible, or in the name of some saint. If any of these oaths are in defense of a lie, it is a mortal sin, but a man may be excused from mortal sin if there was no full deliberation.

But this does not apply to those who have the habit of swearing and do not try to overcome it. They cannot excuse themselves by saying that they did not think of what they were doing, because if a man wills to have a bad habit, he also wills whatever proceeds from that habit. Therefore, one should strive as much as possible to rid himself of this evil habit and when he takes God's name in vain, let him say a prayer or give an alms to the poor, not only as a penance, but also as a reminder to be more careful in the future lest he fall again.

But the worst of all the sins against the name of God is that of blasphemy, a sin very similar to infidelity, despair, and hatred of God. It seems that if the man who blasphemes could do so, he would at that moment kill God. For that reason, St. Augustine states that they who blaspheme Christ do no less to Him now that He reigns in heaven than they would have done when He was on earth. They would have crucified Him.

A third consideration in regard to the external acts of religion is the observance of Sunday, which is set aside so that the faithful will attend church and assist at the ceremonies for the adoration and worship of God. On such occasions the faithful manifest their obedience to God and the Church and stimulate others by their holy example. God has not only told us to honor and adore Him internally, but that we are to observe certain public rites and ceremonies whereby the faithful as a body can make a manifestation of faith.

It is also necessary to observe that servile work is forbidden on Sunday. God did not forbid manual labor on Sunday because labor is evil, but in order that man might be free to observe the holy day. Man is in this world as an exile and he must live by the labor of his hands, but he also needs certain days which he can devote to God. If a man is always employed in earning a livelihood and is always thinking in terms of the body and those things that pertain to this life, he can very easily forget God and his spiritual life. Therefore, he needs certain days on which he can leave his worldly affairs and labors and dedicate a day to the God who made him and sustains him in this life and has promised him eternal blessings.

The Lord wishes us to dedicate the entire Sunday to Him as we have dedicated the other six days of the week to ourselves. He wishes us to glorify Him with hymns and canticles, to do penance for our sins, especially those committed during the past week, to devote ourselves more ardently to prayer, to receive Communion, to give thanks to Him for blessings received, to be especially vigilant in matters of chastity and temperance, to visit and console the sick, to engage in edifying conversations, to teach Christian doctrine to our family, or to occupy ourselves in one or another of the works of charity or piety. This is true sanctification of Sunday. In a word, we should comport ourselves so that there will be nothing in that day that is not good and holy. Otherwise, how can we say that the sabbath is more holy than any other day?

Those who do manual or mechanical work on Sunday or command others to do so without any necessity, but solely for gain, sin against the precept which obliges us to sanctify the sabbath day. If, however, there is necessity, then it is lawful to work on Sunday. In like manner, any work of charity that is performed for our neighbor is also permitted because this precept yields to charity. This is exemplified in the life of Christ when He explained to the Jews what works could be done on the sabbath.[1] But apart from these cases, it is a mortal sin if a man does manual work on Sunday. He not only breaks the Commandment, but he scandalizes others who see him do it.

There are also other ways in which the Sunday observance is broken. Those who, although they refrain from manual labor, do nothing by way of prayer or religious observance and spend the whole day in idleness, or games, or recreation. They are like those Jews who abstained from all work on the sabbath but ate more delicately and did nothing at all toward the glory of God and the betterment of their own souls. It would be better for them not to have a sabbath at all, but to work as on every other day.

But they especially break the Sunday observance who spend the day in banquets, card-playing, drunkenness, dances, and other such things. This is one of the most lamentable things in Christendom: to observe the manner in which Sunday is kept, especially when certain persons put Sunday aside as the day for their carousing and the other evil deeds that they do not have time to commit on other days. As a result, the day which has been set aside by God as the day of prayer and holy works has become for them a day of evil and sin. The day that was meant to be a holy day becomes the one on which more sins are committed than on any other day of the week.

What can we expect from people such as this? What can be expected of a man who takes the day assigned for the service of God and spends it in the service of the devil? God has given you six days of the week for yourself and has reserved but one day for Himself. You not only refuse to give Him this day, but you offer your service to God's greatest enemy. With what kind of a face shall you stand before God

[1] Matt. 12:10–13.

on judgment day? Where, He will ask you, are the gods that you served? Turn to them now and let them help you in the time of your tribulation.

CHAPTER 41 ✍

Obedience to God

THERE are three degrees of obedience to God: obedience to His commandments, obedience to His counsels, and obedience to His inspirations. The first is necessary for salvation; the second is a great help to the observance of the Commandments because it rids the Christian of many obstacles and is a wall of defense for the Commandments. Therefore, he who wishes to be secure in the observance of God's precepts, should, according to his state in life, strive to observe the counsels.

He who wishes to cross the raging current of a river does not attempt to walk straight across the stream, but walks upstream against the current and gradually works his way to the opposite shore. So also, the servant of God will not keep his eyes merely on that which is sufficient for salvation but will try to aim higher, for if he does not succeed perfectly, at least he will be more sure of doing that which is required for salvation.

The third grade of obedience is to follow divine inspirations. The good servants of the Lord not only obey His words, but whatever He manifests to them by signs. But there is always great danger of error in these things and for that reason we should keep in mind the warning of St.

John: "Believe not every spirit, but try the spirits if they be of God." [1] In addition to testing these things by the teaching of Scripture and the saints, it is well to observe this general rule: When there is a choice of performing an action that is purely voluntary or one that is of obligation, that which is of obligation must always take precedence, however excellent and meritorious the purely voluntary act may be. This is the way in which we are to understand the statement of Samuel: "Obedience is better than sacrifices," [2] for God wishes man to obey His word and then he may do what he pleases, as long as it is not against obedience. By works that are of obligation we understand in the first place the observance of the Commandments of God, without which there is no salvation; secondly, obedience to the precepts of those who stand in the place of God, because he who resists these superiors, resists God; thirdly, the observance of those things that pertain to the duties of one's state in life, for example, the duties of the prelate, a religious, or a married person; fourthly, the performance of those works which are not absolutely necessary but assist in the observance of necessary things and thus share to a certain extent in the obligation of the others.

An example will make the matter clear. If a man takes time each day to examine his conscience, he will have a better picture of his life and will be better able to master himself and will be more apt for the works of virtue. On the other hand, if he neglects the daily examination, he soon begins to fall into many imperfections and runs the danger of losing his former good habits. From this he should understand that God calls him to the practice of daily examination because such a practice is helpful to him and without it he becomes worse. This is not to be taken as a precept but as

[1] Cf. I John 4:1. [2] Cf. I Kings 15:22.

something very helpful for him in fulfilling his Christian vocation.

Likewise, if you are a person who always seeks comforts and luxuries and are your own best friend but an enemy of any kind of effort; if you recognize that this prevents you from making spiritual progress by causing you to neglect many virtuous actions because they involve labor; if you fall into many faults because they are delightful, then understand that the Lord is calling you to austerity and mortification of your body as well as the denial of your tastes and appetites. In like manner, you can judge all the activities of your life that are profitable to you and the lack of which cause you spiritual harm. Understand that the Lord is calling you to the observance of the former, though in this as in all other things you should follow the counsel of those who are more experienced. In other words, in making a selection of good works or spiritual practices, a Christian need not always fix his eyes on that which is best in itself, but on that which is best for himself. Many works are excellent, but they are not necessarily the best for you, because you may not have the strength to do them or are not called to do them. Therefore, let each person stay within his calling; let him know himself and seek those things that will be best for him, and not reach forth to that which surpasses his strength. "Lift not up thy eyes to riches which thou canst not have, because they shall make themselves wings like those of an eagle and shall fly toward heaven." [3] Those who do otherwise will merit the reprimand: "You have sown much and brought in little." [4]

Such is the rule that should be observed in regard to voluntary works and those that are of obligation, but we should further observe that some voluntary works may be

[3] Prov. 23:5.   [4] Agg. 1:6.

secret and others public; some may bring honor or delight, and others not. Therefore, if you do not wish to err in these things, you should strive always to be more cautious regarding works which are public than those which are secret, or those which bring honor or delight than those which do not. The reason for this is that self-love is very subtle and is always seeking its own advantage, even in the most holy and noble actions. As a religious once said: "Do you want to know where God is? Where you are not." In other words, that is more surely the work of God where there is no self-interest, because then it is evident that one is not seeking anything but God. I do not say these things so that you will follow this principle in every case, because it may happen that there is more merit in following the other course or a greater obligation to do so in spite of these dangers. I mention this primarily to warn against the snares of self-love so that a man will not always trust it, even if it appears under the guise of virtue.

To these three grades of obedience we can add another which is the most perfect possible conformity to the will of God in all that He ordains in our regard, striving to keep our hearts indifferent to honor or dishonor, good reputation or infamy, health or sickness, life or death. In this fourth degree of obedience one humbly bows his head to all that God decrees, accepting rewards as well as punishments, favors as well as injuries, not looking at what is given, but considering Him who gives and the love with which He gives, for the Father loves His child no less when He chastises Him than when He gives him presents.

He who has reached this fourth degree of obedience will have attained that resignation which is so highly praised by all the masters of the spiritual life. It places a man so definitively in the hands of God that he becomes like a piece of soft clay in the hands of an artist. It is called resignation because the perfect Christian gives himself so completely to God that he no longer wishes to be his own nor to live for himself, but to do all things for the glory of God. He conforms to the most holy will of God in all things and accepts with equanimity all the labors and chastisements that may come to him. He dispossesses himself of self and self-will in order to fulfill perfectly the will of Him whose slave he wishes to be.

Thus, we read of David's resignation to the will of God: "I am become as a beast before Thee and I am always with Thee." [5] And Isaias referred to this when he said: "The Lord God hath opened my ear and I do not resist; I have not gone back." [6] For this perfect obedience one needs not only promptness of will, but also prudence and discretion so that he will not be deceived into doing his own will under the name of God's will. As a general rule, whatever is conformable to our tastes and desires, we should regard with suspicion; whatever is contrary to our desires and inclinations, we may accept without fear.

Obedience is the greatest sacrifice that God exacts of man and the greatest gift that man can give to God, because in this he gives himself. St. Augustine says that it is not for all to say: "I am Thine, Lord," but only for those who have despoiled themselves of self and have abandoned themselves completely to the service of God. This is by far the best preparation for reaching the full perfection of the Christian life, for if man does not resist God but surrenders himself completely, God can easily effect in him all that He desires and can make of him a man after His own heart.

[5] Ps. 72:23.   [6] Isa. 50:5.

CHAPTER 42 🖋

Obedience to Parents and Superiors

WE are obliged to manifest a special reverence for our parents and to strive to repay them for all that they have done for us. They have brought us into the world and, after God, they have given us our very being. They have provided for our needs and have trained us, while they have patiently endured our inconstancy and ignorance and misbehavior. All this is sufficient reason why they should receive from us as great a repayment as we can make for all that they have done for us.

Therefore, we should love them as they have loved us; we should be as solicitous for them as they have been for us. As they have provided for our needs, we should do likewise for them when we are able, and we should ever keep in mind the great love and patience with which they have suffered for us. There is no effort or hardship that their poverty, sickness, or old age can cause us that could ever equal the debt we owe them.

If even the animals show this love for their parents, with what greater reason should human beings do this, especially since God Himself has commanded that this be done. "Honor thy father and forget not the groanings of thy mother. Remember that thou hadst not been born but through them and make a return to them as they have done for thee." [1] Likewise, Tobias admonished his son: "Honor

---

[1] Ecclus. 7:29–30.

thy mother all the days of her life, for thou must be mindful what and how great perils she suffered for thee in her womb." [2] Again, we read in Ecclesiasticus: "Son, support the old age of thy father and grieve him not in this life; and if his understanding fail, have patience with him and despise him not when thou art in thy strength, for the relieving of the father shall not be forgotten." [3]

On the other hand, parents should be mindful of their obligations to their children and the care they should take of them. Let them love their children with all their heart; let them be careful in training them; let them watch over them in the fear of the Lord; let them teach them good manners and habits; and let them treat them with tenderness. St. Paul says: "Fathers, provoke not your children to anger, but bring them up in the discipline and correction of the Lord." [4] Ecclesiasticus says on this same subject: "He that loveth his son frequently chastiseth him, that he may rejoice in his latter end and not grope after the doors of his neighbors. He that instructeth his son shall be praised in him and shall glory in him in the midst of them of his household." [5]

From what has been said it is evident how reprehensible those parents are who, through an indiscreet tenderness, do not correct or punish their children but let them become vitiated by laxity and evil habits. What greater cruelty than to see your own child drowning in a river and rather than pull him out by the hair and cause him pain, you would let him drown? Those parents are no less cruel who, because they are unwilling to correct or punish their children, let them drown in a sea of vices. I do not know the words by which I could fittingly condemn this carelessness. Even the

[2] Tob. 4:3–4.   [3] Ecclus. 3:14–15.   [4] Eph. 6:4.
[5] Ecclus. 30:1–2.

rich man in hell, who was condemned for his avarice, thought of his brothers yet on earth and begged Lazarus to go to them and warn them lest they, too, should be punished in the flames of hell. But if a condemned man had such care for his own, how will they be confounded who on earth do not do as much for their own children? However, the punishment of one's children should be done with discretion and mildness, seeking the proper time and occasion to correct their faults. This should never be done in the heat of anger, but always when one is in control of reason. Above all, parents should see to it that their children are protected against evil companions, excessive recreation, and idleness, which is the scourge of youth, and teach them from their earliest years to fear God, to break their self-will, to abhor lying, not to use the name of God loosely, and not to be gluttonous in eating. One of the best ways of training children in these matters is for the parents themselves to take care that the children see nothing in their own lives that the children are not supposed to do. For children are great imitators, and the actions of their parents are almost a law to the children.

Moreover, let parents provide good teachers and instructors for their children and let them introduce their children at an early age to honest and profitable studies. Let them teach the children how to pray and to be attentive in church and to assist at Mass and other services with recollection and devotion as well as to confess their sins at frequent intervals.

Parents should never treat their children too delicately or fondly nor let them do just as they please, for this is one of the easiest ways to make the child indomitable, self-willed, and sensual. And let parents not lose the splendid opportunity afforded by nature itself for training children well by teaching and correcting and punishing during their tender years, for if the childhood and early youth are not utilized, it is likely that the parents will never succeed in training their children properly. All things have their proper time and season, times when the best can be accomplished, but when that time is past, any efforts that are expended will be wasted and fruitless. The farmer selects the proper time for ploughing and sowing, the fisherman, the proper time for making a good catch. Neither should parents fail to use the time of their children's youth, which is a most propitious time for training them.

The name of father is also given to prelates and priests and all who have the care of souls, and we should therefore mention something of the obligations we have toward such persons. I do not think that anyone would be so ignorant or shameless that he would not recognize his obligation to respect priests and bishops, because if we owe great reverence to our parents, who have generated our bodies, we likewise are indebted to those who nourish our souls with sound doctrine and the administration of the sacraments. St. Paul writes to Timothy: "Let the priests that rule well be esteemed worthy of double honor, especially they who labor in the word and doctrine." [6] And how should reverence be shown to the clergy? We should hold them in high esteem, considering them worthy of the greatest respect; we should love them wholeheartedly and accept their warnings and corrections; and we should contribute toward their sustenance. St. Paul commands this many times: "We beseech you, brethren, to know them who labor among you and are over you in the Lord and admonish you; that you

[6] Cf. I Tim. 5:17.

esteem them more abundantly in charity for their work's sake." [7] "Remember your prelates who have spoken the word of God to you." [8]

On the other hand, the pastors of souls are obliged to exercise great diligence and care over the flock committed to them and to nourish them with sound doctrine and the example of a holy life. St. Paul admonishes: "Take heed to yourselves and to the whole flock wherein the Holy Ghost has placed you . . . to rule the Church of God which He hath purchased with His own blood." [9] And St. Peter writes: "Feed the flock of God which is among you, taking care of it, not by constraint, but willingly, according to God; not for filthy lucre's sake, but voluntarily; . . . being made a pattern of the flock from the heart." [10]

Teachers and masters also share in the duties and cares of parents, for as the parents engender the bodies of their children and the priests provide for their souls, teachers instruct them in various subjects and form good habits in them, especially during their early years. Therefore, children owe a special reverence and respect to their teachers and they should obey them and be grateful for all that they receive from them. At the same time, teachers should take care that they perform their office diligently, that they punish students who are vicious or do evil, that they protect the innocent and weak, and that they take special care not to engender the wrong judgments in these tender minds. Those who are responsible for the hiring of teachers should see to it that they receive a just and fitting salary.

Now we shall say something about the mutual obligations between servants and masters. Servants should love their masters and work for their prosperity. They are to

[7] Cf. I Thess. 5:12–13.   [8] Heb. 13:7.   [9] Acts 20:28.
[10] Cf. I Pet. 5:2.

obey them in all that pertains to their employment and cheerfully fulfill the commands that are given. Moreover, they should come to the aid of their masters in any way that is necessary, whether it be a question of safeguarding their temporal possessions or protecting their good name.

On the other hand, employers should be kind to their servants and employees, provide them with the necessities of life, and pay them a just wage. "If thou have a faithful servant, let him be to thee as thy own soul; treat him as a brother." [11] "Masters, do to your servants that which is just and equal, knowing that you also have a Master in heaven." [12]

All that we have said concerning the obligations of reverence applies also to the aged, for they should be respected by the young. In the first place, we should show them the ordinary marks of courtesy and politeness that are shown to any person of dignity and authority, and we should willingly and humbly seek and accept their counsel and admonitions. Thus, we read in Scripture: "Despise not a man in his old age, for we also shall become old. . . . Despise not the discourse of them that are ancient and wise, but acquaint thyself with their proverbs, for of them thou shalt learn wisdom and instruction of understanding." [13]

Yet, old people should so live and conduct themselves that they are not deserving of rebuke or ridicule when compared with the young. Piety and honesty should be especially manifested in them, both in their words and in their actions. Hence, St. Paul admonishes the aged to be sober, chaste, prudent, sound in faith and love and patience.[14]

[11] Ecclus. 33:31. [12] Col. 4:1. [13] Ecclus. 8:7–10.
[14] Titus 2:2.

CHAPTER 43

Fortitude

THERE are two outstanding difficulties in the acquisition of virtue: distinguishing good and evil and overcoming the latter to attain the former. The one requires great attention and the other demands great fortitude. Whenever either of these elements is lacking, virtue remains imperfect and the effort to attain it is to some extent ineffectual.

The fortitude of which we speak is not the particular virtue which suppresses cowardice and fear, but that general virtue by which the Christian overcomes the difficulties that prevent the practice of the various virtues. Therefore, the spirit of fortitude will accompany the other virtues to clear the way of all difficulties and impediments.

Virtue, as the philosophers tell us, is something difficult, and for that reason true virtue must always call upon fortitude to assist in overcoming difficulties. Fortitude is the spiritual hammer which overcomes the resistance to the acquisition of virtue, and the Christian can do as little without fortitude as a blacksmith without his hammer.

Whether it be a question of fasting, prayer, temperance, obedience, humility, or any other virtue, one always encounters difficulties in the practice of a given virtue because of self-love, temptations from others, the allurements of the world, or for some other reason. If fortitude is lacking, what can one accomplish, even if he has the greatest love and esteem for virtue? He will be as helpless as if he were bound hand and foot. Therefore, if you desire to advance in virtue, be mindful of what God said to Moses: "Take this rod in thy hand, wherewith thou shalt do the signs." [1] That is to say, by the rod of fortitude you can overcome all difficulties which the enemy or the love of your own flesh shall put in your way and will enable you to emerge victorious in this glorious enterprise.

It is necessary to mention here a great deception that often befalls those who begin to serve God. Sometimes they read in spiritual books how great are the consolations of the Holy Ghost and how sweet charity is and they think that the whole path to perfection is filled with delights and that there is no effort or fatigue involved. As a result, they prepare themselves for it as for something easy and pleasant and do not arm themselves for entering battle. They do not realize that while the love of God is in itself very sweet and delectable, the way to perfect charity is arduous, because to attain it, one must completely conquer self-love, and this involves a constant struggle against self. Thus, Isaias says: "Shake thyself from the dust; arise, sit up, O Jerusalem." [2] In other words, the soul must shake off the dust of worldly affections and attachments and arise from its sins before it can enjoy the pleasure of seating itself in charity. However, God bestows marvelous consolations on those who faithfully struggle and on all those who trade the delights of earth for the joys of heaven. But if this barter is not made and a man does not want to surrender his spoils, this celestial refreshment will not be given to him. For we know that the heavenly manna was not given to the children of Israel until they had finished the grain that they had brought with them out of Egypt. [3]

Those who do not fortify themselves with courage are incapable of attaining what they seek and until they are

[1] Exod. 4:17.   [2] Isa. 52:2.   [3] Exod., chap. 16.

properly armed they will never find it. They should understand that rest is won only with effort, the crown is gained only after the battle, joy follows tears, and the most sweet love of God is gained only when one spiritually hates himself. That is why Scripture so often condemns and severely censures sloth and indifference and praises fortitude so highly, because the Holy Ghost knows what a great impediment the one is to virtue and what a great help the other is.

But you may ask what means are to be used in order to acquire the virtue of fortitude, since it will surely be as difficult to attain as any of the other virtues. The first step is to consider the value of fortitude, for surely it must be of great worth if it helps us to attain the inestimable treasure of the other virtues. If you do not believe this, then tell me why worldly men flee so much from virtue. It is for no other reason than the difficulties and labors involved, so that the slothful man says: "Better is a handful with rest than both hands full with labor and vexation of mind." [4] But if one has the fortitude to overcome sloth, the whole kingdom of the virtues is won. The kingdom of heaven is won only by the courageous. Moreover, fortitude conquers self-love, and when self-love is vanquished, the love of God reigns in its stead. "He that abideth in charity, abideth in God and God in him." [5]

The acquisition of fortitude is also aided by the example of the servants of God who live in poverty, hunger, sickness, or who endure voluntary mortifications. Some of them love hardship and asceticism so dearly that they search out the monasteries of greatest rigor, seeking hunger, poverty, and the cross and abnegation. And what is more contrary to the desires of the world and the delights of the sensate

[4] Ecclus. 4:6.　　　　　[5] Cf. I John 4:16.

man? Such a life is a contradiction to flesh and blood but it is in complete accord with the spirit of the Lord.

More particularly, the example of the martyrs is a condemnation of our comfort and luxury. Think of the sufferings and torments through which they won the kingdom of heaven. Scarcely a day passes that the Church does not propose to us in the martyrology the example of these martyrs. Each day there is read to us the account of some servant of God who suffered death by fire, by drowning, by torture, by being beheaded or strangled, by being dismembered, shot with arrows, stoned, or suffered death in some other cruel and terrifying manner. And though any one of these things is more than human endurance can stand, some of the martyrs were miraculously kept alive so that they could endure even greater torments before their death.

Yet, the martyrs had bodies no different from our own. The same God was their helper as He is ours, and they sought no other glory or reward than the one that has been promised to us. If they could endure so much for the love of God, how is it that we do not for the same love mortify our evil desires? If they died of starvation, can we not fast for one day? If they persevered amidst excruciating suffering, shall we not spend one hour on our knees in prayer? If they willingly submitted their bodies to be dismembered and tortured, shall we not restrain our passions and base instincts? If they spent weeks and months in dark prisons, shall we not spend a little time each day in the solitude of our chamber? If they accepted the pain of the scourge on their shoulders, shall we not discipline ourselves to carry the cross that God has placed on our shoulders?

If these holy examples do not suffice to awaken in you a

desire to strive for Christian fortitude, lift your eyes to
the holy wood of the Cross and see who it is that there endures the cruel torments of love. "Think diligently on
Him," says St. Paul, "that endured such opposition from
sinners against Himself, that you be not wearied, faint-
ing in your minds. For you have not yet resisted unto
blood, striving against sin." [6] The example of Christ crucified is a terrifying example no matter from what aspect
we consider it. If we think of the labors, there were none
greater; if we consider the Person who suffers, there could
be none more noble; if we think of the cause for which He
suffered, it was not for any fault of His own, for He was innocent, nor was it for any necessity of His, for He is the
Lord of all creation. He suffered purely out of goodness
and love. His body and soul suffered such torments that all
the sufferings of the martyrs and of all the men of the world
could never equal His suffering. This was a suffering that
caused astonishment in heaven and made the earth quake.
How can a man be so insensible that he does not react to
that to which inanimate creation reacted? Christ Himself said that it was fitting that He suffer these things, because He came into the world to lead us to heaven. But the
way of Christ is the way of the Cross and He has led the way
so that we would have heart from His example to follow
His footsteps.

Who will be such an ingrate and such a lover of his own
ease that when he sees the Lord and His faithful followers
pursuing the way of the Cross, he would spend his life enjoying luxury and ease? When David told Urias to rest in
his own home after returning from the wars, the holy captain replied: "The ark of God in Israel and Juda dwells
in tents, and my lord Joab and the servants of my lord abide

[6] Heb. 12:3-4.

upon the face of the earth, and shall I go into my house to eat and to drink and to sleep with my wife? By thy welfare and by the welfare of my soul, I will not do this thing." [7] Why do not you have the same compassion for Christ when you see Him suffering on the cross? The Ark of God endures passion and death, and do you seek comfort and rest? He who is the manna of angels, tasted vinegar and gall for your sake, and will you run after sensual pleasures and delights of the palate? He in whom are all the treasures of wisdom and knowledge is reviled and taken for a fool, and will you seek the honor and praise of men?

If such was the life of the saints and of Him who is the Saint of saints, I do not know by what right or title any Christian can claim the privilege of reaching the same goal as they did by traveling along the path of pleasure and comfort. Therefore, if you wish to be a companion of the saints in glory, you must also be their companion in hardship and suffering; if you wish to reign with them, you must first suffer with them. Above all, remember the inspiring words of Christ: "If any man will come after Me, let him deny himself and take up his cross daily and follow Me." [8]

[7] Cf. II Kings 11:11.   [8] Luke 9:23.

CHAPTER 44 🖋

Martyrdom

NO man could be so insensible as not to be moved by the examples of martyrdom that we have mentioned. When since the beginning of time have persons suffered with such fortitude and joy? If these things had taken place in a savage country where the people do not have so great a fear of death, it would not be so unusual, but the persecution of the Christians has been carried on in all the nations and cities of the world, especially in such centers as Rome, Alexandria, and Antioch. Moreover, if all the martyrs had been robust men, there would be less reason for astonishment, but old men, young boys and girls, delicate women, and persons from every walk of life and every profession offered their bodies to the persecutors.

Aristotle says that the worst of all terrors is death, which all animals naturally fear and abhor. But man especially fears death because his flesh is much more delicate and his imagination more vivid for picturing the agony of pain and the loss of life. If a man has been sentenced to death, there is no labor or danger that he will not face in order to escape it, even if it means abandoning home and wife and children, for self-preservation is one of the strongest instincts of nature. But there is something even more fearful than death, and it is the torments that various persecutors invented to overcome the constancy of the martyrs. They did not intend to kill, but to torture, and in so doing, they killed the Christians not once, but many times, and they tormented not one member of the body, but all the members. It takes but the slightest discomfort to cause pain to the body, but the persecutors, enraged at seeing themselves withstood by women and children, used all their ingenuity to find ways and means of inflicting the greatest possible torture.

Is it not to be marveled at that women and young maidens should have hastened to their torture as if to a wedding feast and that they should even have vied with one another to be the first to fall under the sword? St. Euphemia complained that whereas she was of noble birth, others were martyred before her. What has become of the law of nature? Where is the power of self-love? Where is the natural fear of death that is common to all living things? Were not these bodies of the same constitution as our own? Were they not as delicate and sensitive as ours?

What did you see, O glorious martyr, when amidst your sufferings you vanquished suffering, when in prison you were more free than those who had imprisoned you, when in chains you were less bound than your captors, and when judged you were above those who had sentenced you? You looked upon your wounds as flowers, your blood as the royal purple, and your martyrdom as a most pleasing sacrifice that you offered to God.

And you, delicate virgin, who has armed you with such fortitude that you are stronger than steel? Your body dismembered, you remain intact; your flesh consumed, your virtue remains untouched. Your body was torn, but your soul was never vanquished.

How is it possible that so admirable a deed as martyrdom should not be the result of some special cause? An act so far above the laws of nature must have a supernatural cause, for the philosophers tell us that effects must have causes proportionate to themselves. How was it possible for St. Eulalia, a thirteen-year old girl, to suffer a variety of torments with such joy if she had not been the recipient of special help from the Holy Ghost? How could a mother like St. Felicitas see her own children martyred before her eyes and all the time encourage them to suffer and then to accept martyrdom herself? Where was the love of a mother for her children? If God was so pleased with Abraham's willingness to sacrifice his only son, what must have been His divine pleasure with a mother who gladly sacrificed her seven children? And if the mother of the seven Machabees was so highly praised for the sacrifice of her sons, does this woman of the New Testament merit any less praise? And how could either of these mothers have performed so heroic an act without the special help of God? What bravery can compare with the constancy and fortitude manifested by so many mothers and maidens who have died for Christ?

What greater heights than martyrdom could human nature attain? How could a creature of flesh and blood better prove its faith, obedience, and love? What sacrifice is more acceptable to God? Let the heavens and earth be silent; let the splendor of the sun and moon and stars be still; let the angels cease their praise of God in comparison with the glory that the martyrs give to God. For what do these others do but recognize God as their Creator, without having a rebellious flesh that draws them away from their sacred duty? And although the goodness and beauty of the Creator is more perfectly manifested in the angels, this is a pure gift of God, but the martyrs, under the influence of grace, freely laid down their lives for God.

CHAPTER 45 ✍

Patience

SOLOMON invites us to the practice of patience when he says: "My son, reject not the correction of the Lord, and do not faint when thou art chastised by Him, for whom the Lord loveth, He chastiseth, and as a father in the son He pleaseth Himself." [1] St. Paul develops this teaching at length in his Epistle to the Hebrews: "Persevere under discipline. God dealeth with you as with His sons. For what son is there whom the father does not correct? But if you be without chastisement, whereas all are made partakers, then you are sons of another father, but not of God. Moreover, we have had fathers of our flesh for instructors and we reverenced them. Shall we not much more obey the Father of spirits that we may live?" [2]

These words clearly demonstrate that it is part of the office and duty of fathers to correct and chastise their children and it is the duty of children humbly to bow their heads and accept the chastisement as a great blessing and a sign of the love of the paternal heart. The only Son of God taught us this lesson when St. Peter tried to prevent His arrest: "The chalice which My Father hath given Me, shall I not drink it?" [3] It is as if Jesus had said: "If this chalice had come from another hand, there would be reason to refuse it, but since it comes from the hand of My Father, why shall I not drink it, without wanting to know anything more than that it comes from Him?"

In times of peace some souls think they are perfectly sub-

[1] Prov. 3:11–12.　　[2] Heb. 12:7–9.　　[3] John 18:11.

missive to the heavenly Father and conformable to His will, but in time of adversity they prove how deceptive was their conformity and submission, because it failed them when it was most needed. Such is the case with those who are weak and cowardly. In times of peace they show great spirit, but when the time of battle draws nigh, they lose their courage.

It will be helpful to realize that all the labors of this life do not begin to compare with the glory that can be won through them. So great is the joy of heaven that if we were able to taste of it for but an hour, we would gladly embrace all the labors of the world and reject all its delights in order to possess it. St. Paul tells us that present tribulation is light and momentary, but it works for us an eternal weight of glory.[4]

Consider also that when things prosper with you, they frequently smother the soul with pride, while adversities purify the soul with sorrow. In prosperity your heart is lifted up, but in adversity the heart is made truly humble; in prosperity the soul is interested only in self, but in adversity it becomes mindful of God; in prosperity good works are often neglected, but in adversity the sins of many years are atoned for and the soul is preserved from further falls. If sickness befalls you, believe that the Lord knows the evils you would commit if you were in good health and therefore He makes you incapable of doing those things. It is much better to be broken by bodily suffering than to remain healthy in iniquity. Jesus has said that it is better to enter eternal life lame or crippled than to be cast into eternal fire sound of body and with all one's limbs intact.

Our merciful Lord does not delight in sending us tor-

[4] Cf. II Cor. 4:17.

ments and afflictions, but He desires that those of us who make ourselves ill through the delights of this world should convalesce through suffering, and those of us who fall through unlawful acts should rise again by being deprived even of those things that are lawful. Thus does the Lord vent His anger in this life so that He will not have to do so in the next. Now He mercifully uses rigor so that later He will not have to take just revenge.

You can see from this how diligently the Lord cares for you when He does not let you out of His hand nor give you free rein to satisfy your evil desires. Physicians readily grant every request of those whose cure is despaired of, but if there is still hope of a cure, they make the patient adhere to a strict diet and refrain from anything that may prove harmful. So also, parents are very careful of the amount of money that they give to their children, although later on these same parents will bequeath to their children all of their possessions. In like manner does the heavenly Physician and Father treat us.

Consider the numerous and grave sufferings that Christ endured from the very persons He had come to save. How patiently He turned His face to those who spat on Him, how silently He endured the cruel scourging, how meekly He bowed His head to receive the crown of thorns, how submissively He tasted of the vinegar and gall, with what patience and love He suffered the death of the cross. Then, wretched sinner, do not think it rigorous or severe that you must suffer the chastisements that He rightly inflicts on you for your sins. Much better to suffer patiently in this life than to endure the torments of the life to come, for the sufferings of this life can serve as atonement for sin and a source of merit, while the sufferings of the next life are without fruit or merit. And whether you will or not, those sufferings will come to you that God has willed for you and you cannot avoid them.

In order to acquire and preserve patience, the Christian should always be prepared for any adversity or affliction, from whatever source it may come. What else can be expected from a world that is so evil, from a flesh that is so fragile, and from the devils who are so envious of our spiritual progress? The prudent man will walk cautiously and well-armed, like one who travels through enemy territory. If he does so, he will bear his burdens and afflictions with a lighter heart because he is prepared for them, and when evils befall him, he will understand that God is asking a sacrifice of him.

When a man understands that afflictions can come to him from either God or man and he disposes himself to accept them with all humility and patience, resigning himself to the will of God and accepting his trials as if they come from the hands of God, let him know that his sacrifice will be most agreeable to God and that he can merit as much by his promptness of will as by the actual suffering. This, indeed, is one of the principal duties of the Christian, as St. Peter reminds us when he says that we should not be discouraged in our afflictions because we have been deputed for this.

Let the Christian realize, therefore, that in this world he should be like a rock that is constantly buffeted by the waves but remains constant and unmoved. Let him strive to cultivate perfect patience by passing from the first degree, in which he bears labors and afflictions patiently, through the second degree, in which he desires afflictions for the love of God, to the third and perfect degree, in which he rejoices in his sufferings and afflictions. The first degree was clearly demonstrated in the life of Job; the second, in the desires of the saints for martyrdom; and the third, in the joy of the apostles at being called upon to suffer for Christ.

The third degree of patience does not signify, however, that we should rejoice at the sufferings and afflictions of our neighbor, much less at those of our parents and family or the Church. Charity demands that we rejoice at our own sufferings but have compassion for the suffering of others. In this way charity knows how to weep with those who weep and rejoice with those who rejoice. Moreover, since the third degree of patience is the highest and most perfect expression of this virtue, relatively few souls reach it in practice and therefore it does not bind under precept.

CHAPTER 46 ✍

Chastity

NO matter how weak a man is in the spiritual life, he is obliged to avoid all mortal sin and to be especially vigilant in regard to the sins against purity, which are the most perilous. In one of the first assemblies of the primitive Church a doubt had arisen concerning those who were converted to the faith. The question had been raised concerning their obligation to follow the Mosaic law, and it was decided that they were not so bound, although they were obliged to refrain from the worship of idols, fornication, and eating certain types of meat.[1] It is noteworthy

[1] Acts 15:20.

that special mention was made of fornication. The reason for this was that sins against purity are very easy to commit because in these matters a man is his own enemy. Even if the devil does not tempt from without, concupiscence and evil inclinations frequently arise from within. The inclination of the flesh is so strong that theologians teach that no part of man has been so cruelly wounded by original sin as the sexual instinct. The early Christians understood this very well and for that reason they issued a special warning against the sins of the flesh.

In conformity with this teaching, St. Paul warned the Thessalonians to be vigilant: "We pray and beseech you in the Lord Jesus that as you have received from us how you ought to walk and to please God, so also you would walk that you may abound the more. . . . For this is the will of God, your sanctification; that you should abstain from fornication; that every one of you should know how to possess his vessel in sanctification and honor, not in the passion of lust, like the Gentiles that know not God." [2]

However much a beginner a man may be in the spiritual life, he is obliged to conquer this enemy and preserve chastity. St. Augustine tells us that of all the battles the Christian must fight, the most severe is that against this virtue. It is almost a daily warfare and the losses are very great. What makes it even more difficult is that it is not merely a question of preserving bodily chastity, but also chastity of mind. For that reason the Savior has said: "Whosoever shall look on a woman to lust after her, hath already committed adultery with her in his heart." [3] In God's eyes it is all one, both the external act and the intention to perform the deed, and this is true of both good and evil deeds. Whence, Abraham merited as much a reward by his inten-

[2] Thess. 4:1–5.   [3] Matt. 5:28.

tion to sacrifice his son at God's command as if he had actually performed the deed. Likewise, he sins no less in intending to commit a sin of impurity than in actually performing the action. St. Jerome asks: "Who will glory at having a pure and chaste heart if he does not use all the safeguards to protect this purity?"

The first and best safeguard of chastity is the practice of prayer, which is a general weapon against all the attacks of the enemy. Another safeguard is temperance in food and drink, for if the body is subdued by abstinence and sobriety, the passions are more easily kept under control. Another great help is custody of the eyes, for they are the gates through which impurity enters the soul, as happened when David looked upon Bethsabee. Yet another protection of chastity is to flee the occasions of sin and especially to avoid certain persons who may even be very virtuous in themselves. Indeed, it sometimes happens that persons who themselves are very chaste, unwittingly arouse severe temptations in others. Moreover, St. Augustine says that he has seen persons fall who had the reputation of great holiness. What must be the danger to reeds shaken by the wind when the strong cedars have sometimes been felled by sins against chastity? And if holy persons have fallen because they did not avoid the occasions of sin, what will happen to you, who are much weaker in virtue?

I shall not bring any testimony against you except your own conscience. Examine the secret corners of your heart and see how well you are protecting and preserving your purity. Perhaps you will then have to repeat the words of St. Peter: "Having eyes full of adultery and of sin that ceaseth not." [4] In other words, you may find that you are so ill-provided and poorly armed against sins of impurity that

[4] Cf. II Pet. 2:14.

you have only to look upon something lustful and you desire it. That is why St. Peter says that it is a sin that never ceases, for the man who is not armed against this vice sees occasions of sin on every side and falls frequently.

The vice opposed to chastity is called lust and it signifies an inordinate inclination to sexual pleasures. From this vice flow other pestilential sins such as blindness of intellect, lack of consideration, inconstancy, rashness, self-love, hatred of God, fear of death, and despair of salvation.

If you were to ask how to combat this vice, I would say that first and above all you must understand that the most difficult of all battles is that against lust, and victory is not won as often as one would expect. The devil knows very well that for most Christians the struggle against sensual delights is more difficult than the battle against most of the other vices, because it is fought within a man's own body and victory is much more uncertain. It is more difficult to defend yourself against the enemy who is already within the gates of the city than one who is attacking from outside.

Therefore, great vigilance is required to suppress the concupiscence of the flesh. However, it is important to understand that although concupiscence may be very strong and cause a great disturbance, it cannot overcome you unless you wish to be overcome. Your inclinations and passions are under your control and it is within your power to make your enemy your servant. As long as you do not give consent, all will be well with you, and as often as you resist, so often do you gain a crown.

When lust tempts you, remember that this vice not only stains the soul that has been washed by the blood of the Lamb of God, but it pollutes the body which is a sacred reliquary for the Eucharistic body of Christ. And if it is a great crime to desecrate a material temple of God, what must it be to profane this living temple which is His dwelling-place? So St. Paul warns us: "Fly fornication. Every sin that a man doth is without the body, but he that committeth fornication sinneth against his own body. Or know you not that your members are the temple of the Holy Ghost, who is in you, whom you have from God, and you are not your own? For you are bought with a great price. Glorify and bear God in your body." [5]

Consider also that this vice is very sweet at the beginning, but it has a bitter ending. There is nothing in which a man so easily becomes involved, but once he is ensnared in it, once evil friendships have been established and the veil of shame has been torn aside, who will save a man from that snare?

Realize also the multitude of evils that arise from this vice. It robs the sinner of his good reputation, which is man's most treasured natural possession, for there is no vice as odious as that of lust. It weakens a man's physical strength, gradually destroys his beauty, ruins his good disposition, and sometimes brings on terrible diseases that are as painful as they are repulsive. It destroys the flower of youth and hastens old age; it dulls the sharpness of the intellect and makes a man brutish. It makes a man lose the taste for honest study and pious exercises and he eventually becomes so embroiled in the deeds of lust that he cannot think or talk about anything else. It makes youth foolish and old age wretched. Not content with the evil it causes to the man himself, it consumes his wealth and other possessions in the pursuit for sensual gratification. It leads to gluttony and drunkenness, because men who are carnal are generally great lovers of food and drink. It causes

[5] Cf. I Cor. 6:18–20.

women to become vain and to spend great sums of money on clothing, perfumes, and jewelry.

The more you give your thoughts and your body to sexual pleasures, the less satisfaction you will find in those pleasures, for they do not give satisfaction but only increase the appetite for more. This pleasure, which is so very brief, merits a suffering that is eternal and is, therefore, a poor barter for the peace of a good conscience and the eternal happiness of heaven. As St. Gregory says: "That which delights lasts for but a moment; the torment will last forever."

On the other hand, consider the dignity and beauty of chastity. Those who are chaste in this life are, because of their purity, compared to the angels, because to live in the flesh without doing the deeds of the flesh is more angelic than human. Moreover, virginity gives men a foretaste of the heavenly kingdom and in heaven the virgins will receive a singular reward: "These are they who were not defiled with women, for they are virgins. These follow the Lamb whithersoever He goeth. These were purchased from among men, the first fruits to God and to the Lamb; and in their mouth there was found no lie, for they are without spot before the throne of God." [6]

In addition to this, purity makes men truly Christlike and living temples of the Holy Ghost, for the divine Spirit is a lover of purity and in no soul does He repose more delightfully than in the souls of the pure. For that reason the Son of God was conceived by the Holy Ghost in the womb of a virgin and born of a virgin-mother.

If you have already lost your virginity, then at least learn to be wary of the dangers you have already experienced. If you have not succeeded in keeping your physical nature

[6] Apoc. 14:4–5.

intact, mend it now as best you can and turn back to God after your sin. Occupy yourself more diligently in good works than you did previously. For it sometimes happens, as St. Gregory tells us, that after a fall the soul becomes more fervent, whereas in the state of its innocence it might have remained weak and indifferent. God has continued to protect you in spite of your sins; make amends for the past lest your final state be even worse than the first.

In addition to the common remedies against lust, there are certain particular helps that are efficacious. The first is to resist temptation from the very beginning, for if you do not repulse the enemy at once, he will become more powerful as you become weaker. St. Gregory says that once the desire for sensual delights has taken hold of the heart, it does not let the heart desire anything else. Therefore, reject all carnal thoughts at the very beginning, for they feed evil desires as wood feeds fire. If thoughts are good, they will inflame the soul with charity and holy desires, but if they are evil, they will arouse lust.

It is also necessary to keep custody over the senses, especially the eyes, lest you look upon things that will be sources of temptation. Sometimes a single glance is enough to wound the soul, and since the wanton eye easily arouses evil desires, Scripture warns us: "Look not round about thee in the ways of the city nor wander up and down in the streets thereof. Turn away thy face from a woman dressed up and gaze not on another's beauty, for many have perished by the beauty of a woman, and hereby lust is enkindled as a fire." [7] Remember the example of Job, who was a man of virtue but kept a strict custody over his eyes because he did not trust in his virtue alone.[8] Consider, on the other

[7] Ecclus. 9:7–9.   [8] Job 31:1.

hand, that although David was a saintly man, one glance at a woman led him into such grave sins as adultery, homicide, and scandal.

No less strict should be the custody of the ears. When impure things are discussed in your presence, show by your countenance that this subject is displeasing to you, for people readily talk about those things that others listen to with eagerness. Guard your tongue from any impure speech, because good customs are corrupted by evil conversations. The tongue reveals a man's interior state, for out of the fullness of the heart the mouth speaks. Try to keep your mind occupied with holy and wholesome thoughts and your body with honest duties. St. Bernard says that the devil sends evil thoughts to the idle soul so that even if a man is not actually performing the external acts of sin, he will continue to dwell on evil in his mind.

In every temptation, but especially in temptations against chastity, remember your guardian angel who protects you and the devil who tempts you. They are always watching what you do. But if you would hesitate to perform a base action before another human being, how can you do so in the eyes of your guardian angel and the God who will judge you? Think also of the terror of the final judgment and the horror of eternal damnation, for sometimes we can extinguish the fires of lust by remembering the flames of hell.

As a general rule, avoid conversing alone with persons of the opposite sex who are or may be sources of temptation to you, for the devil is more daring in his insinuations when a man and woman are alone together. Therefore, make it a custom to have a companion when dealing with members of the opposite sex, because the mere fact of your being alone with the other party may incite all manner of evil desires and unchaste thoughts. And do not rely on your virtue or your past victories over temptation, but remember how those old men were inflamed with lust when they gazed upon Susanna.[9] Consequently, avoid every suspicious association with the opposite sex, because merely to be with them may cause you to be tempted, merely to listen to them may arouse evil desires, merely to speak with them may inflame your passions. "Those who dedicate their bodies to chastity," says St. Gregory, "should not dare to dwell with women, because no one can presume that the fire of the passions is totally extinguished."

Avoid also the little gifts and souvenirs as well as visits and letters from women, for all these things can fan the fire of evil desires. If you truly love some virtuous woman, then love her in your heart, without seeking occasions to visit her and under all circumstances avoid becoming familiar with her.

Gaze upon the sorrowful figure of the crucified Christ and observe the welts and wounds that covered His sacred body. Remember that He suffered all this in order to destroy sin. Be ashamed ever to treat your body with delicacy and sensuality when He was treated with such severity and cruelty. And as you gaze upon His torn and lacerated figure, cry out with all your heart: "O God, come to my assistance; O Lord, make haste to help me!"

[9] Dan. 13:8.

CHAPTER 47 ✒

Abstinence and Sobriety

ABSTINENCE is one of the principal virtues required for Christian perfection and it is difficult to acquire because of the disorder in the appetites of our fallen nature. Scripture gives explicit instructions concerning this virtue: "Use as a frugal man the things that are set before thee, lest if thou eatest much, thou be hated. Leave off first, for manners' sake, and exceed not, lest thou offend. And if thou sittest among many, reach not thy hand out first of all, and be not the first to ask for drink." [1]

Hugh of St. Victor treats of the virtue of abstinence in greater detail when he says: "At the time of eating there are two things in which discipline and moderation should be observed, that is, in the food itself and in the one who eats the food. While a man eats he should observe moderation by keeping silence, by custody of the eyes, by proper posture of the body, so that he may refrain from too much talking, not be looking in all directions, and keep the members of his body composed and quiet." Some persons, when they sit at table, manifest their unruly appetite by acting as if the entire meal were for them alone and by various gestures and mannerisms they give evidence of their voracious appetite and their intense desire for food. They attack their food like a soldier attacking a fortress and if they could, they would eat from several dishes at the same time or put all the food into their mouth at once.

If the proper disposition of spirit and correct deport-

[1] Ecclus. 31:19–20.

378

ment are necessary at all times, they are especially so when a person is very hungry or when the food is unusually tasty and appetizing. In these cases there is a greater incentive to gluttony, either because the organism is more receptive to food or the food itself is more savory. St. John Climacus says that gluttony is a type of hypocrisy of the stomach, for at the beginning of the meal a man believes that he could eat everything that is on the table, but after he has eaten a little he finds that his stomach has deceived him and he is satiated with much less than he anticipated.

Gluttony is an inordinate desire for food, and its daughters are: senseless mirth, gossiping, buffoonery, uncleanness, and dullness of the intellect and senses. Christ warned us against this vice in the following words: "Take heed to yourselves, lest perhaps your hearts be overcharged with surfeiting and drunkenness and the cares of this life." [2] And we read in Ecclesiasticus: "By surfeiting, many have perished, but he that is temperate shall prolong life." [3]

Lest you be caught in the snare of this vice of gluttony, understand that many times when the natural appetite for food makes itself felt, the delight which accompanies eating may easily lead you astray. Great caution is necessary to control the appetite and to place sensuality under the control of reason. If you wish your flesh to serve you and to be subject to reason, then subject your reason to God, for the reason must be ruled by God if your sensuality is to be under the rule of reason.

If you are tempted to gluttony, imagine that you have already enjoyed the delight of food and that it is now over, because the pleasure of taste is like last night's dream, which is soon over and easily forgotten. But if you succumb to gluttony, it will leave your mind troubled, for if you per-

[2] Luke 21:34.   [3] Ecclus. 37:34.

form a virtuous deed at the cost of great effort, the labor passes away but the virtue remains, but if you take delight in some sinful deed, the pleasure passes away but the sin remains.

If great caution is required in the matter of eating, it is much more necessary in regard to drink, for one of the greatest enemies of chastity is wine and other intoxicating drinks. St. Paul admonishes: "Be not drunk with wine, wherein is luxury." [4] This is especially true in the case of young people, as St. Jerome says: "Wine and youthfulness are two incentives to lust. Why throw oil on the fire? Why add more fuel to the flames?" Excessive drinking undoes the work of the moral virtues, for their principal function is to control the passions.

Moreover, immoderate drinking easily leads to quarrels, arguments, fights, betrayal of secrets and confidence, and similar disorders, for as the passions are more aroused, the rule of reason is more weakened. To drink a little wine suffices for the needs of the body; to drink a little more than is necessary gives delight and affability; but to go beyond this second stage leads to drunkenness and folly. Hence, when a man is intoxicated, all his judgments and opinions are to be looked upon with suspicion, for as a rule it is not his reason that speaks, but the drink.

It is especially important for a man who has had too much to drink to avoid speaking too much or trusting others too much. Many men have revealed things under the influence of liquor and have soon wished that they had not spoken. Solomon tells us that there are no secrets in the kingdom of wine. Moreover, we should refrain from discussing other people when we are eating and drinking, for it is easy to

[4] Eph. 5:18.

sin against justice through the loquacity that usually accompanies drinking and feasting. St. Augustine was so opposed to this practice of talking about others when at table that he had a short verse printed and placed in view of all who sat at his table: "He who comes here to gnaw at the character of those who are absent, let him know that this table was not set for him."

If you wish an incentive to the practice of temperance in food and drink, consider the singular abstinence of Christ, who fasted in the desert and throughout His life treated His body with great austerity. If He who sustains the angels with His glance and provides for the birds of the air suffered hunger for you, how willingly you should do the same for Him. By what title do you claim to be a servant of Christ if you spend your life eating and drinking, while He suffered so much for your salvation? And if the cross of mortification and abstinence seems heavy, remember the weight of His cross on His shoulders and the vinegar and gall that were given to Him when He suffered from thirst.

Consider also the fasting and abstinence of the monks of the desert, who crucified their flesh and its appetites for the love of God and were sustained for many years on herbs and roots. If they imitated Christ by traveling along the road of mortification, how can you expect to reach heaven along the road of sensual gratification? Does it not seem incredible that a man would risk the torments of hell for some passing delight? Do you not see how foolish you are to treat with such delicacy a body that will one day be consumed by worms, while you neglect the soul that will one day stand before God's judgment seat? Will you starve your soul as you fill your stomach with food and drink? Your body was given you as a help to the soul; you have made it an occasion of sin which will accompany your soul to eternal torment.

Let us now consider the benefits of temperance in food and drink. In the first place, fasting, abstinence, and sobriety are meritorious of grace and glory if they are done for the love of God. They also serve as a means of reparation and atonement for sin whereby we can remit a portion of the debt for which we ask pardon each time we recite the Our Father. Although these benefits are common to all the works of virtue, they are attributed in a special way to fasting, almsgiving, and prayer, for these three works have a special aspect of satisfaction for sin.

If one breaks the civil law, he is obliged to pay the penalty; likewise, if one disobeys the laws of God, he must pay the price. The payment will be made either in this life or in the next, that is, either on earth, in purgatory, or in hell. The soul in hell repays its debt with eternal fire; the soul in purgatory repays with a suffering so intense that St. Augustine says that there is no suffering on earth that can be compared to it, not even the sufferings of the martyrs. But fasting and other bodily austerities, although they are incomparably less than the sufferings of purgatory or hell, can save us from both of those places, because God does not look so much at the actual work that is done, but at the intention and the will to make sacrifice and atonement. Moreover, that which is accepted as a suffering on earth is a voluntary affliction, whereas the pains of purgatory and hell are inflicted by necessity. Therefore, from the viewpoint of merit, the sufferings in this life are much more valuable than the sufferings in purgatory.

Another benefit of fasting and abstinence is that they are excellent predispositions to the awareness of God and the enjoyment of spiritual consolations and these, in turn, wean us from sensual delights. The Holy Ghost is the Consoler and when He sees a soul reject all mundane delights and the pleasures of the flesh, He gladdens it with spiritual joy. For the soul cannot live without joy and if it has renounced the world's delights, it is fitting that it receive a portion of heavenly delight.

Moreover, the practice of bodily austerities renews in our minds the memory of Christ's sufferings. When we are fatigued and hungry, when tasteless food discourages us, when rough clothing irritates the flesh, when we must sleep on a hard bed, or when we suffer any other bodily austerity, we should raise our minds to Christ, who is the symbol of suffering and affliction. Seeing how innocence suffered for malice, justice for sin, holiness for evil, and God for man, we should take courage. Prosperity, on the other hand, easily leads to a forgetfulness of God. "They were filled and were made full, and they lifted up their heart, and have forgotten Me." [5]

Another benefit to be obtained from abstinence and fasting and other austerities is that they help us acquire wisdom and prudence. It is a common doctrine of the saints that gluttony deadens the intellect and the senses, but St. Basil teaches that fasting strengthens the powerful, teaches legislators, is the guardian of the soul, the weapon of the strong, the preserver of chastity, strength in battle, and a garrison of peace. Fasting sanctifies priests, gives gravity to the young, adorns old age, is the ornament of women, and the source of restraint for men. There is no virtue that is not helped in some way by fasting. Christ, when He was about to preach, prepared Himself with fasting and prayer, not because He needed any preparation, but to teach us that

[5] Os. 13:6.

little can be accomplished in the spiritual life without fasting and prayer.

If the Christian faithfully practices fasting and other bodily austerities, he will discover that these are practices in which he most resembles Christ. St. Peter tells us that as Christ suffered in the flesh, we should also suffer with Him, for if we are partakers in His pain, we shall also share in His glory. That is the singular glory of the predestined, who were chosen from all eternity to be made conformable to the image of Christ both in this life and in the next.[6] In this life they will imitate Christ by drinking the chalice of suffering; in the next life they will drink the chalice of His delights. Nor is it necessary to run the risk of becoming Pharisees in the practice of bodily austerities, but let each man become a persecutor of his own flesh.

But some men are so sensate that they are not interested in anything but their own profit. To them also we say that there are many benefits in fasting and bodily austerity. For example, health, life, possessions, honor, and pleasure are the great goods that attract men and each one of these goods is in some way fostered by fasting. Fasting contributes to a longer life, as Scripture promises: "Be not greedy in any feasting and pour not out thyself upon any meat, for in many meats there will be sickness and greediness will turn to choler. By surfeiting, many have perished, but he that is temperate shall prolong life." [7] Think of the monks who never dine on delicacies and you will find that as their fasts are more rigorous, their lives are longer, for they do not overtax the body with foods that are too rich or difficult to digest. So also, fasting is beneficial for the health and sometimes fasting alone will restore health when all medicines have failed.

[6] Cf. Rom. 8:29.   [7] Ecclus. 37:32–34.

As to honor and reputation, who will deny that the temperate man is highly esteemed, while the glutton and the drunkard are pitied and censured? This is as it should be, for what is more brutish than always to be filling one's stomach with food and drink? What is more contrary to man's dignity than excessive food and drink? And even if the glutton or drunkard does not go so far as to lose the use of reason, he will eventually come to a state that is not far removed from madness. What happiness can such men hope to find in these things? A man who wishes to accomplish great things must be able to endure hardship and austerity. Therefore, nothing can be expected of gluttons and drunkards in letters, in war, in business, or in administration and government. If they ever attempt great enterprises they either cannot persevere because such enterprises necessarily withdraw them from excessive eating and drinking, or they will not attempt the tasks at all because they are so enslaved by their vices. Therefore, no man is less to be feared than he who is a glutton or a drunkard. Caesar, when advised by his friends to beware of certain men, replied that he had no reason to fear the drunkards and fat men, but those who are lean and temperate. Later events proved that Caesar was right in his judgment, for temperate and austere men are courageous, but gluttons and drunkards are usually cowards.

There is also a joy in temperance, although one would not think that fasting and abstinence could bring delight. Delight in food does not depend only on the quantity of the food eaten, because large quantities of food cause satiety rather than pleasure. Nature has placed pleasure in eating but too much food can be harmful as well as too little food. Nor does the pleasure of eating come from the quality of the food alone, for we know that when men are sick no food, however savory, is tasty to them. The principal cause of delight in eating is the condition of the organism and the extent of the appetite. When the organ of taste is well disposed and one has an appetite for food, the food is enjoyable. "A soul that is full shall tread upon the honeycomb and a soul that is hungry shall take bitter for sweet." [8] So it is that the poor laborer receives much more enjoyment from his humble fare than the rich man does from his delicacies.

The glutton and the drunkard do not wait for hunger in order to eat or drink, but they eat out of habit rather than necessity. The temperate man, on the other hand, eats because of a need for nourishment. And now consider the temperate man and the glutton after they have eaten. The glutton is disgusted, suffers indigestion, is bloated and flatulent, suffers heartburn and discomfort because of the amount of food he has eaten. He is useless for any kind of intellectual work or meditation. But the temperate man remains light and agile, is capable of doing his work, and is complete master of himself.

Some may say that what we have said is perfectly suited for religious but that it is not expected that people in high places should be advised to practice these austerities in regard to food and drink. By reason of their office and position they must attend banquets and feasts. My answer to them is that they should read the books of Sallust and Livy and see how the Romans conquered and ruled the world as long as they observed temperance in food and drink. Men who had lived on vegetables alone left their ploughs to fight for the Empire. But when abstinence gave place to gluttony, sobriety to drunkenness, chastity to the pursuit of sexual pleasure, the Romans became effeminate,

[8] Prov. 27:7.

corrupted by lust, and vitiated by the idleness that followed years of war. As a result, what they had won by temperance, they lost by their dissolute lives. They who had conquered the nations of the world could not at the end conquer their own lusts and appetites.

This is true not only of the Roman Empire but of every state or nation and every religious order that has lost its primitive observance and austerity. Indeed, St. Jerome points out that this same affliction has befallen the Church of Christ from time to time. If wisdom and prudence are the principal virtues required in rulers and superiors, then the vices most destructive of good government and administration are gluttony, drunkenness, and lust. From all that we have said, it should be evident how important are fasting, abstinence, and sobriety for all Christians, whether as private individuals or as superiors and rulers.

CHAPTER 48 🦢

Christian Modesty

CHRISTIAN modesty requires that nothing in our gait or posture or clothing scandalize or offend anyone, but that everything about us manifest our dignity as Christians. The servant of God should strive to cultivate the gravity, humility, affability, and meekness that will edify others and serve as a good example to them. The Apostle states that the Christian should be the "good odor of Christ" [1] which is communicated to all who come in con-

[1] Cf. II Cor. 2:15.

tact with him. In other words, our bodily actions and posture should be such as are proper to the follower of Christ, so that each Christian will be a kind of silent sermon which leads others to love God by the example of virtue, as Christ recommends when He says: "So let your light shine before men that they may see your good works and glorify your Father who is in heaven." [2]

This does not mean that a man should perform good works for the purpose of being seen by others. St. Gregory says that we should do good works in public in such a way that our intention remains hidden, so that we may give good example to our neighbor by the good deed and may please God alone by our good intention.

The second benefit of Christian modesty is that it is a great safeguard of devotion and custody of the passions and senses. There is such an intimate relation between modesty of deportment and interior custody that the condition of the one will be communicated to the other. If the soul is composed, the body will be composed also; if the body is restless and disordered, the soul will reflect this same restlessness. The one is like the mirror or shadow of the other, for whatever movements you make in front of a mirror, the image in the glass will do the same, and whatever the motions of your body, they will be imitated by your shadow. Hence, it is most rare to find a collected and tranquil spirit in a restless body. As a result, the man who lacks the deportment and gravity that befit his Christian calling will fall into many defects and imperfections.

Thirdly, modest deportment imparts to those in authority the gravity that is due them in view of their office. Such dignity, of course, must be far removed from any trace

[2] Matt. 5:16.

of pride or affectation. Moreover, the dress of a man and his manner of walking and laughing frequently give an indication of what he is. Thus, Solomon says: "As the faces of men that look therein shine in the water, so the hearts of men are laid open to the wise." [3]

Some persons are excessively vivacious, under the pretext that they do not wish to be considered hypocrites. Consequently, they laugh and talk and are such extroverts that they lack all composure and restraint. Let such persons realize that they should not forsake Christian modesty out of respect for the world, for it is not permitted to desist from the practice of virtue out of human respect.

Once the body as a whole has been held in restraint by Christian deportment, it is necessary also to gain control of the senses and especially of the eyes. Persons dedicated to prayer must be most vigilant because the images that enter the mind through the eyes may easily destroy recollection and so disturb the mind that it cannot think of anything else. Hence, it is sometimes necessary not only to keep one's gaze from falling upon things that are unlawful, but even from things of great sensible beauty and attraction, for sometimes things that are not sinful in themselves may become sources of distraction in prayer.

A similar custody should be maintained over the ears because they, too, sometimes admit things that can disturb and distract the soul. The good Christian will not only refrain from listening to injurious or evil speech, but he will not listen to the curiosities and novelties of the world which are of no concern to him. A person who listens to every bit of news and strains to hear everything that is said about every topic must pay for it when he tries later to be

[3] Prov. 27:19.

recollected, for then the things that he has heard will come before his mind and so divert his attention that he cannot think of the things of God.

Of custody of the tongue there is much to say, for we read in Proverbs: "Death and life are in the power of the tongue." [4] The goodness or evil of a man will depend to a large extent on how well he can control his tongue. St. James writes: "Behold also ships, whereas they are great and are driven by strong winds, yet are they turned about with a small helm, whithersoever the force of the governor willeth. Even so, the tongue is indeed a little member and boasteth great things. Behold how small a fire kindleth the great wood. And the tongue is a fire, a world of iniquity. The tongue is placed among our members which defileth the whole body and inflameth the wheel of our nativity, being set on fire by hell. For every nature of beasts and of birds and of serpents and of the rest is tamed, and hath been tamed by the nature of man. But the tongue no man can tame, an unquiet evil, full of deadly poison. By it we bless God and the Father; and by it we curse men, who are made after the likeness of God. Out of the same mouth proceedeth blessing and cursing." [5]

In order to control the tongue in a Christian manner, we should be attentive to four things: what we say, how we say it, when we say it, and why we say it. As to the first, let us keep in mind the statement of St. Paul: "Let no evil speech proceed from your mouth, but that which is good, to the edification of the faith, that it may administer grace to the hearers." [6] Later in the same Epistle he mentions specifically what he means by evil speech: obscenity, foolish talking, and scurrility. [7] Just as the captain of a ship has

---

[4] Prov. 18:21.   [5] Jas. 3:4–10.   [6] Eph. 4:29.
[7] *Ibid.*, 5:4.

the dangerous shoals and reefs marked on his map, so the Christian should take special notice of the various kinds of evil speech so that he can avoid them, and we would add that the custody of speech likewise applies to the conscientious safeguarding of secrets that have been entrusted to us.

As to the manner of speaking, we should take care not to speak with too much tenderness nor with boldness, not too rapidly nor with too much affectation, but always to speak with a certain gravity, affability, meekness, and simplicity. Neither should we be headstrong or too self-confident or over-anxious to express our own opinions, for many times this destroys one's peace of conscience and leads to sins against patience and charity. It is the sign of a generous heart to let oneself be outdone in an argument and it is the sign of a prudent man to follow the advice given in Ecclesiasticus: "In many things be as if thou wert ignorant and hear in silence and withal seeking." [8]

Concerning the time at which we speak, remember that when a fool speaks a wise and profound thought, he is not heeded, because the fool speaks at the wrong time. Lastly, the intention in speaking is important because some persons speak good things in order to appear wise and discreet, while others do the same in order to be considered brilliant and eloquent. The first is hypocrisy and pretense; the second is vanity and foolishness. Therefore, we must see to it not only that our words are good but that our motive is good, seeking always the glory of God and the benefit of our neighbor.

It is also well to consider the person who speaks, for if young men speak when older men are present or if ignorant men speak when wise men are present, it is often better if the speaker had remained silent, for he will be condemned

[8] Ecclus. 32:12.

for presumption and will not be heard. Indeed, it is a great safeguard to love silence because by keeping silent we shall be protected from offending by speech. "Even a fool, if he will hold his peace, shall be counted wise, and if he close his lips, a man of understanding." [9]

Another important aspect of Christian self-control is domination and restraint of the sensitive appetites or passions, of which the basic ones are: love, desire, joy, hate, aversion, sorrow, hope, despair, courage, fear, and anger. The passions are powers that we have in common with the animals and therefore they tend to make us brutish and to draw us away from spiritual things. They are the source of most of the evils in the world and the reason for the condemnation of most of the souls in hell. The passions are another Eve through whom the devil tempts the Adam in us and it is in the passions that the wounds of original sin are deepest.

The passions or emotions are the battlefield of the spiritual life and it requires the whole array of the virtues to subjugate and conquer these enemies and to win the crown of victory. Accordingly, the Christian must be like the driver of a team of horses, who holds the reins in his hands and makes his passions do his bidding rather than to let them follow their own inclinations. This is one of the principal works of the servant of God, and in this he differs greatly from the carnal and sensate man who is moved to and fro by the impulse of his passions. The subjugation of the passions implies holy mortification and self-abnegation.

To control the passions as befits a Christian, each man must know his own temperament and his natural inclinations and dispositions. If he possesses this self-knowledge, he will have one of the strongest weapons against his pas-

[9] Prov. 17:28.

sions. And although he must be vigilant over all the movements of the passions, he must be especially careful of the inclinations to pleasure, fame, and worldly possessions, for these are three principal sources of evil in us.

It is likewise necessary to avoid being self-willed and interested in satisfying one's own appetites and desires. This disposes very easily for a restless spirit and the sins that are common among people who are accustomed to have their own way. Therefore, it is a good practice to deny ourselves sometimes even in regard to those things that are lawful so that we may more easily deny ourselves in regard to things that are unlawful. We must use the same strategy in fighting spiritual battles as men of war use in military battles. We should also occupy ourselves from time to time in humble tasks and lowly offices, without any regard for what the world will say, for the world can do nothing to him who has God as his treasure.

Moreover, since the imagination is the instigator of the passions and is itself very difficult to control, the Christian will also keep a special custody over this faculty. The imagination is like a wayward child which runs here and there before we can bring it back to its rightful place. It will receive whatever is set before it, like a hungry dog that scavenges here and there and eats whatever it finds. It is a free and wild faculty that acknowledges no master and some persons make it worse by treating it like a spoiled child, letting it do whatever it pleases and never suppressing it. Later, when they try to bring the imagination under control, it does not obey but follows its own pursuits.

Once the Christian realizes what a wild beast the imagination can be, let him curtail its freedom and use it only in the consideration of good and holy things. There must be as great a custody of the imagination as there is over the tongue, for both of these powers have a tendency to be indocile and wild. Those who are careless in examining the type of images in their imagination will admit many things into their minds which will impede devotion and lessen the fervor of charity. A wild and restless imagination will also prevent recollection and impede the practice of prayer, but he who is accustomed to keep a close watch over his imagination will be able to persevere in peaceful and devout prayer.

CHAPTER 49 ✄

Anger

ANGER is the inordinate desire for revenge and it gives rise to other sins such as disputes, fights, quarreling, indignation, blasphemy, and hatred. St. Paul warns us against anger when he says: "Let all bitterness and anger and indignation and clamor and blasphemy be put away from you, with all malice. And be kind to one another, merciful, forgiving one another, even as God hath forgiven you in Christ." [1] And Jesus has said: "Whosoever is angry with his brother shall be in danger of the judgment. . . . And whosoever shall say, 'Thou fool,' shall be in danger of hell fire." [2]

When you are tempted to this sin, overcome the temptations by the following considerations: First, consider how even the brute animals live in peace and harmony with those of their own species, but only man, to whom peace

[1] Eph. 4:31–32. [2] Matt. 5:22.

and humaneness are much more proper, gives vent to unreasonable anger and hatred. Secondly, consider that nature has given the various animals weapons for fighting and defense, such as horns to the bull, claws to the cat, the stinger to the bee, and teeth to the dog, but man, who was made for peace and harmony, came into this world naked and unarmed. How contrary it is to man's nature to seek vengeance on another and to try to do harm to another when he must seek outside himself for the weapons that nature has denied him.

Anger and revenge are proper to ferocious beasts, for it is well known that wild animals that have been injured by man have later returned to attack and kill the man who had hurt them. When the passion of anger overwhelms reason and prudence, a man is carried away by the fury of a beast and follows that part of his nature which he has in common with animals rather than that part of him that makes him resemble the angels. And if you say that it is a very difficult task to quell the movement of anger, why do you not stop to consider how God has restrained His just anger against you because of your sins? Were you not listed among the enemies of Christ when He shed His blood for you? Yet see how meekly He endures you even when you renew your sins from day to day. See how mercifully He receives you when you turn back to Him. And if you say that your enemy does not deserve to be pardoned, tell me whether you deserved to be pardoned by God. Do you demand mercy of God and then dare to treat your neighbor in accordance with the strict justice of an eye for an eye and a tooth for a tooth? And even if your enemy does not deserve pardon, remember that as long as you are at enmity with your neighbor, you cannot offer a pleasing sacrifice to God. "If, therefore, thou offer thy gift at the altar, and there thou remember that thy brother hath anything against thee, leave there thy offering before the altar and go first to be reconciled to thy brother, and then coming, thou shalt offer thy gift." [3] So also, St. Gregory says: "The good works that we do are of no value if we do not suffer with meekness the afflictions that befall us."

Consider the man whom you look upon as your enemy. He is either just or unjust. If he is just, there is much reason to lament that you should wish evil to a just man and make an enemy of one who is a friend of God. If he is an unjust man, the situation is no less unfortunate, for you wish to avenge the evil of another with your own evil, for you wish to make yourself his judge and thus punish his injustice with your own injustice. And if it should happen that the injury has been mutual, and he seeks to avenge his injury as you seek to avenge yours, there will be no end of the matter.

How much more Christian it is to follow the advice of the Apostle and to overcome evil with good. [4] It often happens that when a man tries to return evil for evil and is resolved not to be content with anything less than perfect satisfaction, he is himself defeated at the end, for he will be overcome by rage and will fall a victim to his own fury. It is much less a victory to conquer those outside yourself than to subdue the passions that arise within you, and especially when it is the fierce beast of anger. But if you do not control your anger, it will one day rise up so strongly that it will cause you to do something that you will regret bitterly. What is worse, you may not even be aware of the full extent of the evil you have done, because the angry man is convinced that his cause is just and many times he deceives himself into believing that the thorn of anger is the

[3] Matt. 5:23–24.   [4] Rom. 12:19–21.

zeal of justice, thus covering his vice with the cloak of virtue.

One of the surest ways to overcome the vice of anger is to rid yourself of your inordinate self-love and your excessive attachment to the things that pertain to you. As long as you are the victim of your own self-love, you will burst forth into anger as soon as there is the slightest word or action that touches anything that pertains to you. And if you feel that by temperament you are more readily inclined to anger, strive the more diligently to practice patience and try to anticipate the various annoyances that will arise in the midst of your various occupations and duties. If you see the arrow from a distance, it is less likely to strike you and wound you. Therefore, be firmly resolved that when anger begins to seethe within you, that you will say and do nothing. Regard with the greatest suspicion anything that your heart prompts you to do when in the state of anger, even if it appears to you to be most conformable with reason and most just. Delay action until anger has subsided and say a few prayers instead of doing what you feel inclined to do. Indeed, there is no worse time to decide a course of action than when one is angry, and yet there is no stronger desire to do so than when one is angry. For that reason, you must resist this inclination with firm determination, for just as a man who has taken too much wine is not able to defend this action, neither can you justify any commands or advice you may give in the heat of anger.

It is also a good practice for the irascible person to divert his attention to other affairs so that he can avoid the occasions of anger, for if fuel is not added to the fire, the flames soon die out. Moreover, the man who is prone to anger should make positive efforts to love those people with whom he must of necessity associate, for if our endurance of others is not accompanied by love, our apparent patience may easily be turned into rancor and hatred. Thus, St. Paul says that charity is patient, because it loves those whom it endures with patience. It is likewise a laudable practice to yield to the anger of your neighbor, for if you remove your presence from an angry person, you give the anger a chance to spend itself. But if escape is not possible, then answer him with kindness, for a soft answer turns away wrath.[5]

CHAPTER 50

The Grades of Humility

HUMILITY is the foundation of all the virtues and the disposition for the reception of all graces. This doctrine is taught in both the Old and the New Testaments, where grace is promised to the humble, to the little ones, and to the poor in spirit. St. James says that God resists the proud and gives His grace to the humble.[1] The reason for this is that as a man knows himself better, he becomes more humble and more distrustful of self and is moved to place all his trust in God and dispose himself to let God work in him.

To lay the foundations of a building it is necessary first to dig down through the topsoil and loose gravel until one reaches the hard rock that will serve as a firm support. This is what humility does in the spiritual life; it rids the soul of the instability and fickleness of human resources in order to build upon God, who is the firm rock upon which the

[5] Prov. 15:1. [1] Jas. 4:6.

edifice of the spiritual life must be constructed. I say this because some persons who are desirous of making progress in virtue presume too much on themselves and rely on their own efforts without fully realizing that they are doing so. Thus, some rely on their ingenuity, others on their state in life, their knowledge, their naturally good temperament, their chastity, the masters under whom they have studied, the good company they have kept, or the good training they have received. They think that one or another of these things will give them an advantage in the pursuit of virtue over those who lack such qualities. It is true that all these things help in one way or another in the acquisition of virtue, but without grace they are all smoke. Therefore, they who rely on some particular quality and depreciate others who do not possess it are building on sand. He who wishes to construct a solid spiritual edifice should not rely solely on these things but should build on God, who is the cornerstone of the spiritual life. To do this, one needs humility and hope; the first in order to be distrustful of self, and the second in order to trust in God.

There are no limits to God's grace and mercy, for He is infinitely good and infinitely generous. If He does not actually communicate His grace in an infinite degree, it is not because of any defect in God, but because the human vessel is not capable of receiving more. Hence, divine mercy is infinite in itself but limited by reason of the subject in which it is received. But the more the subject is disposed to receive this mercy, the more it will receive. And if you ask what is the best way to dispose oneself for the reception of God's mercy, I shall say that it is by means of the virtues, and especially by humility and charity. The one empties a man of self and the other draws him to God.

In order to reach perfect humility one must usually pass

through the different grades of the virtue. Theologians and spiritual writers have enumerated various degrees of humility, but we shall list only the six principal grades. The first grade of humility is to acknowledge that whatever is good in us comes from God. If all the goods of nature are from God, much more so are those of grace. And as no one can perform any good work without the divine *concursus* of the First Mover, neither can any Christian perform a supernatural work except by cooperating with the First Cause of the supernatural order. Everything in the natural order and in the order of grace must be referred to God; therefore, how foolish they are who attribute to God the works of nature and take credit themselves for the works of grace, which is to take credit for the greater and leave to God that which is less.

No man can say that any good work is his alone and that God had no part in it. "As the branch cannot bear fruit of itself, unless it abide in the vine, so neither can you, unless you abide in Me. . . . Without Me, you can do nothing." [2] St. Paul repeats this doctrine when he says: "Not that we are sufficient to think anything of ourselves, as of ourselves, but our sufficiency is from God." [3] Therefore, whenever you experience a good desire, a holy resolution, or a pious thought, understand that these proceed from God, who wishes to save you and moves you to good works. The truly humble man is not content with knowing this in a purely speculative way, but is as certain of this truth as if it were something he could see with his eyes and touch with his hands. This first grade of humility will make the Christian grateful and devout; grateful for what he has received and prompt to seek that which he lacks. It will arm him against vainglory and human praise so that even when others praise

[2] John 15:4-5.   [3] II Cor. 3:5.

him, he will act as if the praise were directed to God, to whom all praise is due.

The second grade of humility is for a man to realize that whatever he has received from God has not been through his own efforts but through the divine mercy. Some persons realize that all their good is from God, but within their hearts is a tacit conviction that they have attained these things by their own labors and merits, as if it were not true that those very merits are no less a grace and gift of God than the goods that have been obtained through them. Moreover, the value of our good works is not from the works themselves, but from the grace from which they proceed, and grace is definitely a gift of God. Just as paper money has little or no value in itself but only from the denomination with which it is stamped, so the merit of a good work is not from the work itself but from the divine grace which makes it meritorious. Therefore, if anything accrues to us because of our good works, it is always a case of grace being given for grace.

Isaias refers to this when he says: "All you that thirst, come to the waters, and you that have no money, make haste; buy and eat. Come ye, buy wine and milk without money and without any price." [4] This signifies that man has no reason to glory in himself but should realize that what he has of himself is a multitude of sins by which he has merited hell. Everything else, apart from evil, is a gift of grace and the basis of its merit is grace.

But these two grades do not suffice for perfect humility, for there are many persons who acknowledge that all their good is from God and that it is given through grace, but they think they have more than they have or more than their neighbors. They think that the sun rises only in their own

[4] Isa. 55:1.

back yard and not in others. They think that they have more light and more virtue than others and are filled with self-esteem. And the devil can make these persons believe such things in so disguised a manner that they themselves do not realize the deception.

Such was the condition of the Pharisee who thanked God that he was not like other men. In thanking God, he acknowledged that all his gifts were from God, which is the first grade of humility, but he believed that he had goods that he actually did not possess and that he was on that account better than other men, and hence he was lacking in the third grade of humility. The same is true of the wretched person described in the Apocalypse: "I know thy works, that thou art neither cold nor hot. I would thou wert cold or hot, but because thou art lukewarm, and neither cold nor hot, I will begin to vomit thee out of My mouth. Because thou sayest, 'I am rich and made wealthy and have need of nothing,' and knowest not that thou art wretched and miserable and poor and blind and naked." [5]

As a remedy against this condition, we have the third grade of humility, by which a man is aware of the virtues of others and blind to his own and therefore lives in holy fear. Temporal possessions are more secure when they are more closely watched, but spiritual goods are best guarded when least thought of. That is one of the reasons why the Lord sometimes permits His servants to suffer great temptations, for when our weakness and imperfections are brought to our attention, vanity is destroyed.

The fourth grade of humility is necessary because it is not enough that a Christian realize how poor and weak he really is in spiritual goods, but he he must also appreciate that he is overwhelmed with evil. He must acknowledge his self-love,

[5] Apoc. 3:15–17.

his self-will, his unruly passions, and his evil inclinations. This type of knowledge is the loftiest science in the world, for St. Paul tells us that other science puffs up but this knowledge humbles us.[6] Our own efforts do not suffice to give us this knowledge; we need light from heaven so that the cloud of self-love will not obscure the sight of ourselves as we really are. If a judge is very suspect when passing sentence on a friend, how much more suspect is the man who attempts to judge his own case. Therefore, a man must beg light from God and ask for it as insistently as did St. Francis, who frequently repeated the petition: "My God, that I may know Thee and that I may know myself."

The next grade of humility is not only to consider oneself a sinner, but to see oneself as the worst of all sinners. There is no harm in placing oneself beneath all others, but there may be a great deal of harm in putting oneself above others. One of the saints had a most effective remedy against the inclination to place himself above his neighbor and when he was asked how he could possibly believe that he was the worst of all sinners, he answered that he was convinced that if God were to remove His protecting hand, he would be the worst of all men, and if God had given to the worst sinner the many graces and blessings that had been given to him, that sinner would now be much better than himself. Therefore, it is very helpful in attaining the fifth grade of humility to consider frequently the benefits you have received from God and to compare them with your evil inclinations, and you will see that you have not always used God's gifts as they should have been used and that if you were left to follow your evil inclinations, there is no degradation to which you could not descend.

It is also helpful to consider the virtues of the saints who

[6] Cf. I Cor. 8:1.

are now in heaven and of the holy persons who yet remain on earth, for as long as the world exists there will not be lacking Christians in whom the Holy Ghost lives and works. Compare your virtue and holiness with theirs and then humble yourself before God when you see how far you are from their sanctity.

The sixth grade of humility pertains to the exterior manifestations, which should always proceed from an interior humility. True humility of heart is not only a knowledge and depreciation of self, but also an external manifestation of the internal virtue. In other words, he who humbles himself interiorly and considers himself unworthy of all honor and praise should also act that way in his external posture, gait, and facial expression. He should disdain empty titles and academic degrees; he should always take the lowest place; he should not refuse to associate with the simple and lowly; he should discharge humble and hidden duties; he should be mindful that the Son of God came to this earth to serve and not to be served and that one of His last lessons was the washing of the feet of His disciples. But these external acts of humility must be in accordance with the demands of prudence, the dignity of the human person, and the duties of one's office.

Exterior humility should not only spring from the interior virtue, but it should increase the source from which it flows. For that reason St. Bernard says that humiliation is the way to humility. Therefore, if you wish to attain true humility, do not avoid the exercises of humility, for if you do not wish to humble yourself, you will never acquire true humility. And although this self-abasement is laudable in all Christians, it is especially so in persons of high office. Therefore, St. Bernard says that men in high positions should not have vain thoughts but should converse with the humble and the lowly, for this is pleasing both to God and to man. This is the etiquette of the kingdom of God.

By means of these various grades of humility we can approach to the throne of the King of Peace, as St. Augustine says: "Notice, brethren, this great miracle. God is great, but if you exalt yourself He will flee from you; if you humble yourself, He will come to you." The humble man is no friend to self-will; he is neither ingratiating nor too independent. He will always judge and condemn himself and not the deeds of his neighbor, because true humility does not judge the defects of others, but one's own.

The truly humble man prefers to be despised and yet does not try to appear humble. He is subject to all, he obeys all, he honors all, and he never reprehends anyone without just cause. He does not give himself airs, either in speech or in action; he does not resort to hypocrisy; he does not scrutinize the secrets of God out of curiosity; he seeks no recognition or acknowledgment of his goodness; he is not crafty or malicious; he does not rely on himself and his own good works, but all his hope is in God. Yet in all his words and deeds he is ever devout, sweet, affable, and gracious.

O powerful humility, which raises the fallen and enriches the poor; which cures the sick and enlightens the blind! You make the man on earth possess heaven and from the abyss of his sins you lead him to the gates of paradise. The desire that we should be lovers of God brought God from heaven to earth, from the bosom of His Father to the womb of His immaculate Mother, and placed Him in a humble crib and later stretched out His sacred body on the cross. Humility made God man; humility will also make man God.

CHAPTER 51 ✍

Pride

PRIDE is the inordinate desire for one's own excellence. Sometimes it is buried deep in the soul and at other times it is manifested externally. Pride is the mother of all vices, but it particularly engenders the following: disobedience, arrogance, hypocrisy, obstinacy, discord, curiosity, and presumption. For good reason did Tobias counsel: "Never suffer pride to reign in thy mind or in thy words, for from it all perdition took its beginning." [1]

Of all the temptations to which the Christian is exposed, there is none more subtle, more dangerous, and more difficult to recognize than that of pride. Temptations to the other vices, such as those of the flesh, hatred, envy, anger, and desires for vengeance, are clearly seen for what they are. But pride often enters stealthily, flattering a man that he is of much worth, telling him that he is discreet, is deserving of a certain office or position, or that he is much better than other persons, and other things of this type. A man readily believes these things because of the self-love which blinds and deceives him. Hence, pride is one of the greatest pitfalls in the spiritual life.

When this vice tempts you, consider the terrible punishment that was meted out to the bad angels, who became so proud that they were cast out of the company of the good angels. Consider how this vice so perverted the intellect of him who was the prince of angels that he not only became a devil, but the worst of all the devils. And if this

[1] Tob. 4:14.

happened to the angels, what could happen to you, who are but dust and ashes? God is not an acceptor of persons and He does not contradict Himself. He hates pride and loves humility, both in men and in angels. That is why St. Augustine says that humility makes men angels but pride makes angels devils. And St. Bernard says that pride tears down the loftiest to the lowliest, but humility exalts the lowliest to the highest. The proud angels fell into the abyss of hell; the humble man shall be exalted to the very heavens.

Consider also the example of the Son of God, who took upon Himself our lowly nature and was obedient to the will of His Father, even to the death of the cross. Learn to obey; learn to be like the earth beneath your brother's feet; learn that you are nothing but dust. Learn, O Christian, of your Lord and your God, who is meek and humble of heart. If you refuse to follow the example of truly humble men, do not refuse to follow the example of your God, who became man to redeem you.

Look at yourself and you will see so many things that preach humility to you. Think of what you were before your birth, what you are now, and what you shall be after your death. Before birth you were a slimy, nameless matter; now you are a dungheap covered with snow; and after death you will be food for worms. What have you to be proud of? You, whose birth is a fault, whose life is misery, and whose end is corruption! If you take pride in your temporal possessions, wait but a moment. Death will come; that death which makes us all equal. For we were all born in the same condition and we shall all die in the same condition, except that some will have more to account for than others.

Meditate on the words of St. John Chrysostom: "Consider attentively the tombs of the dead and seek there some small trace of their former magnificence and wealth and the pleasures they enjoyed. Tell me, where now are their ornaments and beautiful vesture? Where are their recreations and sports? Where are their companions and the multitude of their servants? The feasts and banquets, the laughter and games, the worldly joys and pleasures, all are ended now. Approach more closely to the tomb and you will see there nothing but a handful of dust and ashes, worms and rotted bones. Such is the end of the human body which has given itself to pleasures and wealth."

And would that this were the only evil, but much more to be feared is the final judgment, the sentence that will be inflicted, the gnashing of teeth, the gnawing worm of conscience, and the fire that never ceases.

Consider also the danger of vainglory, which is a daughter of pride. St. Bernard says that vainglory flies lightly and lightly enters but it is not a light wound that it inflicts on the soul. If men praise you, see whether you deserve praise or not. And if there is a basis for praise, then say with the Apostle: "By the grace of God, I am what I am." [2] Realize also what foolishness it is to measure your worth by the opinion of men, who are inclined to favor those whom they like and criticize those whom they dislike. So fickle are they in their judgment that the very man who praises you today may condemn you tomorrow. If you judge yourself by their speech, sometimes you are great, other times you are less, and again you are nothing, depending upon the changeable mood of men. Therefore, do not measure your worth by the praise that is heaped upon you, but by what you know yourself to be in the sight of God. When others praise you to the skies, listen to what your conscience says of you, for your conscience knows you better than anyone else.

[2] Cf. I Cor. 15:10.

You have no reason to become puffed up with pride; rather, you should humble yourself and give glory to God, for He has given you all that you have. When you accept honor and praise from men, you make yourself the cause of that which should rightly be attributed to God and thus you steal from God that which rightly belongs to Him alone.

If you are ambitious, which is another effect of pride, then think of the great danger and risk that you run by wanting to rule and govern others. How can you govern others if you have not yet learned to govern yourself? How can you render an accounting for many when you are scarcely able to give an account of yourself? Look at the danger for you when you add to the responsibility for your own faults a responsibility for the faults of others. "A most severe judgment shall be for them that rule; for to him that is little, mercy is granted, but the mighty shall be mightily tormented." [3]

Pride has never brought happiness and contentment to anyone. It does not bring God, because God resists the proud and gives His grace to the humble. It does not make the proud man a friend of other proud persons, because the very reason for which one man exalts himself will make others hate him, for they cannot tolerate to see anyone surpass them. Nor will the proud man find peace and contentment with himself, for if he looks at himself honestly, he will recognize his folly and vanity. St. Bernard puts these words into the mouth of God: "O man! If you knew yourself well, you would be discontent with yourself and would love Me; but because you do not know yourself, you are content with yourself and discontent with Me. But the time will come when neither I nor yourself will content you; not I, because you have sinned, and not yourself, because you

[3] Ecclus. 6:6.

will burn forever. Only the devil approves of your pride, because he delights in that which is like himself."

It will also help to humble us if we consider how few merits we have before God, for many times vice puts on the appearance of virtue, or pride destroys works that are good in themselves. The judgments of God are not our judgments, for He is less offended by the humble sinner than by the righteous man who is proud, though it is true that no man can be called righteous if he is proud. And if our good works have been performed with defects or with lukewarmness, we have more reason to ask pardon for them than a reward.

Be fearful of yourself, O Christian! Fear if you are in the state of grace, lest you ever do anything unworthy of grace. Fear if you have lost grace, and make haste to seek it again. Fear after you have regained grace, lest you lose it again. Whatever your state, do not presume on yourself, but be filled with a holy fear of the Lord.

CHAPTER 52

The States of Life

MANY virtues are required for the perfect Christian life but not all the virtues are equally manifested in the lives of holy Christians. Some will be pre-eminent in one virtue and others will especially manifest other virtues. Thus, some persons are more given to the practice of those virtues which pertain to the adoration and worship of God and which are characteristic of the contemplative life. Others will be outstanding in those virtues that pertain to man's relations with his neighbor, and these pertain to the active life. Yet another group of Christians seem to excel in the personal or monastic virtues.

Yet all the virtues are means of increasing grace and some persons will receive grace in one way rather than another. Hence, some Christians make use of fasting, the discipline, and bodily austerities; others give alms and perform the works of mercy; still others practice prayer and meditation, and since there are many types of prayer and meditation, each one should use that which is most profitable to himself.

However, there is a very common error among Christians in regard to the practice of the various virtues. Some persons, when they have made some progress along one of these ways to perfection, think that because they have prospered in that way, there is no other way to advance to God except by the one that they have used and they propose to teach it to all. They may even consider that other persons are deceived and in error if they do not adopt this one way or method, because they are convinced that there is no other road to perfection. Thus, a man who devotes much time to prayer may think that there is no other way to holiness; he who fasts and practices mortification may think that all other exercises are useless; and he who dedicates himself to the contemplative life may think that those who do not do the same are in great danger and he may even go so far as to depreciate the active life. On the other hand, there are some in the active life who do not know from their own experience what transpires between God and the soul during contemplation, whereas they can see tangible results in the active life and the apostolate. As a result, they may be tempted to belittle the contemplative life and merely tolerate the combination of the active and contemplative life, which is called the mixed life. So also, a man who is proficient in mental prayer may consider all vocal prayer as sterile, while he who practices vocal prayer may consider it much more profitable because it is more laborious.

But every tradesman praises his own wares and everyone, wittingly or unwittingly, feels inclined to praise that which he finds most beneficial to himself or that which he does best. The same thing is true in the matter of virtue as in human affairs: each one praises that in which he is a master and tacitly rejects everything else. The orator thinks that there is no other art in the world that compares with oratory; the astrologer thinks there is no other science that approaches the study of the stars and the heavens; the philosopher, the student of Scripture, and the speculative theologian each thinks his science the best.

When it comes to a question of the practice of virtue, the tendency to praise what one knows or does best is more disguised. Each lover of virtue strives to find that which will most readily perfect him and will be the best defense for him in the spiritual life. When he finds that which is most beneficial to him as an individual, he is likely to conclude that it is the best for all. The shoe that fits him comfortably he thinks should fit everyone else. It is because of this tendency that we have so many judgments on the lives and deeds of others. Each one thinks that the other is wrong or is going astray because the second does not follow the same method as the first. St. Paul was very explicit in pointing out to the Corinthians that there is a diversity of graces, but the same Spirit; a diversity of ministries, but the same Lord; and a diversity of operations, but the same God who works in all.[1]

[1] Cf. I Cor., chap. 12.

There is no better cure for this error than that which St. Paul gives in the passage from his Epistle to the Corinthians, in which he reminds them that all gifts and graces, though diverse in themselves, have the same source and origin. So also, through the same baptism they are all members of the same body of which Christ is the head. "For as the body is one and hath many members, and all the members of the body, whereas they are many, yet are one body, so also is Christ. . . . For the body also is not one member, but many. If the foot should say, because I am not the hand, I am not of the body, is it therefore not of the body? And if the ear should say, because I am not the eye, I am not of the body, is it therefore not of the body?" [2] Therefore, there is a certain equality among Christians so that there may be unity and brotherhood, but there is also a certain diversity and variety that are compatible with this unity.

The diversity among Christians springs partly from nature and partly from grace. It springs from nature because although the entire spiritual life pertains to the supernatural order of grace, grace itself is received like water into a vessel, that is, it will adapt itself to the various conditions and circumstances and dispositions of the one who receives grace. Some men are naturally reserved and tranquil and seem more disposed to the exercises of the contemplative life; others are more active and energetic and seem better qualified for the active life; still others are robust and more detached and seem more inclined to the works of penance and austerity.

Here we see again how wonderfully the goodness and mercy of God are manifested, for as He desires to communicate Himself to all, He did not wish there should be only one way of doing this, but that they should be many

[2] *Ibid.*, 12:12–16.

and varied to suit the diversities of individuals. Thus, he who is not inclined in one way, may receive God's grace in another way.

The diversity among Christians also depends on the Holy Ghost, the Author of grace, who desires that there be variety among the servants of God for the beauty and glory of the Church. The perfection and beauty of the human body require various senses and members; so also, the beauty of the mystical body demands a variety of graces and virtues, for if all the members of the Church were identical, how could the Church be called a body? "If the whole body were the eye, where would be the hearing? If the whole were the hearing, where would be the smelling?" [3] Hence, some members of the Church are dedicated to the contemplative life, others to the practices of penance and mortification, others to prayer, to study, or to the spiritual and corporal works of mercy.

A similar variety is found in the various religious orders of the Church. Although they all lead to Christian perfection, each follows its distinctive path. Some go by the road of poverty, others by that of a penitential life, others by the contemplative exercises, others by the active life of the apostolate. And even in the one religious order there is great diversity, for some are chanting in choir while others are hearing confessions, preaching, teaching, writing, or studying in their cells.

Since variety is necessary for the beauty of the Church, why is it that we criticize one another because all do not act in the same way or because one person does not live like another? This is destructive of the mystical body of the Church; it creates discord in the beautiful harmony of the spiritual life. I would be very much in error if I were

[3] *Ibid.*, 12:17.

to condemn someone for not doing as I do. It is as foolish to condemn or criticize others whose circumstances and dispositions are unlike our own as it would be for the eyes to condemn the feet because they cannot see or for the feet to murmur against the eyes because they cannot walk. The value of things is not measured by the effort involved but by their importance.

Therefore, let us leave each one to his vocation and calling. This is what St. Paul advises when he says: "Let not him that eateth, despise him that eateth not; and he that eateth not, let him not judge him that eateth." [4] The musical notes that are written on the line are as important as those that are written between the lines; so also, he who does one thing is as beneficial to the Church as he who does something entirely different.

CHAPTER 53

Action and Contemplation

THE human sciences as a rule admit of both a speculative and a practical aspect. The first pertains to theory and the second to practice and experiment. These two aspects are so different from one another that a man who is proficient in the speculative aspect of a science is rarely proficient in the practical aspect, and vice versa. The same thing is true of the virtues; some are more closely related to the contemplative life, such as prayer, meditation, study, spiritual reading, while others pertain more to the active

[4] Rom. 14:3.

life and the apostolate, such as the works of mercy. Although it is impossible that any of these virtues be opposed to one another, they are nevertheless so different that a Christian is seldom outstanding in the virtues of both the contemplative and the active life.

St. Gregory states that as few men are found to be equally facile with their right hand as with their left, so few men are equally proficient in the exercises of the active and the contemplative life. They who are given more to one type of life do not feel inclined to the other. If they follow the contemplative life, they soar to God like an eagle and converse with Him in prayer, and it is with a heaviness of spirit that they return to earth to treat of worldly matters. On the other hand, those who are drawn to the exercises of the active life may find it very difficult to be recollected for any length of time.

He who wishes to be a perfect servant of God and to be perfectly submissive to the divine will must be prepared for whatever God wills. He must be prepared to soar with the eagles or to walk amidst the pitfalls of this world. He must be ready to repose in God or to work for his neighbor, to enjoy spiritual consolations or to weep over the misfortunes of his brethren, to enjoy the holy leisure of love or to exhaust himself in the labors that charity demands.

The servant of God must be prepared for everything. Even if he should be raised to the heavens in prayer, he must return to earth when he knows that his neighbor needs him and he must assist his neighbor as best he can, not doing what he does for his neighbor precisely because of his neighbor, but because He sees God in his brethren. And even if the Christian loses his spiritual consolations and delights because of the demands of charity toward his neighbor, he does not lose God, for he has merely left God for God. And when the work of the apostolate is completed, he can return to his life of prayer and recollection as if it had never been interrupted. This is the way the servant of God should conduct himself, ever disposed to do God's bidding in either the active or the contemplative exercises and, in the case of the former, hastening back to God as soon as the demands of the apostolate have been satisfied.

CHAPTER 54 ✍

The Evangelical Counsels

IN addition to the precepts and commandments of God which are of obligation for all and suffice for salvation, there are certain counsels for those who wish to walk the road to perfection with greater security. The first of these counsels is that of perfect chastity, which is a virtue proper to the angels and by means of which man avoids a multitude of cares and anxieties which are necessarily connected with the state of marriage and may easily become impediments to perfection. The celibate has only one concern, and that is to take care of himself; the married man has the care of a wife and children, whose sickness or death or misfortune he feels as if they were his own. The celibate is freed of all these anxieties and is therefore more free to give himself entirely to God, to the study of wisdom, to the practice of prayer, and to meditation on the divine truths.

A second counsel is that which the Savior gave to the rich young man when He told him to sell all his goods, give to the poor, and follow the Master.[1] This counsel of poverty frees a man from the anxieties and vexations connected with the administration of worldly goods so that he can give himself more completely to the things of God.

A third counsel is to do good to those who do us evil and to pray for those who persecute and calumniate us. In doing this we become worthy children of our heavenly Father, who makes the sun shine on the just and on sinners. God wishes us to imitate His mercy toward sinners, not only by helping them in their grave need, but by enduring them with patience, urging them to repentance, and arousing them to sorrow for their sins. God also wishes us to imitate His liberality and generosity. If we are injured, we should not become indignant, but the more our enemies persist in insulting and injuring us, the more we should strive to do good to them.

Yet another counsel is to perform the works of mercy, not only in cases that are of obligation or precept, but when we are in no sense obligated to do so. This counsel is so proper to the Christian life that scarcely any other virtue is as highly recommended to us as is mercy and scarcely any other vice is so strongly condemned as inhumanity. Thus, when speaking of the day of judgment and the terror of sinners and the confidence of the just, Christ spoke only of mercy and inhumanity.[2]

The last evangelical counsel that we shall mention is that of frequent prayer. St. Paul would wish us to pray always and in every place. Since fallen human nature is so weak and slothful, the Christian must call upon God to cure the wounds of his soul and give him the fervor needed for observing the Commandments. "I have lifted up my eyes to the mountains, from whence help shall come to me. My help is from the Lord, who made heaven and earth."[3]

---

[1] Cf. Matt. 19:21.   [2] Cf. Matt. 25:40.   [3] Ps. 120:1.

From what has been said, we can understand that there are two ways of living the Christian life: by observing the Commandments or by adding to this the observance of the evangelical counsels. This double aspect of the Christian life is symbolized by the two types of sacrifice in the Old Testament. In one form of sacrifice only the fat and entrails of the animal were destroyed, but in the other type of sacrifice the entire animal was offered as a holocaust. So also, the Christians who live according to the Commandments keep the law of charity and spend their lives fulfilling their obligations and helping to take care of the needs of their neighbor. But the Christians who live according to the counsels try as far as possible to live detached from the affairs and interests of the world and to give themselves completely to God through an ardent and constant love. Such was the life of the saints, who were exiles or pilgrims in this life but whose conversation and thoughts were in heaven. Blessed are they who live in this manner, for they are living sacrifices to God; they are holocausts of love.

CHAPTER 55

Duties of State

HAVING spoken of the duties and obligations of Christians in general, we must now speak briefly of the duties of the various states of life. Each Christian is bound by laws and precepts according to his state in life or his vocation in the Church. Some are prelates, some are subjects, some are married, and others are religious, and each one is obliged to fulfill the duties peculiar to his state.

The prelate, as St. Paul tells us, should exercise his office with all solicitude. Solomon issued the same command when he said that such persons should realize the responsibility of their office and be conscientious in the fulfillment of their duties and obligations. Persons in authority usually exercise special solicitude when they are dealing with something of great value or when great danger threatens, but since nothing is more valuable than souls nor are any dangers more perilous than those which beset the Christian life, prelates and superiors of all kinds should understand how great is the charge that has been laid upon them.

The subject, on the other hand, should not consider his superior as a man, but as one who takes the place of God and who is on that account deserving of reverence. One should obey his superior with the same promptness that he would manifest if God Himself were issuing the command, for when we obey our lawful superiors we are obeying God. But obedience itself admits of three different grades: the performance of the work commanded, the performance of the work accompanied by conformity of will, and the performance of the work together with conformity of will and judgment. Some subjects do the external act of obedience but they neither agree with the judgment of the superior nor do they conform their will to his; others obey with a good will but they do not consider the command of the superior to be prudent; still others suppress their own judgment in the service of Christ and obey the superior as they would obey God, that is, with a good will and without making any judgment on the command itself. Our obedience to superiors should be in conformity with the words of Christ: "He that heareth you, heareth Me." [1] As for those who find obedience difficult, let them

[1] Luke 10:16.

remember the words of Scripture: "Your murmuring is not against us, but against the Lord." [2]

The married woman should look first to the care of the home, provision for her family, satisfaction of her husband, and all that pertains to the duties of a wife and mother. Only after she has fulfilled the obligations of a wife and mother can she give herself to devotions and pious exercises, for her first duty is to fulfill the obligations of her state in life.

Parents should always keep in mind the severe punishment that God inflicted on Heli because he neglected to reprimand his sons for their evil ways. He does not deserve the name of father who has brought children into the world but does not prepare them for heaven. Let the father correct, punish, and advise his children and keep them from evil companions; let him entrust them to good teachers and train them from their youth to fear God and keep the Commandments. A man is not a true father if he does no more for his children than animals do for their offspring. To be a father means to be a Christian father, a father who has brought forth his children to become citizens in the kingdom of heaven.

Let the good Christian, whatever his state in life, be most solicitous in doing God's will in all things and in fulfilling the duties of his state in life. This is the very basis and foundation of the Christian life.

PRAYER TO OBTAIN VIRTUES

O God, all powerful, who knowest all things, who hadst neither beginning nor end, who dost give, preserve, and reward all virtues; deign to make me steadfast on the solid foundation

[2] Exod. 16:8.

of *faith,* to protect me with the impregnable shield of *hope,* and to adorn me with the wedding garment of *charity.*

Give me *justice,* to submit to Thee; *prudence,* to avoid the snares of the enemy; *temperance,* to keep the just medium; *fortitude,* to bear adversities with patience.

Grant me to impart willingly to others whatever I possess that is good, and to ask humbly of others that I may partake of the good of which I am destitute; to confess truly my faults; to bear with equanimity the pains and evils which I suffer. Grant that I may never envy the good of my neighbor, and that I may always return thanks for Thy graces.

Let me always observe discipline in my clothing, movements, and gestures. Let my tongue be restrained from vain words, my feet from going astray, my eyes from seeking after vain objects, my ears from listening to much news. May I humbly incline my countenance, and raise my spirit to heaven.

Grant me to despise all transitory things, and to desire Thee alone; to subdue my flesh and purify my conscience; to honor Thy saints and to praise Thee worthily; to advance in virtue, and to end good actions by a happy death.

Plant in me, O Lord, all virtues, that I may be devoted to divine things, provident in human affairs, and troublesome to no one in bodily cares.

Grant me, O Lord, fervor in contrition, sincerity in confession, and completeness in satisfaction.

Deign to direct my soul to a good life, that what I do may be pleasing to Thee, meritorious for myself, and edifying to my neighbor.

Grant that I may never desire to do what is foolish, and that I may never be discouraged by what is distasteful; that I may never begin my works before the proper time, nor abandon them before they are completed.

Grant me, O merciful God, that what is pleasing to Thee, I may ardently examine, truthfully acknowledge, and perfectly accomplish for the praise and glory of Thy name. Regulate my whole life, O God, and let me know Thy will that I may fulfill it; give me the grace to do that which is necessary and profitable for my soul.

Grant, O Lord my God, that I may not fail in prosperity or in adversity, avoiding pride in the former and discouragement in the latter. May I rejoice in nothing but what leads to Thee, grieve for nothing but what turns away from Thee. May I wish to please no one but Thee.

May I despise, O Lord, all transitory things and prize only that which is eternal. May I shun any joy that is not Thee; may I wish for nothing outside of Thee. May I delight in any work undertaken for Thee and tire of any repose which is without Thee. Grant me, O my God, to direct my heart toward Thee, constantly to grieve for my sins, and to amend my life.

Make me, O Lord, my God, obedient without contradiction, poor without depression, chaste without corruption, patient without murmuring, humble without pretense, cheerful without dissipation, sorrowful without despair, serious without constraint, prompt without levity, God-fearing without presumption, correcting my neighbor without haughtiness, and edifying him by word and example without hypocrisy.

Give me, O Lord God, a watchful heart, which no curious thought will turn away from Thee; a noble heart, which no unworthy affection will drag down; a righteous heart, which no irregular intention will turn aside; a firm heart, which no tribulation will crush; a free heart, which no violent affection will claim for its own.

Grant me, finally, O Lord my God, intelligence in knowing Thee, diligence in seeking Thee, wisdom in finding Thee, perseverance in trusting Thee, and the confidence of finally embracing Thee. Let me accept Thy punishments as a penance for my sins, and enjoy Thy benefits by grace in this world, and Thy blessedness by glory in the next. Who livest and reignest true God, forever and ever. Amen.

(St. Thomas Aquinas)

Appendix ✍

Chapter 1: *Introducción al símbolo de la fe,* Part II, chapter 2.

Chapter 2: *Guía de pecadores,* Book I, Part III, chapter 28.

Chapter 3: *Guía de pecadores,* Book I, Part III, chapter 38.

Chapter 4: *Guía de pecadores,* Book I, Part III, chapter 29; Book II, Part II, chapter 19.

Chapter 5: *Compendio de la doctrina cristiana,* Part I, chapter 11.

Chapter 6: *Guía de pecadores,* Book II, Part I, chapter 12; *Memorial de la vida cristiana,* Treatise II, Part I, chapter 3; Part II, chapter 2; *Compendio de la doctrina cristiana,* Part II, chapter 12; *Doctrina espiritual,* Treatise V.

Chapter 7: *Compendio de la doctrina cristiana,* Part II, chapters 21 and 22.

Chapter 8: *Guía de pecadores,* Book I, Part II, chapter 18.

Chapter 9: *Compendio de la doctrina cristiana,* Part II, chapter 13.

Chapter 10: *Compendio de la doctrina cristiana,* Part II, chapter 1.

Chapter 11: *Guía de pecadores,* Book I, Part I, chapter 5; *Memorial de la vida cristiana,* Part II, Treatise V, chapter 1; *Introducción al símbolo de la fe,* Part IV, chapter 12.

Chapter 12: *Adiciones al "Memorial de la vida cristiana,"* chapter 22.

Chapter 13: *Introducción al símbolo de la fe,* Part II, chapter 1.

Chapter 14: *Introducción al símbolo de la fe,* Part II, chapter 2.

Chapter 15: *Introducción al símbolo de la fe,* Part II, chapter 27.

Chapter 16: *Introducción al símbolo de la fe,* Part II, chapter 30.

Chapter 17: *Compendio de la doctrina cristiana,* Part I, chapter 3.

Chapter 18: *Introducción al símbolo de la fe,* Part II, chapter 30.

Chapter 19: *Introducción al símbolo de la fe,* Part IV, dialogue 11.

Chapter 20: *Guía de pecadores,* Book I, Part II, chapter 17; *Introducción al símbolo de la fe,* Part II, chapter 15; *Compendio de la doctrina cristiana,* Part I, chapter 4.

Chapter 21: *Adiciones al "Memorial de la vida cristiana,"* chapter 1.

Chapter 22: *Memorial de la vida cristiana,* Part II, Treatise VII, chapters 1 and 2; *Adiciones al "Memorial de la vida cristiana,"* chapter 22; *Introducción al símbolo de la fe,* Part II, chapter 14.

Chapter 23: *Guía de pecadores,* Book I, Part II, chapter 14.

Chapter 24: *Adiciones al "Memorial de la vida cristiana,"* Part I, chapter 2.

Chapter 25: *Memorial de la vida cristiana,* Part II, Treatise VII; *Adiciones al "Memorial de la vida cristiana,"* Part I, chapters 3 and 5; Part II, chapters 10 and 11.

Chapter 26: *Compendio de la doctrina cristiana,* Part II, chapter 20; *Adiciones al "Memorial de la vida cristiana,"* Part I, chapter 3.

Chapter 27: *Guía de pecadores,* Book I, Part II, chapter 16.

Chapter 28: *Libro de la oración y meditación,* Part III, Treatise III.

Chapter 29: *Compendio de la doctrina cristiana,* Part II, chapter 23; *Sermón de las caídas públicas.*

Chapter 30: *Guía de pecadores,* Book II, Part I, chapters 7 and 9.

Chapter 31: *Guía de pecadores,* Book II, Part II, chapter 15.

Chapter 32: *Guía de pecadores,* Book II, chapters 9 and 11 (*texto primitivo*).

Chapter 33: *Guía de pecadores,* Book II, Part I, chapter 5.

Chapter 34: *Guía de pecadores,* Book II, Part I, chapter 5.

Chapter 35: *Guía de pecadores,* Book II, Part I, chapter 11; *Compendio de la doctrina cristiana,* Part II, chapter 9.

Chapter 36: *Introducción al símbolo de la fe,* Part I, chapters 8 and 38; *Libro de la oración y meditación,* Part II, chapters 1, 2, and 3.

Chapter 37: *Libro de la oración y meditación,* Part I, chapter 1; Part III, chapters 1 and 2; *Memorial de la vida cristiana,* Part II, Treatise V, chapters 2 and 4.

Chapter 38: *Memorial de la vida cristiana,* Treatise IV, chapter 3; Treatise VI, chapter 3; *Libro de la oración y meditación,* Part I, chapters 4, 9, and 10; *Doctrina espiritual,* Treatise I, chapter 15.

Chapter 39: *Libro de la oración y meditación,* Part II, chapter 5.

Chapter 40: *Introducción al símbolo de la fe,* Part IV, dialogue 10; *Guía de pecadores,* Book II, Part I, chapter 11; *Compendio de la doctrina cristiana,* Part II, chapters 3 and 4.

Chapter 41: *Guía de pecadores,* Book II, Part II, chapter 17.

Chapter 42: *Compendio de la doctrina cristiana,* Part II, chapter 1.

Chapter 43: *Guía de pecadores,* Book II, Part II, chapter 23.

Chapter 44: *Introducción al símbolo de la fe,* Part II, chapter 25.

Chapter 45: *Guía de pecadores,* Book II, Part II, chapter 17.

Chapter 46: *Sermón de las caídas públicas; Guía de pecadores,* Book II, Part I, chapter 6; *Compendio de la doc-*

trina cristiana, Part II, chapter 16.

Chapter 47: *Guía de pecadores,* Book II, Part I, chapter 8; Part II, chapter 15; *Libro de la oración y meditación,* Part III; *Compendio de la doctrina cristiana,* Part II, chapter 18.

Chapter 48: *Guía de pecadores,* Book II, Part II, chapter 15.

Chapter 49: *Guía de pecadores,* Book II, Part I, chapter 9; *Compendio de la doctrina cristiana,* Part II, chapter 19.

Chapter 50: *Adiciones al "Memorial de la vida cristiana,"* Part II, chapter 15.

Chapter 51: *Guía de pecadores,* Book II, Part I, chapter 4; *Compendio de la doctrina cristiana,* Part II, chapter 14.

Chapter 52: *Guía de pecadores,* Book II, Part II, chapter 21.

Chapter 53: *Adiciones al "Memorial de la vida cristiana,"* Part II, chapter 19.

Chapter 54: *Introducción al símbolo de la fe,* Part II, chapter 5.

Chapter 55: *Guía de pecadores,* Book II, Part II, chapter 18.

If you have enjoyed this book, consider making your next selection from among the following . . .

Prices guaranteed through December 31, 1995.

Miraculous Images of Our Lady. *Cruz* 20.00
Raised from the Dead. *Fr. Hebert* 15.00
Love and Service of God, Infinite Love. *Mother Louise Margaret* . 10.00
Life and Work of Mother Louise Margaret. *Fr. O'Connell* 10.00
Autobiography of St. Margaret Mary 4.00
Thoughts and Sayings of St. Margaret Mary 3.00
The Voice of the Saints. *Comp. by Francis Johnston* 5.00
The 12 Steps to Holiness and Salvation. *St. Alphonsus* 7.00
The Rosary and the Crisis of Faith. *Cirrincione & Nelson* 1.25
Sin and Its Consequences. *Cardinal Manning* 5.00
Fourfold Sovereignty of God. *Cardinal Manning* 5.00
Dialogue of St. Catherine of Siena. *Transl. Algar Thorold* 9.00
Catholic Answer to Jehovah's Witnesses. *D'Angelo* 8.00
Twelve Promises of the Sacred Heart. (100 cards) 5.00
St. Aloysius Gonzaga. *Fr. Meschler* 10.00
The Love of Mary. *D. Roberto* 7.00
Begone Satan. *Fr. Vogl* 2.00
The Prophets and Our Times. *Fr. R. G. Culleton* 11.00
St. Therese, The Little Flower. *John Beevers* 4.50
St. Joseph of Copertino. *Fr. Angelo Pastrovicchi* 4.50
Mary, The Second Eve. *Cardinal Newman* 2.50
Devotion to Infant Jesus of Prague. *Booklet* .... .75
Reign of Christ the King in Public & Private Life. *Davies* 1.25
The Wonder of Guadalupe. *Francis Johnston* 6.00
Apologetics. *Msgr. Paul Glenn* 9.00
Baltimore Catechism No. 1 .... 3.00
Baltimore Catechism No. 2 .... 4.00
Baltimore Catechism No. 3 .... 7.00
An Explanation of the Baltimore Catechism. *Fr. Kinkead* 13.00
Bethlehem. *Fr. Faber* 16.50
Bible History. *Schuster* 10.00
Blessed Eucharist. *Fr. Mueller* 9.00
Catholic Catechism. *Fr. Faerber* 5.00
The Devil. *Fr. Delaporte* 5.00
Dogmatic Theology for the Laity. *Fr. Premm* 18.00
Evidence of Satan in the Modern World. *Cristiani* 8.50
Fifteen Promises of Mary. (100 cards) 5.00
Life of Anne Catherine Emmerich. 2 vols. *Schmoger* 37.50
Life of the Blessed Virgin Mary. *Emmerich* 15.00
Manual of Practical Devotion to St. Joseph. *Patrignani* 13.50
Prayer to St. Michael. (100 leaflets) 5.00
Prayerbook of Favorite Litanies. *Fr. Hebert* 9.00
Preparation for Death. (Abridged). *St. Alphonsus* 7.00
Purgatory Explained. *Schouppe* 13.50
Purgatory Explained. (pocket, unabr.). *Schouppe* 7.50
Fundamentals of Catholic Dogma. *Ludwig Ott* 20.00
Spiritual Conferences. *Tauler* 12.00
Trustful Surrender to Divine Providence. *Bl. Claude* 4.00
Wife, Mother and Mystic. *Bessieres* 7.00
The Agony of Jesus. *Padre Pio* 1.50

Prices guaranteed through December 31, 1995.

Prices guaranteed through December 31, 1995.

Brief Catechism for Adults. *Cogan* 9.00
The Cath. Religion—Illus./Expl. for Child, Adult, Convert. *Burbach*. 9.00
Eucharistic Miracles. *Joan Carroll Cruz* 13.00
The Incorruptibles. *Joan Carroll Cruz* 12.00
Pope St. Pius X. *F. A. Forbes* 6.00
St. Alphonsus Liguori. *Frs. Miller and Aubin* 15.00
Self-Abandonment to Divine Providence. *Fr. de Caussade, S.J.* ... 16.50
The Song of Songs—A Mystical Exposition. *Fr. Arintero, O.P.* ... 18.00
Prophecy for Today. *Edward Connor* 4.50
Saint Michael and the Angels. *Approved Sources* 5.50
Dolorous Passion of Our Lord. *Anne C. Emmerich* 15.00
Modern Saints—Their Lives & Faces. *Ann Ball* 18.00
Our Lady of Fatima's Peace Plan from Heaven. *Booklet* .... .75
Divine Favors Granted to St. Joseph. *Père Binet* 4.00
St. Joseph Cafasso—Priest of the Gallows. *St. John Bosco* 3.00
Catechism of the Council of Trent. *McHugh/Callan* 20.00
The Foot of the Cross. *Fr. Faber* 15.00
The Rosary in Action. *John Johnson* 8.00
Padre Pio—The Stigmatist. *Fr. Charles Carty* 13.50
Why Squander Illness? *Frs. Rumble & Carty* 2.00
The Sacred Heart and the Priesthood. *de la Touche* 7.00
Fatima—The Great Sign. *Francis Johnston* 7.00
Heliotropium—Conformity of Human Will to Divine. *Drexelius* ... 11.00
Charity for the Suffering Souls. *Fr. John Nageleisen* 15.00
Devotion to the Sacred Heart of Jesus. *Verheylezoon* 13.00
Who Is Padre Pio? *Radio Replies Press* 1.50
Child's Bible History. *Knecht* 4.00
The Stigmata and Modern Science. *Fr. Charles Carty* 1.25
The Life of Christ. 4 Vols. H.B. *Anne C. Emmerich* 55.00
St. Anthony—The Wonder Worker of Padua. *Stoddard* 4.00
The Precious Blood. *Fr. Faber* 11.00
The Holy Shroud & Four Visions. *Fr. O'Connell* 2.00
Clean Love in Courtship. *Fr. Lawrence Lovasik* 2.50
The Prophecies of St. Malachy. *Peter Bander* 5.00
St. Martin de Porres. *Giuliana Cavallini* 11.00
The Secret of the Rosary. *St. Louis De Montfort* 3.00
The History of Antichrist. *Rev. P. Huchede* 3.00
The Douay-Rheims New Testament. *Paperbound* 13.00
St. Catherine of Siena. *Alice Curtayne* 12.00
Where We Got the Bible. *Fr. Henry Graham* 5.00
Hidden Treasure—Holy Mass. *St. Leonard* 4.00
Imitation of the Sacred Heart of Jesus. *Fr. Arnoudt* 13.50
The Life & Glories of St. Joseph. *Edward Thompson* 13.50
Père Lamy. *Biver* 10.00
Humility of Heart. *Fr. Cajetan da Bergamo* 7.00
The Curé D'Ars. *Abbé Francis Trochu* 20.00
Love, Peace and Joy. (St. Gertrude). *Prévot* 5.00
The Three Ways of the Spiritual Life. *Garrigou-Lagrange, O.P.* ... 4.00

At your Bookdealer or direct from the Publisher.

Prices guaranteed through December 31, 1995.